Introduction
to Comparative
Politics

Introduction to Comparative Politics

Regimes and Change

SECOND EDITION

Roy C. Macridis

and

Steven L. Burg

Department of Politics
BRANDEIS UNIVERSITY

New York   San Francisco   Boston
London   Toronto   Sydney   Tokyo   Singapore   Madrid
Mexico City   Munich   Paris   Cape Town   Hong Kong   Montreal

Sponsoring Editor: Lauren Silverman
Project Coordination: Spectrum Publisher Services, Inc.
Cover Design: Mina Greenstein
Production: Michael Weinstein
Compositor: Kachina Typesetting, Inc.
Printer and Binder: R. R. Donnelley & Sons, Company
Cover Printer: Phoenix Color Corp.

Introduction to Comparative Politics, Second Edition

Library of Congress Cataloging-in-Publication Data

Macridis, Roy C.
    Introduction to comparative politics: regimes and
change / Roy C. Macridis and Steven L. Burg.
        p.   cm.
    Includes bibliographical references and index.
    ISBN 0-673-52035-8
    1. Comparative government.   I. Burg, Steven L.   II. Title.
JF51.M323   1991
320.3—dc20   90-44998
                                                        CIP

31 32 33 34 35 -DOC- 06 05 04 03

Contents

Preface

This is a radically revised edition of *Modern Political Regimes: Patterns and Institutions*, which came out four years ago. While it continues to focus on institutions—"commonly agreed patterns of political behavior"—this edition also attempts to analyze and describe the processes by which regimes undergo rapid transformation.

The book is now divided into four major parts. In the first, we provide a general framework for the comparative study of political regimes. In the second part of the book, we focus on democratic regimes. We deal with the major institutional structures that can be traced to nineteenth-century liberalism; structures which have undergone profound changes in response to expanding popular participation and economic modernization that together produced increased state intervention in order to bring about social equality. Because of the adaptability of Western democratic regimes, they have proven remarkably durable. But this has not been the case with authoritarian regimes. In the third part, we describe the features of such regimes, emphasizing their great variety and devoting particular attention to a type of regime which has dominated the stage of world politics for so long—the totalitarian regime. Today, however, all types of authoritarian regimes are in disarray. To paraphrase Marx, it is the specter of liberalism that haunts them all!

In the fourth and final part of the book, we identify the major categories of analysis by which the process of regime change takes place. Drawing on European, Mediterranean, and Latin American experience, we review the "breakdown" of democratic regimes, and the "liberalization" and "democratization" of authoritarian regimes. We devote special attention, however, to the historic processes of change in the Soviet Union and Eastern Europe that are unfolding even as we write these words.

The collapse of the "old order" in the USSR and Eastern Europe is only a necessary condition for rapid change. It is still uncertain whether such change will produce democratic regimes in these countries. But the questions we raise in this volume, and the framework for understanding what we offer in it, are intended to provide students of politics with a basis for some tentative and qualified insights into the prospects for democracy in each case.

We present this new volume in the same spirit in which the first edition was written—not only to provide the student a panorama of the institutional configurations of our political universe, but also to raise questions about regime performance, legitimacy, and change.

We would like to thank the following reviewers for their insightful comments and suggestions: Jutta A. Helm, Western Illinois University; Eric Nordlinger, Brown University; and Gerard F. Rutan, Western Washington University.

R.C.M.
S.L.B.

Part One

Introduction

Ours is a world of nation-states. People are grouped together into separate geographic boundaries, living under their own political regimes—that is, under the sets of rules, procedures, and understandings that shape the relationship between rulers and ruled in each state.

There are many types of politial regimes. In every state there are a variety of political institutions—executive organs, a legislative body, a political party or parties, administrative bureaucracies, to mention a few—that perform the allotted tasks and roles involved in governance. Even when institutions carry the same label, we find great variation in their roles and their performance; political parties or legislatures, for example, play different roles in different states. Each political regime—that is, the particular combination of institutions, rules, and procedures in a given state or states—is shaped by the particular historical, cultural, economic, social, and interactional factors that determine the political behavior and attitudes of both the rulers and the ruled.

The arrangements which define particular political regimes vary most noticeably with respect to four broad characteristics:

1. the organization of political power
2. the forms of political participation
3. the organization and articulation of interests
4. the configuration of political rights

1

Regimes also vary notably in the depth of their legitimacy, the degree to which they are institutionalized and, therefore, their stability. As a result of these differences, political regimes change. Over time, the changes that take place may be so great as to alter the very nature of the political regime. And it is precisely these changes from one type of regime to another that are among the most interesting political phenomena to study.

Our political world is thus one of great variety. It is a source of pleasure and wonder to the traveler and the historian, as Herodotus found out so many centuries ago, but a virtual nightmare for those who try to impose some order on the profusion of regimes and on the confusion their differences entail. As we look at the world around us, from China and the Soviet Union to England, the United States, or Switzerland, is it possible to find general patterns—common characteristics and styles—that will enable us to separate some regimes from others? And, as democracies give way to dictatorships, or authoritarian and totalitarian regimes undergo democratization, can we identify the boundaries which distinguish one "type" of regime from another?

Our first job in the comparative study of political regimes is to develop some general concepts that will help us find the fundamental similarities and differences that are necessary to arrive at some descriptive generalizations. Only then can we ask the proper questions about political organization and political behavior. Unless we establish a framework within which we can identify similarities and differences, classify political regimes, and generalize about them, we will not succeed in the attempt to understand our political universe.

1

Political Regimes: A General Framework

Introduction

To establish a general framework of comparative analysis, let us begin at the abstract level of system theory. A political system consists of *functions* and *structures*. *Functions* refers to the things that have to be done. *Structures* refers to the institutions, the mechanisms, the arrangements, and the procedures through which these things are done. System theory suggests the major functions of a political system and their interrelationships and interdependence, but only in general terms. These are:

1. Generate commonly shared goals. To do so, a political system must provide for socialization; i.e., for the common acceptance by the population of the goals and the institutions through which these goals are to be realized. This concept underlines the importance of commonly shared ideas or the existence of a prevailing ideology.
2. Provide mechanisms for decision making, including both decision-making institutions and agreed-upon rules of procedure.
3. Provide for the ways and means whereby decision makers are selected, together with the rules for their succession.
4. Establish mechanisms for the articulation and aggregation of those interests that must be taken into account in the determination of policy.

5. Maintain order by defining agreed-upon rules of political behavior, and providing for effective means of enforcing them.
6. Be capable of self-preservation.[1]

All political regimes attempt to perform these functions through the institutions they establish. Different types of political regimes differ in the particular ways and means by which these functions are structured and patterned into institutions and procedures, and in the way such institutions and procedures relate to one another.[1]

There are four major interacting processes that characterize all political systems. It is the differences among these that we will use to distinguish political regimes. They are:

1. The organization of command—in essence the state and its agencies—what we often refer to as "the government"
2. The organization of consent
3. The configuration of interests
4. The organization of rights

The Organization of Command

The Role of the State

Politics and the study of political regimes are concerned primarily with power and its exercise. Command, imperium (what the Greeks called "kyrion"), souverain, and sovereignty are the terms we most frequently come across to denote the existence of political power within a given territory. As a noted British author wrote more than a half century ago, "The state consists of a relatively small number of persons who issue and execute orders which affect a larger number in whom they are themselves included; it is of the essence of its character that, within its allotted territory, all citizens are legally bound by those orders."[2] In the language of system theory, the state makes "authoritative decisions"; that is, decisions expected to be obeyed and enforced.

The state differs from all other associations in a great number of ways: First of all, it is all-inclusive. Some of us may be members of a Catholic or Unitarian church; some of us may belong to a trade union or the American Medical Association or the Chamber of Commerce; others are proud members of the Elks or the Lions; but all of us are in the state.

Second, the purposes of the Elks, the Lions, the Catholics, the Unitarians, or the American Medical Association are special purposes,

---

[1]For a discussion of the structural-functional approach that has mesmerized teachers and students for the last thirty years, see David Apter, *Introduction to Political Analysis* (Boston: Little, Brown, 1982), unit VI, pp. 377–451; also Gabriel Almond and G. Brigham Powell, Jr., *Comparative Politics: A Developmental Approach* (Boston: Little, Brown, 1981).
[2]Harold Laski, *The Grammar of Politics* (London: George Allen and Unwin, 1925), p. 295.

usually narrow in scope. The purposes of the state, however, are far more encompassing than those of all other associations combined. The state rules on matters such as defense, order, and social justice. Harry Eckstein waxes enthusiastic, very much in the spirit of Aristotle, when he writes that in the last analysis the state represents the principle of justice: "It is the only awesome power we have"![3]

Third, individuals can move from one association to another or withdraw from all or any of them. But it is extremely difficult to move out of the state into which you are born, even if that state places no legal restrictions on emigration.

Fourth, you can disobey the rules and regulations of an association, and nobody will bother you except your friends or your conscience. You are free to comply or not. But you do not have the same freedom when it comes to the tax collector, the judge, or the traffic light. The state possesses what no other association has: the right to use force to secure compliance. It sanctions its decisions with force and enjoys a monopoly over the use of force in the territory it controls.

Finally, while the state can use force, it also must rely on emotional supports and loyalty. The modern state, except in some extreme and usually short-lived cases, requires widespread consent and popular support in order to have its decisions obeyed without resort to coercion. The implicit ability to employ force is usually enough to insure against the few who refuse to comply. As long as the majority of its citizens comply, the state can function with a minimum of force. But, if the majority do not comply, then the state cannot survive for long.

Major Organs of Command

Despite the many differences, the formal organs—but not, of course, the actual political practices—most commonly associated with the command structure appear to be similar in virtually all political regimes: an executive body at the top, and administrative or bureaucratic agencies through which it carries out policy subordinate to it; a legislative body to make laws; and a judiciary to apply and settle disputes about the law. In almost all regimes, there is a functional division of judicial, legislative, and executive power, and separate institutions correspond to these functions. Another similarity is that their relationships are arranged by a constitution: A written (but occasionally unwritten) set of rules that sets forth the limits of power, the manner in which power will be used, and the responsibilities and freedoms of the citizens. Actual practices and especially the relative power and autonomy of these elements of com-

---

[3]Harry Eckstein, "On the Science of the State," *Daedalus* (Fall 1979), 18; also Eric Nordlinger, *On the Autonomy of the Democratic State* (Cambridge, Mass.: Harvard University Press, 1981). According to Nordlinger, however, there is nothing awesome in the state. It is but another actor that manipulates the political forces. It is not the embodiment of justice.

mand vary greatly among different regimes. Even within a single state, changes in these relationships over time may produce a change in regime.

Governing Elites

In studying the command structure and the institutions and agencies operating within it, we do not limit ourselves to those persons officially elected or appointed. In most political regimes the decision makers—generally the officials who hold responsible positions (they issue and execute orders)—are part of what may loosely be called the governing elite. All discussions about elites begin with the pithy statement of the Italian sociologist Gaetano Mosca: There is "a class that rules and a class that is ruled." This division is a universal phenomenon. The ruling class is "always the less numerous, performs all political functions, monopolizes power and enjoys the advantages that power brings."[4] The "other" class, the ruled, consists of the great majority of people.

To many people, this statement is unduly cynical. It is difficult to reconcile it with democracy, where the majority are supposed to govern and where egalitarianism is the dominant concept. Nonetheless, if we study the organization of contemporary societies, we find that they are all stratified by status, power, and wealth: the few are at the top and the many are at the base. Also, there are oligarchic tendencies present in all organizations. The few invariably assume positions of authority and command, whether in business organizations, educational institutions, trade unions, political parties, or fraternal associations. In all organizations and especially in political ones, including the political party and the state, there is what another author called, in a famous phrase, an "iron law of oligarchy."[5]

A group of people with the power to make others conform to its preferences and to prevent others from following preferences contrary to its own is an elite. An elite can act *directly*, by occupying the decision-making organs and shaping policy and policy outcomes. In this case it assumes the status of a political elite. But it can also exercise its power *indirectly*, by influencing the political leaders who make policy. In the past, powerful industrialists were reputed to have operated behind the scenes of government, and it has been said that they pulled the strings: J. P. Morgan or the Rockefellers, for instance, or the "two hundred families" that ruled France, or Krupp, the German industrial magnate who exclaimed gleefully in 1932 "we have hired Herr Hitler." Today, in many democracies, big corporations and multinationals are often alleged to be exercising the same influence. There are also other elites to be reckoned with: the high clergy, university presidents, the military,

---

[4]Gaetano Mosca, *The Ruling Class* (New York: McGraw-Hill, 1939).
[5]Robert Michels, *Political Parties: A Sociological Study of the Oligarchical Tendencies of Modern Democracy* (London: Collier Books, 1962).

managerial groups, labor union leaders, owners and directors of the media, leaders of mass organizations and, of course, the wealthy. In liberal democratic regimes there are many competing elites. In authoritarian regimes, the more dominant role of the state and of those who control it reduces the power and influence of all others. Milovan Djilas, the Yugoslav communist leader who broke with the party and became a leading critic of communism, spoke of the political, administrative, and managerial leaders of the totalitarian Soviet Union, united in the Communist party of the Soviet Union, as a "new class": a new oligarchy who ruled over the many, so that communist regimes were also divided between the "powerful" and the "powerless."[6]

Elites propagate ideas that allow them to maintain as well as legitimize their position. For an elite to maintain its position, it helps to have a common *ideology*. Differences, cracks, and splits in the ideology invariably suggest lack of cohesiveness. They herald a crisis. The existence of a coherent, agreed-upon ideology is prima facie evidence of unity and potentially great power in relation to society. Where it cannot be found, we may infer that the elite is divided, in conflict, or in the process of rapid internal transformation. The ideology held by ruling elites with regard to socioeconomic modernization is particularly critical in assessing its survival or not.

The monopoly of power exercised by an elite is determined by the degree to which decision making is reserved to state organs or by how much participation in the authoritative decision-making process is extended to individuals and groups outside the elite. The scope of participation outside the elite, in turn, reflects the degree to which constraints or limitations have been imposed on the elite.

Constraints often appear in the form of *guarantees for the governed* that limit elite power and qualify the monopoly of power. Such constraints and qualifications have developed throughout the world in the last two centuries. These guarantees consist not only of things that the elite cannot do but also of what the governed *can* do and what sanctions the people can impose upon the elites. We will pay particular attention to the institutionalized procedures through which members of the elite can be sanctioned.

If the existence of an elite is a universal phenomenon, its power relative to the rest of society and the guarantees available to the governed to protect them against the elite become crucial variables in any comparative survey. But the arguments that some regimes are elitist and others are democratic, that in some the people govern while in others it is the bosses who rule, miss the point. The point is that there are elites in *all* regimes. But regimes differ, often fundamentally, in how inequality is perceived, how it is maintained, what privileges are bestowed on some, and what deprivations others suffer. In sum, if there are elites every-

[6]Milovan Djilas, *The New Class* (New York: Praeger, 1957).

where, some are more powerful than others, and some regimes are more elitist than others. Likewise, while the many are ruled every-where, in some regimes they are a little more powerful than in others.

Thus, the study of the elite will almost always provide us with insight into perhaps the most important characteristic of the command structure: the distribution and limits of power. Just how much influence elites have over the authoritative decision-making process in any given regime is generally reflected in the organization of consent, the con-figuration of interests, and the organization of rights; in short, in the relationship between state and society.

As we examine various types of regimes, we will try to identify the decision-making elite: officials in government and the most powerful groups in society operating within or behind the government. We will try to find out what distinguishes the elite of one regime from that of another, and what institutional devices different elites use to organize their powers.

The Organization of Consent

A medieval French writer wrote that oxen are bound by their horns and people by their words and wills. The structure of command is fun-damentally a matter of fashioning relationships that will allow some to command with the expectation of being obeyed. It is more a matter of values, myths, symbols, and habits than force.

A political regime needs supports in order to maintain itself and to survive over a given period of time. Supports consist of the positive orientations and attitudes of the citizenry with regard to their political regime. They may be addressed, wholly or in part, to the community of people—the "nation"— encompassed by the state; to the particular political regime within the state; to a particular government in power; or to a given policy or policies or policy outcomes. Supports are usually broken into two major types: affective (or diffuse) and instrumental (or specific).

Affective and Instrumental Supports[7]

Affective supports are the diffuse or generalized attachments the pop-ulation has for the political community and, perhaps, the regime. Those who sing the national anthem during their morning shower obviously

[7]We are following an argument closely associated with the work of David Easton. See in particular his articles, "An Approach to the Analysis of Political Systems," *World Politics* 9 (April 1957), pp. 383–400; and "A Reassessment of the Concept of Political Support," *British Journal of Political Science* 5, 1975, pp. 435–457. See also the discussion of political support in Steven L. Burg and Michael L. Berbaum, "Community, Integration, and Stability in Multinational Yugoslavia," *American Political Science Review* 83, 2 (June 1989), pp. 535–554.

have a deep affective orientation for their country and its political regime. The opposite of this is found in those who dream and plot to destroy it. It takes many years to develop such deep emotional attachments, usually as the result of socialization in childhood and continuing socializing forces in adulthood. Once established, such feelings can become crystallized or hardened in political attitudes and behavior and create a firm foundation for the continuing survival of the regime.

In contrast to affective supports, instrumental supports are very specific. They are generated primarily by utilitarian considerations. They relate to the satisfaction of personal interests and to the realization of personal goals and demands. In short, they are the product of a regime's own performance. A regime that has maintained order, provided important services, kept the people out of war or did not lose one, preserved individual security and rights, and allocated resources evenly and generously will be accepted and respected and supported by most. The people give support in return for what they are getting. It is a quid pro quo arrangement. It is a case of "I'll do something for my country if my country does enough for me." In other words, acceptance of the regime is conditional. Instrumental support, therefore, is more subject to rapid erosion than affective support and is a less powerful basis for the survival of a regime.

When both affective and instrumental supports go hand in hand, the extent and intensity of consent to and acceptance of the regime is likely to be very wide and deep. The opposite is equally true: If the regime is not valued and does not provide adequate services, its legitimacy is very uncertain. More intriguing are the cases where there is tension between affective and instrumental supports.

When a regime performs well but is not valued (i.e., when affective support is low but instrumental support is strong) there may be a gradual increase in popular acceptance until the regime becomes legitimized. Prosperity and well-being may satisfy all but the most deeply opposed. Such continuing opposition tends to arise out of two types of sources: deeply felt attractions for another type of regime, as among democratic dissenters in authoritarian regimes and radical revolutionaries in democratic ones, and the nationalism of ethnic, linguistic, or racial minorities. The latter, in fact, is quite common in multiethnic states and represents a powerful force for political change. In virtually all other cases, instrumental support generated by positive regime performance can, with the help of ongoing socialization, be converted into affective support. This, in fact, explains the survival of many nondemocratic regimes.

While regimes based on instrumental support may be vulnerable to the effects of declining performance, those that enjoy deep affective supports are less so. Take the 1929 depression in the United States. Can such a failure impair affective supports? How fast? We frankly cannot answer this in the abstract. It all depends on how deep and time-honored the affective or diffuse supports have been and on how serious and lasting the crisis facing a regime is. In societies where legitimacy is not deep and a regime has shown only marginal performance, a crisis, such as war or an economic depression, may unhinge the regime. Conversely, in societies where both legitimacy and performance (in other words, both affective and instrumental supports) have been strong for a long time, nonperformance and the resulting waning of instrumental supports may not affect legitimacy even if the problem continues for a fairly long time. In 1929 and throughout the economic depression, few Americans turned against their government or the Constitution. However, in Germany, in 1933, three years after an equally severe economic depression, the Germans had toppled their democratic constitution. The American political regime had a thick cushion of legitimacy and managed to withstand the crisis; not so the German democratic constitution—it was replaced by the Nazi dictatorship. Some regimes can afford mistakes and even prolonged periods of nonperformance; in others, the cushion of legitimacy is but thin ice on which they skate at their own peril.

Even for political regimes that have enjoyed legitimacy for a long time there is a point of crisis. The combination of conflict over domestic civil rights and widespread resistance to the growing war in Vietnam (1960–1973) gave rise to the first serious political crisis in the United States since the Civil War; many people turned not only against their government but against the political institutions—against the political regime and the Constitution. In the case of a regime whose affective support is tenuous, a sharp decline in performance may erode instrumental support enough to bring on crisis. The onset of mass demonstrations and ethnic violence in the Soviet Union under Mikhail Gorbachev, the outbreak of political unrest in Yugoslavia in the post-Tito era, and the series of dramatic regime changes in Eastern Europe in 1989 and 1990 for example, seem to be attributable, at least in part, to such conditions.

When people accept the regime they live in even though they do not agree with some specific policy decisions, we call the regime consensual, or "legitimate." It is based on shared wills and shared values between those who make decisions or "authoritatively allocate values" in the command structures and the population at large. The people consent rather than obey, and those who make decisions need exercise only their authority, not their power.

There are four processes associated with the organization of consent:

1. Socialization
2. Representation
3. Participation
4. Mobilization

(1) *Socialization* comprises the various processes through which loyalties and attachments to a political regime and its institutions are developed. It plays a crucial role in the development of support. The family, the school, and various associations propagate values consistent with the goals and the institutions of the given regime.[8] An ideology is often propagated as a means to rationalize the existing political regime. By the time most children become adults, they have been imbued with the prevailing ideology and are ready to give their support. Habit is equally important: the sheer imitation of the elders; the doing of things the way they are done by others; the tendency to follow peer groups or to act in accord with neighbors and friends or other reference groups; all these factors shape and crystallize orientations and loyalties vis-à-vis the political regime. Specifically how different regimes socialize the young and the citizens, or how they fail to do so, is a matter we will examine when we discuss individual cases. The socialization process in general, however, is necessary for the maintenance of any political regime, regardless of the specific methods used.

(2) *Representation*, at least in theory, puts elected representatives in charge of the command structure. In democratic regimes, representative assemblies speak for the whole and are beholden to the whole. In obeying, therefore, the citizenry simply obeys decisions made by delegates they themselves have chosen. In nondemocratic regimes, the popular legitimacy or authority of such institutions is limited.

(3) *Participation* provides an active communication and interaction between the citizenry and those in command positions. In democratic regimes, the citizenry organizes and agitates and talks about everything from trash collections to a nuclear freeze. Associations promote various points of view on domestic and foreign policy questions. And through a political party or even without one, people exert all sorts of efforts (and often expenditures) to ensure that those who reach a position of command are those they want elected. Even in nondemocratic regimes, participation—even if restricted—is an important foundation of political order. Of all the agencies that provide for such participation, in democratic and nondemocratic regimes alike, the political party is considered to be the most important one.

(4) *Mobilization* is often used to denote the awakening of political involvement of people who had remained disenfranchised or alienated. For instance, nationalism and national independence movements mobilized the masses in Europe in the nineteenth century and throughout the Third World after World War II. It brought them into politics. But the word can also be used, and we use it in this sense, to denote intensive participation: a great commitment and sustained activity, a deep in-

---

[8]Kenneth Langton, *Political Socialization* (New York: Oxford University Press, 1969); Richard E. Dawson and Kenneth Prewitt, *Political Socialization* (Boston: Little, Brown, 1969).

volvement. Such participation may arise spontaneously, out of personal interest, or it may be encouraged by political activists seeking to enhance support for their cause. Thus, one might say that organized groups, such as those that support and oppose abortion in the United States, mobilize the population into political action. They spur citizens to intensive political activity. The issues raised by the war in Vietnam spontaneously mobilized many millions of Americans into political action, as did legislation prepared by the French socialist government that appeared to interfere with the autonomy of Catholic schools. Gorbachev's calls for *glasnost* (openness), *demokratizatsiia* (democratization), and *perestroika* (economic restructuring) have led to an explosion of spontaneous popular political activity in the Soviet Union. In the Soviet and other communist systems, the Communist party led efforts to mobilize the population into controlled activities that supported these regimes. The downfall of communism in Eastern Europe was brought about by the sudden increase in mass political activity, organized from below, which followed the onset of glasnost and which could not be contained by existing institutions. When we use the term "mobilization," we refer to such intensive participation, whether spontaneous and initiated from below or initiated and orchestrated from above.

The Configuration of Interests

Within a political regime various actors, both groups and individuals, seek to articulate their various interests. They have certain expectations, they make certain demands, and they seek the realization of their needs and desires. The term *interests* should be defined in the broadest possible sense: material interests; family interests; professional interests; religious convictions; and heartfelt values such as honor, patriotism, rights, and humanitarian considerations.

Interests speak through organizations, usually associations and groups. Groups are generally identified and defined in terms of some shared objective traits such as tribal membership, occupation, age, religion, or ethnic identity. Associations are formally constituted and organized by individuals in order to protect their common interests: the American Association of Retired Persons, the NAACP, the NAM, the AMA, and the AFL-CIO are a few examples.[9] Such associations may be formed voluntarily, as in democratic regimes, or they may be established by the state itself, as in some nondemocratic regimes. Political

[9]For interest group analysis, especially with reference to American politics, one should consult the pioneering works of Pendleton Herring, especially his *Group Representation Before Congress* (1929; rpt. New York: Russell & Russell, 1967). See also Arthur F. Bentley, *The Process of Government* (New Brunswick, N.J.: Transaction Books, 1983) and David Truman, *The Governmental Process* (New York: Alfred A. Knopf, 1947).

parties are associations that bring many interests together into a general purposive activity. The party expresses these interests, reconciles those that conflict, and synthesizes them in support of common policy goals. In democratic regimes, the formal party platform embodies the goals to be pursued by the party leader if that party should assume control of the command structure. In nondemocratic regimes, parties also devise such programs and attempt to implement them.

The configuration of interests in any regime is greatly affected by the levels of economic and social modernization. Economic development—the change from simple agricultural societies to more complex industrial ones, and especially the shift from low to high technologies—produces new groups that expand the basic social categories associated with early industrialization. The division between working class and peasantry is supplemented by the rise of intellectual strata, technical and scientific specialists, administrative and bureaucratic functionaries, and many other specialized groups. This dual process of structural differentiation and functional specialization arising out of the modernization process increases the number of groups and interests with which individuals become identified and, therefore, increases the number of potential bases for their political mobilization.[10]

Modernization produces increased material wealth for the population. Improving standards of living produce the expectation of further improvements. This "revolution of rising expectations" increases the level of popular demands placed on regimes to continue to produce material benefits. Where the distribution of wealth is uneven, inequality itself produces demands for greater equality.

The social foundation of this process is the spread of education; at first, simple literacy, but at later stages of modernization, specialized higher education. With increasing education come new values and increasing demands upon the political order from the population; demands for greater personal freedom, greater political liberty, increased material prosperity, and a more egalitarian society. Such established mechanisms of social control as churches, trade unions, and schools lose their effectiveness, and the regime is compelled to create new bases for its legitimacy. If it is to do so, a regime must deal with the most central issue in political development: the institutionalization of popular participation. Political parties represent the most widespread agencies not only for *mobilizing* participation, but for *institutionalizing* it, as well.[11]

---

[10]For a summary of the political challenges inherent in the modernization process, see Leonard Binder, "The Crises of Political Development" in Leonard Binder et al., *Crises and Sequences in Political Development* (Princeton, N.J.: Princeton University Press, 1971), pp. 3–72.

[11]For an extensive treatment of the institutionalization of participation, see Samuel P. Huntington, *Political Order in Changing Societies* (New Haven, Conn.: Yale University Press, 1968).

The Organization of Rights

Individual rights have traditionally been defined as individual claims *against* the state. Originally they were the claims against absolutist monarchies: freedom to think, to worship, to form associations, to be immune from arrests, to have the right to a fair trial, to be presumed innocent until found guilty. However, since World War II, claims *for* services—especially claims for health services, welfare arrangements, education, and employment—have also come to be regarded as rights. In this case, people expect these services to be provided by the government. They feel that they are entitled to them. The first are, strictly speaking, referred to as *individual rights* or civil rights; the second, inasmuch as they involve groups and the provision of material and economic services for them, are referred to as *social rights*. Finally, there are also *political rights*: to vote, run for office, or organize political associations and political parties. Political regimes vary in their relative emphasis on individual rights, social rights, and political rights. Some emphasize all three; others, one or two. But few regimes fail to pay attention to any. The particular protections they provide and the values that are attached to them are a matter for empirical study of particular political regimes.

Political Regimes: Two Major Models

In all political regimes there is constant flux in the relationship between command, consent, interests, and rights. We have sketched out the elements of a political regime in Figure 1.1. There is a constant interaction and tension between the various groupings and associations and the command structure. Relationships among the executive, the administration, the legislature, and the judiciary also shift and change. In

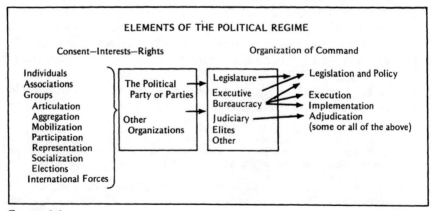

FIGURE 1.1

democratic regimes, "presidential government" and "congressional government" may alternate over time. In one period "the party is king"; in another, "the party is over." Legislative supremacy may give place to cabinet supremacy; political leaders may be replaced by so-called experts or "technocrats." In nondemocratic regimes, an autocrat may give way to collective leadership, or political parties may grow in importance as popular support wanes. In every regime, political institutions gain or lose autonomy in their relationships with social, economic, or other organizations. The role of the army, the party, the state, the trade unions, the clergy, and other institutions may change. In democratic regimes, the influence over decision makers exerted by political associations and groupings—lobbies, single-issue associations, political action committees, and others—waxes and wanes, depending on the issues involved, the amount of popular support they can mobilize, and even the personal convictions of the decision makers themselves. Even in nondemocratic regimes there may be a wide variation in the range of participation by groups, associations, and institutions, in the level of popular support and consent, and even in the organization of rights.

All we can do, therefore, is identify the predominant institutional patterns and relationships that distinguish major regime "types." In a changing world, particular attention must be paid to the boundaries between types: How much change must take place before one type of regime is transformed into another? We shall do so in terms of the four basic categories we set forth above: the organization of *command*, the organization of *consent*, the configuration of *interests*, and the organization of *rights*.

Democratic vs. Authoritarian

In this book we focus on two major types of political regimes: democratic and authoritarian. They correspond to major descriptive generalizations based on the criteria set forth, i.e., the different ways in which command, consent, interests, and rights are organized. In doing so, we shall be defining the relationship between the state and society in each.

Our descriptive generalizations reach out to identify only general characteristics, not detailed profiles. As we will see, there are significant variations from one democratic regime to another, and there are a great variety of authoritarian regimes. One type of authoritarian regime will be given separate and more detailed, treatment: the totalitarian regime. Although the totalitarian regimes seem to be approaching extinction rapidly, the differences between them and other authoritarian regimes are especially important. For the amelioration of totalitarianism would appear to be a prerequisite for the eventual democratization of such regimes.

The Democratic Model

In democratic theory (and, to varying degrees, in democratic regimes) there is a sharp distinction made between state and society. The basic assumption is that in society individuals are free, rational, independent entities, born with inalienable rights to life, liberty, and property. Individuals seek fulfillment in religious, artistic, economic, and many other forms of expression, and the state permits the existence of outlets for achieving these aspirations. Relations among individuals and the associations they form are based on equality: there is no subordination of one to another. Since associations and groups are freely formed and remain free and independent of each other, they denote a pluralistic pattern, allowing a great variety of forms of expression. Morality and the "good life" are what individuals decide they are; people pursue their own interests. They are each armed with a little pocket calculator, so to speak, figuring out what is pleasurable and good (in the most material but also in the loftiest sense of those words) and what is painful or bad, pursuing the one and avoiding the other without any outside interference.

According to this liberal democratic model, the state—the command structure—has one single narrow function: to preserve order. It has the right to use force but only to prevent violence and to provide us the opportunity to "do our thing." The state has no overriding ethical purpose. It cannot decide what is true or false, moral or immoral. Individuals, as members of the society, consent to form a state when they agree to set up a constitution that spells out the organization of the state, the limits of its power, and the rights to be preserved. After they have set up a constitution that defines the organization of individual rights and sets limits to state action, they return to their pursuits in society with the knowledge and the guarantee that they will be able to live in peace and tranquility.

This democratic model stacks the cards on the side of the individuals and the associations they voluntarily form, which represent the creative forces of progress and change. The state is their creature, dependent upon society for its existence and limited by the established rules. Thus, while society is *independent* of the state, the state is *dependent* upon society. The individual is sacred; the state is a necessary evil, like an insurance policy we take against the many hazards that confront us.

Despite many profound and radical social and economic changes that have accounted for drastic reconsiderations of this model, it still remains the true one for most liberal and democratic regimes. Institutional arrangements continue to safeguard individual rights and the pluralism of groups and interests. The political "rules of the game" distinguish sharply between what belongs to the state (and comes under the purview of its activities) and what belongs to individuals, including their free and spontaneous world of social life. Democracy from liberalism to socialism has continued to emphasize (despite growing interdependencies between the state and society and the growing scope of state action, especially in the economy, the *separateness* between the state and society.

A democracy limits the power of its decision makers. First of all, the command structure is ordered in such a way that the decision makers cannot make arbitrary decisions; they are bound by an established legal order. The element of separateness that we just mentioned ensures that the political power given to the decision makers will be a *limited* power. Second, those who occupy the command structure are held responsible for their decisions. They can tax and they can drop an atom bomb, but they will be held *accountable* for what they do. Periodic and free elections, among many other mechanisms, institutionalize this accountability.

The Authoritarian Model

Authoritarianism and the various forms of authoritarian regimes continue to be an expression of the oldest and, some would say, the most corrupt aspect of political life: rule by force. In fact, authoritarianism is a catch-all name for political regimes that we are all more or less familiar with: autocracy, tyranny, satrapy, dictatorship, absolutism, bonapartism, despotism, military rule, junta, oligarchy, "political bossism," theocracy, and even outright gangsterism. They all provide for command arrangements that concentrate power and force in the hands of one or a few leaders who rule without much regard for the organization of consent, with little or no regard for the organization of interests, and needless to say, without respect for individual rights.

Thus, the authoritarian model advances a diametrically different view of the relationship between the state and society (individuals, groups, and associations) than the democratic one. The command structure—and all the means through which it is organized and through which it manifests itself—is controlled by a political elite, to the exclusion of all others. In its most extreme form, the state dominates society. It constrains initiative, it defines what is true and what is false, it establishes official organizations to control all social activities: economic, cultural, religious, even familial. In some instances this control is exercised directly, in others it is exercised through a single political party. Table 1.1 summarizes the differences between authoritarian and democratic regimes.

In this way, authoritarian regimes manipulate and determine the organization of interest, the organization of consent, and the organization of rights. In its most extreme form, the authoritarian regimes makes individuals, groups, and associations "march in step" for the attainment of a prearranged purpose. In some authoritarian regimes (which we

TABLE 1.1   Authoritarian and Democratic Regimes

	AUTHORITARIAN	DEMOCRATIC
1. Limitation on command structure	Little to none	Many
2. Effective responsibility	None	Considerable to great
3. Organization of command structure:		
State	Yes	State and state agencies
Bureaucracy/military	Yes	Subordinate
Individual leader	Yes	Collective/elections
Police, force, intimidation	Yes	Subordinate
4. "Penetration" (inclusiveness) of society by political organs*	Complete to selective	Limited
5. Mobilization for supports*	Induced/variable	Spontaneous
6. Official ideology*	Varies in strength and mobilization	Weak
7. Parties*	Single or none	Many
8. Individual rights (protection)	Virtually none	Yes

*It is primarily with regard to *penetration* of the society, *mobilization* of supports (through the single party) and the *official ideology* that distinctions have been made between *authoritarian* and *totalitarian* regimes. The essence of totalitarianism lies precisely in the full penetration and mobilization of the society in the name of an official ideology disseminated and imposed through the single party; many authoritarian regimes—especially dynastic and military regimes—fail to do so.

identify as totalitarian), there is a high level of *social mobilization* aimed at creating popular support. But in most authoritarian regimes there is no attempt to mobilize the population. In fact, the authoritarian leader and his supporters attempt to prevent the populace from becoming too active; they seek to protect and perpetuate the status quo. They are satisfied to rule a passive and obedient populace over which they hold the instruments of force: the army, the secret police, the tax collector and, not infrequently, the economy.

Bibliography

Almond, Gabriel, and Sidney Verba. *The Civic Culture.* Princeton, N.J.: Princeton University Press, 1963.

Almond, Gabriel, and G. Bingham Powell. *Comparative Politics: System, Process and Policy.* Boston: Little, Brown, 1981.

Apter, David. *Introduction to Political Analysis*. Cambridge, Mass.: Winthrop/Boston: Little, Brown, 1982.

Bill, James A., and Robert L. Hardgrave, Jr. *Comparative Politics: The Quest for Theory*. Lanham, Md.: University Press of America, 1982.

Blondel, Jean. *World Leaders: Heads of Government in the Postwar Period*. Beverly Hills, Calif.: Sage Publications, 1980.

————. *Comparative Political Institutions*. New York: Praeger, 1973.

Davis, Morton R., and Vaughan A. Lewis. *Model of Political System*. New York: Praeger, 1971.

Easton, David. *A Framework for Political Analysis*. Chicago: University of Chicago Press, 1979.

Eckstein, Harry, and David Apter. *Comparative Politics: A Reader*. Glencoe, Ill.: The Free Press, 1963.

Finer, Samuel H. *Comparative Government*. London: Penguin Books, 1970.

Friedrich, Carl J. *Man and His Government: An Empirical Theory of Politics*. New York: McGraw-Hill, 1963.

Holt, Robert T., and John E. Turner. *The Methodology of Comparative Research*. New York: The Free Press, 1970.

Macridis, Roy, and Bernard Brown (eds.). *Comparative Politics: Notes and Readings*. 7th ed. Belmont, Calif.: Brooks/Cole Publishing Co., Wadsworth Inc., 1990.

Mahler, Gregory S. *Comparative Politics: An Institutional and Cross-National Approach*. Cambridge, Mass.: Shenkman Publishers, 1983.

Michels, Robert. *Political Parties: A Sociological Study of Oligarchical Tendencies in Modern Democracies*. (Originally published in German in 1911); rpt. London: Macmillan, 1962.

Mosca, Gaetano. *The Ruling Class*. Trans. by Hannah Kahn. Westport, Conn.: Greenwood Press, 1980.

Putnam, Robert D. *The Comparative Study of Political Elites*. Englewood Cliffs, N.J.: Prentice-Hall, 1976.

Taylor, C. C., and O. A. Jodich. *World Handbook of Politics and Social Indicators*. New Haven, Conn.: Yale University Press, 1983.

Tilly, Charles (ed.). *The Formation of Nation States in Western Europe*. Princeton, N.J.: Princeton University Press, 1975.

Part Two

Democratic Regimes

Introduction

Writing some seventy years ago, Lord Bryce saw in democracy a form of government compatible with "human nature," moving gradually but inexorably onward in the countries of the "civilized world" and beyond.[1] Yet, not more than thirty-five political regimes qualified in the 1980s as genuinely democratic. Only in recent years has a strong movement in the direction of democracy once again appeared in Latin America, Southern Europe, and Asia. Even in Eastern Europe, the Soviet Union, and China, democratic aspirations seem to be stirring among peoples long subjected to authoritarian and totalitarian rule. Broken and delayed as it may have been since Bryce wrote, the "march" in the direction of democracy may be on again. The end of the century may coincide with the triumph of democracy.

"Democracy" literally means "government of the people." It consists of the fundamental political equality and participation of all individuals in the political process and guaranteed individual freedom. Democratic regimes are characterized by free competition for political power among autonomous and organized groups arising spontaneously out of society. This competition is carried out through political parties

[1]Bryce, *Modern Democracies* (New York: The Macmillan Co., 1924).

and open elections that determine the relative popular support of each competitor. Those who win this competition, however, remain accountable to the entire electorate.

Constitutional Order

The two basic premises of democracy are the establishment of *limitations* on the state and its agencies and the *responsibility* of ruling elites to the people at large. Limitations are always procedural and often substantive as well. *Procedural* limitations relate to the manner in which the powers of the state are exercised, i.e., how certain things are done. *Substantive* limitations relate to specific issues, such as individual or associational rights that are considered beyond the jurisdiction of the state. They are "things that the state cannot do." Responsibility is a far more elastic concept. It is the holding of officials accountable, politically or legally, for their acts. It is associated with an independent judiciary, representative government and, of course, competitive elections.

In democratic regimes both limitations and responsibility are set forth in broad outlines in a constitution. All democracies operate under a set of rules agreed upon and generally accepted by the people. Constitutions define the ends and limits of government and the means, the processes, and procedures through which they will be attained. A constitution is the fundamental law in the sense that its violation will be sanctioned by courts or by other means.[2]

In virtually all democracies, constitutions are written documents.[3] But they are always qualified or modified by conventions, understandings, and judicial interpretations. Thus, the United States Constitution can hardly be understood without going over the interpretations and reinterpretations of the Supreme Court. England, on the other hand, has no formal written document that we can call a constitution, except for some basic enactments of Parliament that provide for individual rights and the organization of governmental powers. France, in contrast, has had many written constitutions. The most recent one is the constitution of 1958, which established the current regime, the Fifth Republic. Most of the democracies established in the Mediterranean and the Third World have promulgated constitutional documents.

In every constitution there is a statement about individual rights. The first ten amendments to the U.S. Constitution that were adopted along with the original document, as well as the thirteenth, fourteenth, and fifteenth amendments, list rights of individual or associational life

---

[2]On representation, limitations, and responsibility, see Carl J. Friedrich, *Constitutional Government and Democracy*, 4th ed. (Waltham, Mass.: Ginn & Blaisdell, 1968).
[3]For some constitutional texts and an introduction to the characteristics of the unwritten English constitutional arrangements, see Samuel H. Finer, *Five Constitutions: Contrasts and Comparisons* (London: Penguin Books, 1981).

that cannot be impaired or invaded by government. The same is true of the French Declaration of the Rights of Man, which dates back to 1789 and which has been incorporated in all subsequent French republican constitutions (First, Second, Third, Fourth, and Fifth Republics), and in virtually all other European democratic constitutions. Today most political regimes have endorsed the United Nations Universal Declaration of Human Rights (1949).

Organization of Power

If constitutions spell out individual rights, they also organize and structure the political regime. Aristotle defined a constitution (the supreme law) as the "ordering of the commonwealth"—the command structure, linked with the organization of supports and consent. All democratic constitutions assign specific roles and powers to various organs and define them with regard to the powers and roles of the others. The major roles, functions, and powers of the political system are apportioned among three types of institutions: executive, legislative, and judicial. In some democratic constitutions, specific groups such as political parties, the military, or economic councils are allotted a share of the power to make decisions or to participate in the process by which decisions are made.

Generally speaking, a constitution implicitly or explicitly establishes a hierarchy of powers. In most democratic regimes the people hold sovereign power, delegating it to their elected representatives under specific conditions. In Britain, for example, the Parliament is supreme and all other powers are subordinate to it. In France, the situation is less clear: for some matters the National Assembly is supreme; for others it is the president of the Republic; and there are some matters that can only be decided authoritatively by the people in a referendum. In the United States the executive, legislative, and judicial institutions comprise three separate "branches" of government. Each branch checks, or limits, the powers of the others, even at the risk of a stalemate. Only one institution has the power to resolve all conflicts authoritatively, as well as interpret the contemporary meaning of the Constitution itself: the Supreme Court. In no other country does the judiciary enjoy as much authority and power as in the United States. But the practice of judicial review has been gaining strength—notably in France, the German Federal Republic, and other European countries.

Responsibility

It is not enough to organize governmental institutions, apportion the functions of the political system and the powers of the state among them, and structure their relations. It is necessary to make sure that the people who occupy the roles assigned to them will operate according to the rules and will perform their tasks in the manner the constitution sets forth. Since the beginning of the nineteenth century, those who have had legislative or executive power—presidents or prime ministers, and their subordinates—have been held responsible to elected representative assemblies and to the people as a whole. In presidential systems, the president must answer directly to the people through periodic elections. It is only under very special circumstances, for breaking the law or treason, that the president can be removed from office by the legislature or special courts. In all parliamentary regimes, which include most of the contemporary democracies, the prime minister faces the same constraints and is directly responsible to the legislature, which can turn his government out of office at any time by means of a vote of "no confidence," and at election time to the people as a whole.

In summary, a constitution defines rights, organizes the structure of command, and sets specific limitations on the major organs of government by establishing in various ways the responsibility and accountability of officeholders to freely elected representative assemblies (whose members are themselves responsible to their constituents) and, ultimately, to the people.

In this part we shall discuss contemporary democratic regimes in terms of the basic categories we have set forth: the organization of command in Chapter 2, the organization of consent—participation, political parties, elections, and voters—in Chapters 3 and 4, and the configuration of interests and organization of individual rights in Chapter 5.

2

The Democratic Organization of Command

Introduction

The command structure comprises the many officials, elected and appointed, organized in numerous agencies, who have the power to make decisions and to implement them. They issue "commands" in the form of laws, executive orders, rules, and regulations. They have the power to send the army abroad, to use force at home, to tax, and to spend money. These are awesome powers, which appear to be antithetical to individual and associational freedoms. In order to preserve these freedoms, democratic regimes develop explicit rules of responsibility and accountability. They also limit the powers of the command structure as a whole: They build dams and fences and obstacles to their exercise. "Liberty," wrote Thomas Hobbes, is "power cut up in pieces."

In democracies, as in no other political regimes, the command structure is carefully circumscribed and meticulously surrounded by institutional safeguards against those who trespass into areas of decision making outside their allotted field or who attempt to use short cuts in making decisions. This is what makes our discussion of the command structure in democratic regimes both difficult and fascinating. It is almost as if the combined ingenuity of every person writing about democracy or living in a democracy or preparing a democratic constitution was applied to avert the possibility that some officeholders would abuse the office and the powers associated with it. James Madison wrote that "if men were angels no government would be necessary. If angels were to govern men, neither external nor internal controls on government would be necessary."[1] Because we are not angels and because we do need a government, democratic regimes are characterized by stringent efforts to keep the devils out, or, if they sneak in, to make it impossible for them to prevail.

The Executive Branch

In almost all democratic regimes, there are two basic ways of organizing the executive branch: the presidential form and the parliamentary form, often referred to as cabinet government. A few democratic regimes combine some of the characteristics of a presidential system with those of a parliamentary system, as is particularly the case with the French constitution of the Fifth Republic. The prototypes we will discuss (because they are the oldest form of presidential and parliamentary governments) are the United States and England, respectively. We shall also examine the characteristics of the French "semi-presidential" system.

Cabinet Government[2]

In parliamentary regimes, the legislature makes the laws, controls the finances, appoints and dismisses the prime minister and his fellow ministers (the cabinet), and debates public issues. Parliament is supreme. Yet, because of the development of strong and disciplined parties and the support they give to their leaderships, the relationship between executive and legislative institutions has changed over time. It is the cabinet that now initiates legislation and makes policy. Government measures (government bills) have precedence over any other business and their passage is virtually a formality. The majority party in the legislature votes for the measure proposed by its leadership, i.e., the prime minister and the cabinet. The opposition party or parties are given time to criticize. But after the allotted time for debate has been spent, only a few days at most, a vote in favor of the government bill invariably follows.

Thus the parliamentary regime has in fact become transformed into a cabinet government, wherein the leadership of the majority party and its leader, the prime minister, control the command structure. As Walter Bagehot wrote, "The . . . secret of the English constitution may be

[1]James Madison, *The Federalist Papers*, no. 51, edited by Clinton Rossiter (New York: New American Library, 1961), p. 322.
[2]The classic statement of the cabinet government is Walter Bagehot, *The English Constitution* (Oxford: Oxford University Press, 1936), originally published in 1867.

described as the close union, the nearly complete fusion, of the executive and the legislative powers. . . . *The connecting link is the Cabinet.*"[3] The supremacy of the legislative institution has become transformed into the supremacy of the executive in a manner that even an American president would covet. But in order for this type of command structure to be established and maintained, certain conditions must obtain:

1. The political parties must be well disciplined; their members in Parliament must vote as one. Cross-voting, or voting with the opposition against one's own party and government, must be the exception.
2. The parties must be few in number. Parliamentary regimes with many political parties often fail to provide strong and stable cabinet government, since there will tend to be no clear majority to support it, unless (as notably in the Scandinavian democracies) a broad consensus develops within which parties cooperate and manage to form and support stable coalitions.
3. The right to dissolve the Parliament and call for a new election must be given explicitly and unequivocally to the prime minister. It is a weapon that commands discipline.
4. The party that wins a majority in parliament must also win a majority of the popular vote, not a mere plurality. In a parliamentary majority based on a mere plurality of the popular vote, the effectiveness of the cabinet—the command structure—may become weakened. People will dispute its right to act as if it represented the majority.
5. Finally, to preserve the rights of the minority, as well as a continuing commitment to democratic procedure, it is expected that neither one of the major parties will retain a majority and, therefore, control over parliament and government for too long a time. In any democratic regime, permanent minority status will tend to erode the commitment of the minority to democratic procedure. In most parliamentary regimes, the major parties, or party blocs, alternate in office.

The Organization of the Cabinet   Over time the cabinet and the prime minister have emerged as quasi-independent policy-making institutions. Furthermore, the prime ministership itself has become institutionalized: it has become a complex but adaptable institution comprising bureaucratic agencies that give to it a structure with an identity separate from the cabinet's. At the same time, the cabinet as a whole has grown more complex with the development of cabinet committees and specialized coordinative, information, and research agencies designed to assist the prime minister and cabinet in the formulation and coordination of policies. One source of the power of the prime ministership is its control over the agenda of the cabinet meetings and cabinet committees.

[3]Bagehot, *The English Constitution*, p. 67.

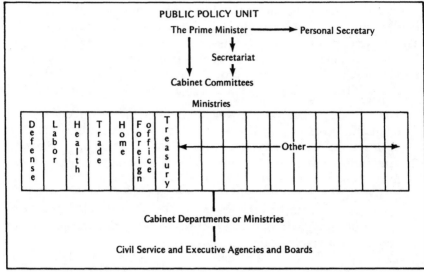

FIGURE 2.1

The power of prime minister and cabinet has been further reinforced by the development of a cabinet secretariat.[4] The secretariat is an office composed of a group of high-ranking civil servants attached to the cabinet, whose duties are to keep minutes of the cabinet meetings, coordinate the work of the cabinet committees, record and communicate the decisions taken, help the prime minister prepare the agenda for the cabinet meetings, and circulate the agenda to the cabinet members in advance of the meetings. It also provides the prime minister and the cabinet members with information to assist the prime minister in supervising the implementation of policy. (See Figure 2.1.)

The Chancellor in the Parliamentary Regime of the FRG

How to reconcile strong executive leadership with democratic and parliamentary institutions was the major preoccupation of the framers of the Basic Law (the constitution) of the Federal Republic of Germany (FRG), which was expected, at the time it came into force in 1949, to apply eventually to a reunified Germany. The framers had two precedents in mind: that of the Weimar Republic (1918–1933) and Hitler's later (1933–1945) authoritarian rule. The Weimar Republic combined a strong presidency directly elected by the people with a prime minister (chancellor) and a cabinet holding office at the pleasure of the legislature

[4]See Samuel H. Beer, *The British Political System* (New York: Random House, 1974), chap. 2, especially pp. 39–40.

(the Reichstag). An extreme proportional electoral system allowing for the representation of minuscule parties made it impossible for majorities to be formed. Hence there were constant cabinet crises and short-lived coalitions that could not govern; the result was the increasing appeal to presidential prerogatives and emergency powers that ultimately facilitated Hitler's coming to power and his centralizing, authoritarian governance. How to maintain the democratic principles and practices of Weimar while removing the authoritarian elements and electoral mechanisms that had paved the way for Hitler was the major task for the framers of the Basic Law.

The answer was to (1) strip the president of all personal prerogatives and powers and provide for a small electoral college for his election so that he could not pretend to speak on behalf of a popular majority; (2) attempt to eliminate the sources of multipartisanship by tightening the electoral system to make it impossible for parties with less than 5 percent of the vote to win any seats; and (3) to strengthen the position of the prime minister (the chancellor). *Kanzeldemokratie* was the term used to denote a strong chancellor within a democratic and parliamentary institutional context. The chancellor can be nominated only by an absolute majority in the lower house, the Bundestag. The first one—some say the greatest chancellor thus far—Konrad Adenauer, was nominated by a margin of one vote! Once elected, a chancellor cannot be overthrown unless an absolute majority votes against him on the question of confidence and votes also for his successor.[5] In this manner, cabinet crises, so frequent in the Weimar Republic, have been avoided. The stability of the chancellor and the cabinet have been the highest among the democratic regimes in Western Europe: six chancellors between 1949 and 1990, as opposed to nine prime ministers in England between 1945 and 1990, and ten prime ministers in France under the Fifth Republic (1958–1990). (See Figure 2.2.)

Endorsed by a majority the chancellor and his cabinet govern with the support of Parliament. Thanks to the changes in the electoral system, the number of parties have been reduced. There are two major parties—the Social Democrats and the Christian Democrats—and until the early eighties, only one "third" party—the Free Democrats (Liberals), with about 8 to 12 percent of the vote. More recently, a fourth party, the Greens, has emerged and gained strength; and in the last few years an extreme right-wing party, the Republicans, has also surfaced, gaining 7 percent of the vote in the European election of June 1989. Thus far, the Liberals have allied themselves sometimes with the Christian Democrats and sometimes with the Social Democrats to participate in and support a cabinet.

---

[5]It happened only once. In 1982 the Free Democrats split from the coalition they had formed with the Social Democrats and voted against the chancellor, Helmut Schmidt.

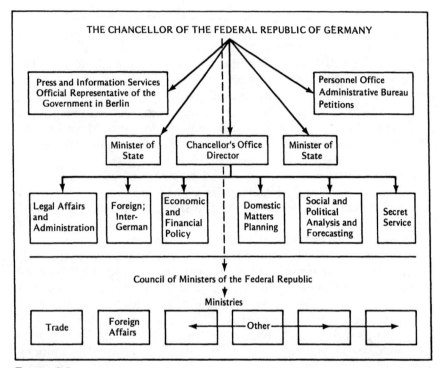

THE CHANCELLOR OF THE FEDERAL REPUBLIC OF GERMANY

Press and Information Services Official Representative of the Government in Berlin

Personnel Office Administrative Bureau Petitions

Minister of State

Chancellor's Office Director

Minister of State

Legal Affairs and Administration

Foreign; Inter-German

Economic and Financial Policy

Domestic Matters Planning

Social and Political Analysis and Forecasting

Secret Service

Council of Ministers of the Federal Republic

Ministries

Trade

Foreign Affairs

Other

FIGURE 2.2

The Bundestag remains a strong legislative body. Investigating committees scrutinize the activities of the cabinet and its ministers and play an important role in initiating and amending legislation and budgetary matters. The system has increasingly developed in the direction of the British cabinet system. Federalism and judicial review institutionalize strong constraints against governmental authority. With the prospects of German reunification, it is expected that the Basic Law will become the constitution of a reunited Germany and the institutions and practices of the FRG will assure a stable, strong, but also responsible governmental authority with strong representative assemblies and respect for individual freedoms.

Presidential Regimes

In all presidential regimes the president is at the top of a vast and sprawling executive institution with special and personal powers. In the United States, these powers derive directly from the Constitution and from the fact of the president's election by the people.[6] According to the Constitution, the president is:

[6]The classic statement on the powers of the presidency is Edwin S. Corwin, *The President: Office and Powers*, 5th rev. ed. (New York: New York University Press, 1984).

1. *Commander-in-Chief.* He (or she) is responsible for the preparedness of the armed forces, their equipment, their strategy, and their use.
2. *Foreign Policy Negotiator.* The president establishes the broad objectives of the nation's foreign policies in time of war or peace.
3. *Manager-in-Chief.* The president's constitutional obligation to see that the laws are faithfully executed places him in control of the administrative apparatus of the federal government. It is for the president to make certain that everything in the executive branch is being done efficiently and expeditiously, but also legally.
4. *Party Leader.* The president automatically becomes the leader of the political party under whose label he was elected. He is, therefore, a partisan figure, responsible for the party program and concerned with the party's political welfare and electoral strength.
5. *Spokesman of the Public Interest.* Although formally elected *indirectly* by the electoral college, the president is effectively elected directly by the people as a whole and is the only governmental official responsible to the whole electorate. This fact provides him with the basis for political leadership. The president, when he chooses to do so, can claim to speak on behalf of the nation and act in accordance with what he considers the national interest. He is able to invoke his status as representative of a national constituency, while the people's elected representatives in the House and the Senate represent only local and state interests. This gives the president considerable leverage over political opponents in the legislative branch. But to the extent that the president also acts as partisan leader of his party, he weakens this leverage. Thus, these two roles, national and political, are usually in conflict.
6. *Broker of Ideas and Policies.* Presidential pronouncements and policies attract public attention. By virtue of the attention devoted to presidential activity in the national media, a president can focus national attention on issues of his own choosing. He can marshal opinion in one direction or another, mobilize public support, and orchestrate the expression of consent.

The Organization of the Presidency

In the last fifty years or so the presidential structure has grown as rapidly as the policy-making functions of the presidency. Figure 2.3 reflects the formal organizational structures under the control of the president. The president is at the very top of the executive branch with his own office, the executive office of the president. He is assisted by a personal staff, the White House office. The executive office consists of a number of agencies and committees that guide, regulate, and supervise the various departments or act directly on his behalf. Some provide research and information, others coordinate and decide on major poli-

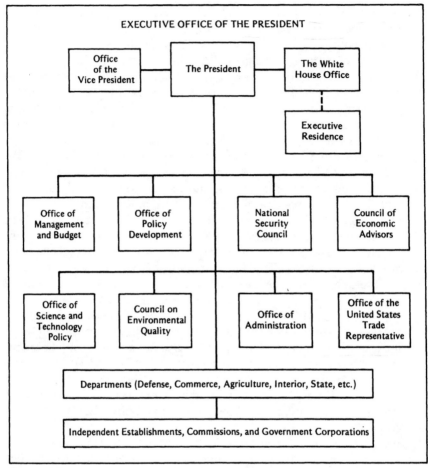

FIGURE 2.3

cies and provide the major policy guidelines. They all speak *to* the president, but more frequently they speak *for* him. They have become semi-autonomous executive bodies, a division of labor and of tasks, that no president could ever fully control. An enormous delegation of responsibility is therefore implicit in the structure of the presidency and the offices it comprises.

The Semi-Presidential, Semi-Parliamentary Regime

The framers of the constitution of France's Fifth Republic (endorsed on September 28, 1958) sought to redress the two major problems that had afflicted French republican regimes in the past: an all-powerful legislature and an executive (the prime minister and the cabinet) that lacked stability and autonomous powers. In fact, the executive was dominated by the legislature. In order to eliminate these two problems, the French introduced an independent and strong presidential component, reinforced the powers of the prime minister and the cabinet, and reduced those of Parliament. The French constitution is thus both presidential and parliamentary.[7]

The Presidential Sector

The French president today holds supreme executive power. He is no longer only the symbolic head of the state; he embodies executive leadership. He is given personal and discretionary powers that no other president holds in any presidential system, even in the United States. He can dissolve the legislature at any time for any reason and call for an election; he can submit proposals to a referendum and, if the proposal is accepted by the electorate, it supersedes existing legislation; he can appoint and remove the prime minister and has broad appointive and dismissal powers over all cabinet ministers and top officials in the army and civil service; he formulates the broad policy guidelines that the prime minister and the cabinet must follow; he is in charge of foreign policy and defense and conducts negotiations himself; he presides over the meetings of the council of ministers. Under certain circumstances, he has the power to declare a state of siege and to govern by executive order. He is elected directly by the people for a seven-year term and is eligible to seek an additional seven-year term. Direct popular elections entitle him to speak on behalf of a national constituency, and he cannot be removed by the legislature. He cannot even be impeached. He can be tried by a special tribunal only if he has committed treason or criminal acts defined by the Criminal Code.

The Prime Minister and the Cabinet

In addition to the presidency, there is also a cabinet led by a prime minister. According to the constitution, the prime minister "determines and conducts the policy of the Nation and is responsible before the Parliament." Special recognition is accorded to the prime minister. He "determines the policy of the nation." He "assures the execution of the laws and exercises the rule-making power." He determines the composition of his cabinet, presides over its meetings, and directs the administrative and executive agencies of government. He defends his policy before the parliament, answers questions addressed to him by its members, states the overall program of the government in special program-

[7]The best discussion of the constitution of the French Fifth Republic is Jean-Louis Quermonne, *Le Gouvernement de la France sous la 5ième République*, 2d ed. (Paris: Dalloz, 1983).

matic declarations, and in general governs as long as he and the cabinet enjoy the confidence of a majority in the National Assembly (the lower house of the legislature).

Thus, this semi-presidential, semi-parliamentary regime divides its executive into two parts: the major part is the presidency, the lesser one is the cabinet. The cabinet is the creature of the president, executing his major policy guidelines: financial, economic, social, strategic, and foreign policy. Any disagreement between the prime minister and the president is resolved quickly, as has been the case a number of times, with the resignation of the prime minister and the nomination of his successor by the president.

Presidential Dominance

The French regime has evolved increasingly in the direction of presidential dominance. The president decides on policy issues without consulting his prime minister and cabinet. The "office of the presidency" is staffed with experts who elaborate and make policy and through whom the president directs the activities of the ministries. He meets with the cabinet not to reach collective decisions but to hear views before deciding himself. The president has also assumed an increasingly larger political role: he has intervened actively in legislative elections by asking the people to vote for his supporters—his party—in order to gain a majority.

The dominance of the presidency has been translated into the growing institutionalization of the office along lines similar to that of the American presidency. As shown in Figure 2.4, within the Elysée (the equivalent of the White House), the French president disposes of a personal staff, technical advisers, his own cabinet, and a large number of people in the general secretariat through which the ministries, the agencies of economic planning, the nationalized industries, welfare and social security services, employment, and defense and foreign affairs come under presidential scrutiny. Policy originates at the Elysée and the president has the authority and the means to check that his policy is implemented by the prime minister, the cabinet, and all subordinate governmental agencies.

F2.4

While encouraged by the provisions of the constitution, presidential dominance has come about primarily because of extra-constitutional and political reasons. Since the inception of the 1958 constitution, coherent, comprehensive, and disciplined political parties have developed in France. Ultimately the Gaullists and their allies stood on one side and the Socialists and their allies on the other to form a two-party bloc system. For almost twenty-five years the Gaullists dominated the legislature and supported the prime minister and the cabinet appointed by "their" president. The president's government enjoyed majority support in the National Assembly. In 1981, the political winds shifted, but

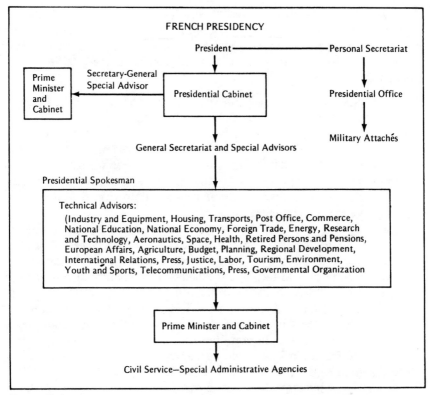

FIGURE 2.4

the powers of the presidency remained. The Socialist candidate won the presidency, and he immediately dissolved the National Assembly and called for an election by which a Socialist majority was returned in the National Assembly. This majority supported the new president and his prime minister and cabinet. A deadlock between a newly elected president and the legislature was thus averted through the mechanism of dissolution.

The political dominance of the presidency and the president was eroded as a result of the 1986 legislative election. The Socialists and their allies were defeated, depriving President Mitterrand of majority support in the National Assembly. The legislative majority came into the hands of the center-right parties, forcing the president to designate their leader, Jacques Chirac, as prime minister. A period of "cohabitation" followed, with the prime minister, supported by a majority in the National Assembly, and the president representing rival party blocs. The second and even more severe blow was what amounted to the president's defeat in the legislative elections of June 1988. President Mitterrand won an impressive victory and a reelection as President of the Republic in May. But after dissolving the assembly and calling new elections in the hope of electing a Socialist majority, his party fell short by a handful of deputies. The dissolution mechanism thus failed in this instance. However, the constitutional provisions allow the prime minister and the cabinet to govern and even legislate as long as there is no majority *against* them, even if there is no majority *for* them. Two of these provisions follow.

1. The prime minister can put the question of confidence on his legislative texts. They can be rejected or amended only if a motion of censure is introduced and is passed by an absolute majority of the National Assembly—289 votes. The text becomes law *unless there is an absolute majority against it*. This procedure has been used a number of times to enact important legislative matters; e.g., nationalizations and privatizations and electoral reform. Both Socialist and Conservative prime ministers have used it.

2. The prime minister can ask the National Assembly for authorization (article 38) to legislate by executive order *(ordonnance)* on certain matters. He does so by asking for the enactment of a "framework law" to be implemented by *ordonnances*. If the National Assembly is unwilling to oblige, then the prime minister will combine his request with the question of confidence. The only way for the National Assembly to reject the law of authorization, therefore, would be to introduce and pass a motion of censure, as described above. Otherwise, the framework law will be passed, and the *ordonnance* issued and signed by the President of the Republic will have the force of law. In short, as long as there is no absolute majority in the National Assembly to overthrow the prime minister, he and the president can govern.

The French semi-presidential system appears more flexible than the American, and thanks to it, its parliamentary component is more responsive to the majority of the electorate. However, what if a legislative majority is elected that is opposed to the President of the Republic? Will the president be able to defy a hostile majority in the legislature, or will he submit to it? Will the regime be able to overcome and survive a prolonged deadlock, as the American regime has learned to do? Is it possible to envisage a long "cohabitation" between an incumbent president and a hostile majority in the legislature—so common in the United States—or will a confrontation between the two become unavoidable?

Presidentialism: Diffusion and Distortion

Presidential regimes have grown rapidly in a number of countries, and in some parliamentary regimes the position of the president has been strengthened. Many Latin American regimes have adopted, at least in form, the American presidential system. Virtually all the former French colonies copied the French semi-presidential constitution of 1958.

But the diffusion of the presidential form amounts also to its distortion. Conceived in the United States and much later in France to operate in the context of democracy and a two-party or multiparty system, it has been only too frequently used to accentuate the concentration of political power (often absolute power) at the expense of democratic institutions and individual liberties. For example, in Latin America "presidentialism" has been adopted by military dictatorships: the military leader who takes power simply proclaims himself president. Similarly, presidential government has been used in single-party regimes. Mexico is the best illustration of a presidential single-party regime: it has been in operation for over fifty years. In the former African colonies of France, presidential power has amounted to the concentration of power and arbitrary rule in the hands of one individual or, at best, a small group. Presidentialism has been used as a device to control the centrifugal forces, to mitigate fragmentation, and to provide for unifying symbols. It has functioned as an instrument of authoritarian governance rather than in the democratic context envisioned in the United States and in France. In only a few instances, such as Portugal, Austria, and Finland, have presidential or semi-presidential arrangements led to the consolidation of democracy. They may yet play the same role in Latin America and Africa, in some of the emerging democracies in Eastern Europe, and especially in the Soviet Union, where reforms to strengthen presidential power have been explicitly compared to the U.S. and French constitutions (see Chapter 8).

The Bureaucracy

Today, the bureaucracy is an essential part of the command structure in all developed societies, whatever the political regime. It has become institutionalized in well-organized, permanent organs that carry on the activities and services of the modern state, from defense to welfare and education. State bureaucracies comprise departments, regulatory agencies, commissions, bureaus, public corporations, and nationalized industries and employ a sizable portion of the work force. Contrary to the view that policy making is the job of elected and responsible officials and that the bureaucracy only implements and executes, the bureaucracy is an integral part of policy making, deliberation, and legislation. The operations of the bureaucracy cut across the major functions of government, legislative, executive, and judicial, and often integrate them into a functioning entity. The bureaucracy deliberates and legislates, organizes and represents interests, adjudicates conflicts, and has wide discretionary powers in the provision of services without which our rights would be seriously undermined. In terms of sheer presence and numbers, it overshadows all other organs of the state.

Policy Making

The distinction between those who implement policy (the bureaucrats) and those who make it (the political leaders in the executive branch or the legislature) is no longer tenable. In any democratic society, or for that matter in any other contemporary political regime, bureaucrats directly influence policy not only because of the information and advice they provide during the formulation of policies but also because the bureaucratic organizations and the civil servants manning them are explicitly empowered to make policy. They in fact legislate.

Legislation

Bureaucracies are among the most important rule-making organizations of the modern state. They can fix prices and wages, decide on social security adjustments, determine the rules on labeling products, allow or disallow the sale of drugs, regulate transportation and fix its rates, determine unemployment compensation benefits, and establish environmental rules and restrictions. In short, they set rules and standards that affect our everyday lives. This indeed covers a vast area of delegated or administrative rule making, and it involves discretion, judgment, initiative, and knowledge.

But that is not all. Quite frequently, legislation enacted by the legislature is itself initiated and/or prepared by the relevant bureaucratic organizations. It may include major legislative reforms, the reorganization of the civil service, the development of institutions and policies for economic planning, the reorganization of branches of the executive, the establishment of new ministries and departments, the development of national health insurance plans, the initiation of major energy policies, the reorganization of the foreign service, the setting of subsidies for industries and agriculture, and even the preparation of the budget. The expertise and training of the bureaucrats entitles them to receive special attention from the political leaders. In practice, the lines between policy making (formally entrusted to the latter) and policy implementation (for which the former are responsible) are very much blurred. As a result, there is one question that is constantly being raised about the nature of the bureaucracy: Is it representative?

Representation

Bureaucrats are not elected; they are appointed. They are not supposed to respond to constituencies of voters; they are supposed to serve the elected officials who are their political masters. As the leaders of executive agencies, they are not supposed to have their own policy commitments but are supposed simply to execute policies determined by others. They are not supposed to seek rewards beyond those that the recognition of loyal service (merit promotions and a good salary) entitles them to. They are supposed to be men and women who fulfill their obligations without regard to their private political passions and preferences.

These generalizations hardly apply to contemporary democracies. The distinction between what is *public* and what is *private* is no longer clear. Bureaucracies and private interests both have the same areas of concern. They have, in the words of Charles Merriam, common areas of "cooperation and cohesion in the common cause and on a common basis in many fields of common action."[8] Such cooperation and cohesion is nowhere seen more clearly than in the economic and social areas, where the bureaucracy and a host of private interests come together in the drafting and implementation of policy. Public officials and private interests that may be affected by decisions meet to discuss them. The proliferation of advisory bodies is the order of the day. The French Economic Plan, for example, consists of literally thousands of such committees, organized on both a territorial and a functional basis. In the United States, there are 1,500 advisory committees in the federal government. On every policy issue, discussions in the public bureaucracies of the modern democratic regimes will include representatives of private groups. There is an institutionalized dialogue in which either the civil service or the private sector takes the initiative. These advisory committees, and the participation they afford to organized social interests, give the bureaucracy a representative character.

Constituency Building "Constituency" usually refers to the territorial unit from which an individual representative in a legislature is elected. But bureaucratic organizations have their own constituencies as well. These consist of the organized interests with which the organization interacts through the regulation process. Bureaucratic organizations go out of their way to establish direct links with these interests, of which advisory committees are but one form. In fact, the strength of a given bureaucratic organization, as well as its effectiveness, depends on the relations it establishes with its interest constituency; and, equally to the point, the welfare of the interests involved depends in turn on the relationships they have established with the bureaucratic organization that regulates or serves them. Bureaucracies, therefore, represent and often organize interests. They speak for a given segment of the public and can claim a representative function just as legitimate and powerful as that of the legislature.

[8]Cited in Mark Nadel and Francis E. Rourke, "Bureaucracies," in Fred I. Greenstein and Nelson W. Polsby (eds.), *Handbook of Political Science*, vol. 5 (Reading, Mass.: Addison-Wesley, 1975), p. 407.

Thus, the bureaucracy overlaps with the legislature, the executive, and the judiciary. It initiates and makes policy; it represents and speaks for a great variety of interests; it integrates interests and makes policy with them and for them; it is given a wide discretion in implementing policy; and it adjudicates conflicts between individuals and the state or among competing parties and interests. The bureaucracy is therefore not adjunct or subordinate to the state; it is an integral part of the command structure. The relative scope of its discretionary powers, especially its coercive powers, corresponds to the authoritarian component that exists in all democracies. It is a component that may grow beyond control. One of the most important problems facing democratic regimes today, therefore, is how to reconcile the power of the bureaucracy with the preservation of democratic values in the policy process.

The Configuration of the Elite[9]

The elite, as we noted, consists of individuals and groups that directly and indirectly influence the policy makers: the executive branch, the administration, the lawmakers, and even the judges. Elites are the social matrix within which the government officials operate.

In democratic societies there are many groups and literally millions of people who exercise influence and hence command deference. Not only do they have access to policy makers, but policy makers—the *political* elite—often defer to them. They also directly influence the attitudes of the people who defer and listen to them. Such an elite could be exceedingly powerful if it were unified and if it functioned on behalf of one single purpose. But what characterizes the configuration of the elite in democracies is its *heterogeneity:* there are many and different groups that compose it.

Heterogeneity

The elite is divided and holds different positions on many issues. Sometimes the differences are between just two groups: this is typically the situation of trade union leaders and the managers of a company. Sometimes the differences coincide: some groups are for a given policy, others are against it. For example, groups favoring more defense spending and less welfare cluster against those who favor more welfare and less defense spending. Sometimes the differences are sharp and pit a given elite against government officials; for example, the business and industrial groups who oppose higher income taxes. Ideologies can splinter

[9]Two contrasting points of view about the elite in democracies are presented in Robert A. Dahl, *Who Governs: Democracy and Power in an American City* (New Haven: Yale University Press, 1961), and C. Wright Mills, *The Power Elite* (New York: Oxford University Press, 1956).

the elite into many groups, as in the case of groups who have strong feelings about particular issues, such as peace, nuclear weapons, environmental policies, economic controls and planning, or abortion.

Competitiveness

In democracies there is a genuine competition for influence, resources, and power among elite groups. It often amounts to a political contest that pits one array of elite groups against another or that cuts across the elites themselves. The rules of competition, however, also determine its limits. Competition is almost always about increments, not wholes; it is about something, not everything. It relates to policy shifts and policy outputs that by and large do not affect the existing status quo. Even when a cluster of elite groups is united on one side of an issue and is pitted against a cluster that opposes it, competition does not involve the destruction of one or the other; it is at most a confrontation, more often an accommodation, hardly ever a war. Even when the differences that separate groups appear to be irreconcilable, they hold each other at bay.

Shifts and combinations, shufflings and reshufflings of elite groups with regard to electoral choice, policy making, and allocation of resources very often create a situation where various combinations counter others. The idea of countervailing power (e.g., trade unions against management or the church against the state) is the societal equivalent of checks and balances. No single dominant group within the elite can gain a monopolistic position. A convergence of positions might occasionally develop, but it is a convergence that amounts to a temporary agreement of some groups and always carries the seeds of divergences. In other words, even if a power elite consisting of the most important groups is dominant for a period of time, it constantly faces the prospects of dislocation. It is at best only a coalition. Whatever consensus it might be able to fashion and impose is in the long run no more than tentative.

Openness

Elite groups disappear and new ones come upon the scene. The immigrant, the technician, or the corporate manager replaces the native-born family, the property owner, or the family firm. New techniques create new social groups and new skills replace the old. New technology spawns a brand-new class of managers and officers in the defense establishment to replace the old. Deference for elite groups shifts and changes as their respective positions change in terms of status, income, and skills. Also, even within a single elite group, the door remains open for outsiders. Ethnic minorities move up into important political positions; disfranchised segments of the population gain political power; the children of workers go on to higher education, which gains them entrance to professional elite groups and the status that goes with them.

With all these changes the elites are always in a state of flux, and while their dominant position may appear to be solid, in reality it is never secure. There was a time when only the sons of the nobility could occupy positions in the British Foreign Office, which was once referred to as the "outdoor relief department of the British aristocracy." There was a time when the Lowells and the Cabots controlled the economy and the politics of New England. No longer.

Economic development and social modernization precipitate the formation of new socioeconomic and professional groups whose skills and value to the regime merit them elite status. The status of established groups are undermined as the status quo weakens. Old values and beliefs disappear, and new ones develop.

In a democratic regime, characterized by an open elite and increased differentiation of the elite into many groups, these changes become reflected in the composition of the political elite. Through the electoral process, the composition of representative institutions comes to reflect the distribution of groups and values in the population. Through the executive agencies and bureaucracies, the administrative elite comes to reflect the distribution of skills and values necessary for keeping the economy and society functioning smoothly. The relative openness of the institutions comprising the organization of command to entry by new elites is one of the hallmarks of the democratic regime.

This argument cannot be pushed too far, however, because there are limits to openness; i.e., to accessibility and circulation. Even in the most open democratic regimes, elites set up barriers to entry by newcomers. They establish their own codes and standards that exclude others. Even newcomers who possess valued skills or other resources may not be able to compete with the advantages of those with inherited wealth, status, and power.

With open circulation there is also a great deal of horizontal mobility among different elite groups. A person belonging to one elite group may move to another. A general may seek and win the presidency; a lawyer may become a politician and in turn may shift to corporate management; members of the clergy have joined political parties and been elected to office; army officers have moved to managerial positions; and astronauts have given up the search for the stars to seek political stardom. There are, however, limits to horizontal mobility even in the democratic regime.

Limitations on the Command Structure

The executive and the bureaucracy, and the broader societal elite within which they operate, are the major forces, organs, and instruments of decision making in the democratic regime. They govern. But they do so under a set of limitations.

One of the most widespread methods of limiting the substance of power is to divide it. Power can be divided territorially, functionally, and among institutions.

Territorial Division of Command: Federalism

A federal system is one where the power to command is divided between a common government for the whole territory and separate governments for subordinate constituent territories.[10] The common government is allotted a set of powers to be exercised over all citizens, while other powers are given to the individual constituent territories. The powers given to the common government are "delegated," while those reserved to the constituent units are "residual." The distinguishing feature of the federal division of power is that the powers of the constituent units are autonomous and significant; the constituent governments make policy on a number of important issues and play an important role in the society.

The federal government is usually empowered to act for defense, foreign affairs, currency and banking, postal services, and commerce and trade between the constituent territories, or states. The states are usually granted most other powers. Often some of the powers of the federal government can be exercised concurrently with those of the states, and there can be overlap, conflict, or cooperation.

Besides the United States and Switzerland, we find federal arrangements in many democracies, including the Federal Republic of Germany, Canada, India, and Australia. In some federal systems the jurisdiction of the federal government is clearly circumscribed, and the residual powers that belong to the individual states are extensive and exclusive. In the United States, judicial interpretation has widened the scope of the power of the federal government, although judicial interpretation may be swinging back in the direction of restricting federal power. The federal and constituent governments of a federation may also develop a cooperative relationship, in which the states implement policies that are decided upon and financed by the federal government.

In all federal systems there is a second legislative chamber, an upper house: the Senate in the United States, the Bundesrat in West Germany, the Council of States in Switzerland. These bodies represent the constituent units that comprise the federation. Each individual state in turn has its own legislature and executive to deal with all matters under its jurisdiction. Legislation or constitutional amendments that affect the powers or the representation of the states must be approved by the second, or federal, chamber.

[10]The characteristics of federalism are explored in Arthur W. Macmahon, Ed., *Federalism Mature and Emergent* (New York: Russell and Russell, 1962), and Carl J. Friedrich, *Trends of Federalism in Theory and Practice* (New York: Praeger, 1968).

One of the many reasons for the division of power along federal lines is the existence of ethnic pluralism. Where a state comprises diverse ethnic populations settled in compact territories, the establishment of constituent units corresponding to ethnic patterns of settlement provides both substantive and symbolic mechanisms for the representation of ethnic groups and identities. While intended to provide for political integration of the whole, the federal organization of a multiethnic regime also provides a ready basis for the emergence of separatist political movements in the constituent territories.[11] Canada, India, and Switzerland are examples of this kind of federalism. In Quebec, ethnic-based claims to autonomy threaten the very survival of the Canadian regime. Elsewhere, as in the Soviet Union, Yugoslavia, and Czechoslovakia, the combination of ethnic diversity and federal structures are complicating the already complex process of regime change.

Functional Federalism

This involves the delegation by the state of independent powers and functions to certain public agencies or corporations. Special agencies are set up to perform such functions as regulating radio and television broadcasting, administering public universities, providing urban transportation, overseeing public utilities, or regulating the monetary system. These agencies are sometimes subject only to the overall supervision of the central authority, and they sometimes operate under a charter that grants them the broadest autonomy in managing the activities entrusted to them. Public corporations, many nationalized industries, and supervisory and regulatory boards, all of which abound in modern industrialized democracies, carry on the activities and responsibilities delegated to them independent of the legislature and the executive. While such autonomous functional entities limit the powers of government institutions, they soon become little governments in their own right, often without the well-institutionalized mechanisms of accountability that constrain elected officials.

Decentralization

Decentralization is the process whereby the national or central government delegates a number of functions and duties to subordinate local units and to their elected representatives. These usually involve such local matters as running the schools, taking care of city and municipal roads, providing fire services, raising and spending revenues, promoting tourism, and establishing health clinics. Though these powers are delegated by the legislature and technically can be revoked by it at any

[11]See "Federalism and Ethnicity," special issue of *Publius: The Journal of Federalism* 7, 4 (1977).

time, the role of local government and its agencies becomes institutionalized and cannot be easily dismantled. These local powers in turn check the central authority. They lead to the creation of powerful institutional enclaves which once erected cannot be easily invaded. Decentralization to the local, urban, or regional level is closely associated with ideas of self-government. It is an expression of the right of people to take care of their own affairs in matters that directly concern their community. It has been very much in evidence in many European states: in the Federal Republic of Germany (perhaps soon in a single unified Germany), in Italy, in England, and even in France where in 1982 there was a radical overhaul of territorial arrangements that established genuine self-government in departments and regions and granted local and regional representative councils certain autonomous powers and some independent financial resources.

Separation of Powers: Checks and Balances

Federalism divides power within the same territory between the central government and the individual states that constitute the federation. Separation of powers divides the command structure at the top. It allots the power to command to different and competing institutions: the legislature, the executive, and the judiciary. Whether the division is adopted in order to assign functionally distinct tasks to different organs or simply to split power in order to weaken it, the result is the same. The concentration of political power is avoided.

The "checks and balances" characteristic of the United States are inherently associated with the separation of powers. They arise out of the institutionalization of overlapping powers in the main organs of government, allowing them to block each other in the adoption and, especially, the implementation of decisions. Checks allow one power to directly make its weight felt upon another. In the United States, the legislature may impeach the president, members of the executive, or the judiciary; in parliamentary systems, the executive may dissolve or adjourn the legislature, and the legislature may vote the government out of office. The president may veto legislation, but his veto can be overriden by a reinforced majority in the legislature; one legislative assembly can withhold its ratification of the decisions of the other.

In both federal and unitary democratic regimes, a way of limiting legislative power, hence "checking" a given majority, is to establish two legislative bodies and require their concurrence in legislation—a *bicameral* system. One body, referred to as the lower house, is elected directly by the people; the second, the upper chamber, is hereditary or appointed or elected indirectly on the basis of special qualifications and arrangements. In most parliamentary regimes the roles and powers of the upper chamber have been sharply reduced. In Great Britain, for instance, the House of Lords has lost all powers over budgetary and fiscal matters, and it cannot block legislation passed by the House of Commons for more than nine months. In the FRG, on the other hand, the powers of the second chamber—the Bundesrat—remain substantial: their consent is needed when the powers of the states (the Lander) are involved or when virtually any bill dealing with finances arises. In France the lower house (the National Assembly) can override the upper chamber (the Senate) if it votes a bill on three separate occasions and at the request of the prime minister. Some democracies have dispensed altogther with an upper chamber; for example, Spain and Greece.

It is only in the United States that the upper chamber (the Senate) maintains powers equal to and in certain matters even greater than the House of Representatives. The origins of this division of power are to be found in the social, economic, and political differences among the former colonies and in the desire by their representatives to the Constitutional Convention to preserve as much autonomy as possible while establishing a union.

Referendum

The institution of the popular referendum constitutes an additional check on government power by creating a powerful instrument for expressing the popular will on controversial issues and increasing the potential electoral vulnerability of officials who disregard it. The referendum is common in the states of America and at both the federal and cantonal levels in Switzerland. In France, it has been used only occasionally (six times) since 1958, and only on one occasion in Great Britain. It is provided for in a number of democratic constitutions, including some of the most recently drafted; for example, those of Portugal, Greece, and Spain. The constraint on government power posed by the referendum becomes even more powerful when it is initiated by the people, something that can be done in the United States (but only in the states themselves) and in Switzerland, where either a certain number of cantons or a certain percentage of eligible voters have the power to initiate a referendum.

Tenure Limitations

One of the most direct limits on the powers of the ruling elite is the establishment of limits on tenure in office. Many democratic regimes at different levels of government have adopted constitutional provisions that prevent an incumbent president, governor, mayor, or even legislator from running for re-election to the same office after serving a given number of terms. An extreme example of such a limit is found in

Mexico, where the incumbent president is not permitted to stand for re-election after his single six-year term expires. A spectacular case was that of the Second French Republic in 1848. The president, like the Mexican president today, was ineligible after his first term. Louis Napoleon Bonaparte, who was elected in 1848, could not run again, but he did not wait long. In 1851 he became an emperor! Thus, in certain unusual instances, a limit on re-election may tempt ruling elites or ambitious political leaders to overthrow the democratic regime rather than restrain them. The more frequent liability of such arrangements, however, is that the inability to stand for re-election so weakens an official that he or she becomes ineffective, especially during the last years in office.

Recall

In some democracies, elected officials may be recalled from office. A petition requiring a number of signatures of eligible voters, a majority as a rule, may suffice. In other instances, such a petition may have to be endorsed by the legislature. Used from time to time in a number of states of the United States and cantons of Switzerland, recall is potentially a powerful deterrent to actions by state officials, including even the governors of states, and a method available to the electorate to redress immediate grievances against officeholders. It is for the electorate the equivalent of impeachment and, if successful, forces the officeholder out. In no democracy today has the practice of recalling an elected member of parliament become institutionalized, even though the idea has been frequently entertained and the practice even occasionally allowed.

Amending the Constitution

Officials in both the legislature and the executive often fret about the limitations that are imposed by a constitution, and they may wish to amend it so as to lift the offending restrictions. All democratic regimes, therefore, make amendments difficult by establishing special procedures and requiring extraordinary majorities for their adoption. Sometimes a referendum is needed, sometimes two-thirds of both chambers must agree; in federal systems, the concurrence of more than a majority of the states is required. In the United States, two-thirds of both houses and three-quarters of the states must assent. In all cases, the amendment process is designed to require a long time and the consolidation of a powerful and large majority before it can succeed. There may even be some provisions that cannot be amended at all, such as those concerning individual freedoms in the constitution of the Federal Republic of Germany (Articles 1 to 18) and the "republican" form of government in France and elsewhere.

The obstacles to amending a constitution dampen the temptation of officeholders to reshape it to their own will. Where the ruling elite remains unhappy with the constitution but cannot muster enough support to change it, two alternative paths remain open. The first is simple subversion of the constitution. Even in an open, democratic system, the complexities of modern bureaucratic government, accompanied by the protective shield of secrecy surrounding issues alleged to involve the national security, provide ample resources for a determined group of elites to carry out activities that violate the spirit, if not the letter, of the constitution. In the United States, recent examples include both the Watergate scandal of the Nixon years and the so-called "Irangate" scandal of the Reagan years, each of which, when uncovered, revealed the great extent to which the preservation of democratic values depended on the moral commitment of the elite and on an alert public. The second is to convince the people of a needed change, which can often be a long and uncertain process.

Judicial Review

Whatever the limitations imposed on the organization of command and the elites that staff it, they are not worth much unless those who ignore them can be sanctioned and the improper decisions they make can be set aside. The existence of an independent body authorized to assess the activities of the elite (in democratic regimes it is the judiciary) remains one of the most important vehicles for enforcing the limitations imposed upon those in command.[12]

In almost all democratic regimes the courts are the guardians of the constitution against any violations by anybody in the command structure. They maintain the limitations the constitution imposes with regard to both the exercise of power and its substance. But judicial review varies from one country to another. In the United States, any and every act of the command structure *at any level* can be challenged as unconstitutional in the courts. A court can decide whether an act of the federal, state, or local government conforms to the federal constitution or, in the case of state and local actions, to both the state and federal constitutions. The courts monitor the federal, state, and local organizations of command and protect individual rights.

[12]The best argument in favor of comprehensive judicial review in the United States remains the decision of Chief Justice Marshall in *Marbury v. Madison* (1803), in Robert Cushman, *Leading Constitutional Decisions*, 14th ed. (New York: Appleton-Century-Crofts, 1971), pp. 1–11. See also Mauro Cappelletti, *Judicial Review in the Contemporary World* (Indianapolis, Ind.: Bobbs-Merrill, 1971), and Martin Shapiro, "Courts," in Fred I. Greenstein and Nelson W. Polsby (eds.), *Handbook of Political Science*, vol. 5 (Reading, Mass.: Addison-Wesley, 1975), pp. 321–372.

In most other democracies only special courts can hear cases involving the constitution and can do so only about special provisions of the constitution. Some deal with the federal structure, as in Switzerland, others with both the federal structure and individual freedoms, as in West Germany. Judicial review is compartmentalized, and special courts are established to pass judgment on questions of constitutionality. In France, review for constitutionality is limited and is undertaken by a special body, the Constitutional Council, which was established by the constitution of 1958. Originally, its major role was to supervise the relations between executive and legislature in order to prevent the encroachment of the legislature on the powers of the prime minister, the cabinet, and the presidency. But in the last decade it has expanded its scope to include the protection of individual rights.

Judicial review of the constitutionality of laws or executive decisions can be considered comprehensive when anybody can raise it, and for any reason. This is the case in the United States. In other democratic regimes a challenge can be raised only by special bodies. In France, only the President of the Republic, the presidents of the National Assembly and the Senate, the prime minister, or any sixty members of either the National Assembly or the Senate can call for judicial review.

In finding an act of the legislature or the executive to be unconstitutional, the courts in some democracies are empowered to declare such acts null and void. Their decision not only suspends the application of a law but destroys it. The effect of the decision is to nullify the law. In other regimes, however, the decision simply suspends the promulgation of the law and invites the legislature to reconsider and redraft it.

Judicial review is not a feature of every democracy even though it has been adopted by a growing number. In Great Britain, for example, judicial review for constitutionality is not permitted. Because the fundamental principle of the British regime is the supremacy of Parliament, the courts must enforce all legislative enactments. This provision considerably strengthens the powers of the Cabinet.

We should conclude this chapter by returning to Thomas Hobbes's pithy statement: "Liberty is power cut up into pieces." Our survey indicates the ingenuity of the citizenry of the democracies in attaining this goal, and suggests a message for the countries where authoritarian regimes still hold sway (even if many appear to be weakening). In order to be harnessed to democratic values and practices, power must gradually lose its monopoly, centrality, and comprehensiveness, and for this to come about, many of the constraints we have discussed must be institutionalized. It will take time and effort.

Bibliography

On Democratic Institutions

Andrews, William G. *Presidential Government in Gaullist France*. Albany, N.Y.: State University of New York Press, 1982.

Berkeley, Humphrey. *The Power of the Prime Minister*. London: George Allen & Unwin, 1968.

Blondel, Jean. *The Organization of Government: A Comparative Study of Governmental Structures*. Beverly Hills, Calif.: Sage Publications, 1982.

Corwin, Edward S. *The President: Office and Powers*. 5th rev. ed. New York: New York University Press, 1984.

Dahl, Robert A. *A Preface to Democratic Theory*. Chicago: University of Chicago Press, 1970.

Friedrich, Carl J. *Constitutional Government and Democracy: Theory and Practice in Europe and America*. 4th ed. Waltham, Mass.: Ginn & Blaisdell, 1968.

Hamilton, Alexander, James Madison, and John Jay. *The Federalist Papers*. New York: New American Library, 1961.

Jennings, Ivor. *Cabinet Government*. Cambridge: Cambridge University Press, 1959.

King, Anthony (ed.). *The British Prime Minister: A Reader*. London: Macmillan, 1969.

King, Anthony. "Executives," in Fred I. Greenstein and Nelson W. Polsby, eds., *Handbook of Political Science*, vol. 5. Reading, Mass.: Addison-Wesley, 1975, pp. 173–243.

Lipset, Seymour Martin. *Political Man: The Social Bases of Politics*. New York: Doubleday/Anchor, 1963.

Macridis, Roy C., and Bernard E. Brown. *The De Gaulle Republic: Quest for Unity*. Westport, Conn.: Greenwood Press, 1980. Originally published in 1962.

Neustadt, Richard. *Presidential Power: The Politics of Leadership*. New York: John Wiley & Sons, 1960.

Nordlinger, Eric A. *On the Autonomy of the Democratic State*. Cambridge, Mass.: Harvard University Press, 1981.

Powell, G. Bingham, Jr. *Contemporary Democracies: Participation, Stability and Violence*. Cambridge, Mass.: Harvard University Press, 1984.

Quermonne, Jean-Louis. *Le Gouvernement de la France sous la 5ième République*. 2d ed. Paris: Dalloz, 1983.

Rose, Richard, and Ezra Suleiman. *Presidents and Prime Ministers*. Washington, D.C.: American Enterprise Institute, 1980.

Rossiter, Clinton. *The American Presidency*. New York: Harcourt Brace, 1956.

Sartori, Giovanni. *Democratic Theory*. Westport, Conn.: Greenwood Press, 1973. Originally published in 1962.

Schweitzer, C. C., D. Karsten, et al. (eds.). *Politics and Government in the Federal Republic of Germany: Basic Documents.* Frankfurt: Berg Publishers, 1984.

Smith, Gordon. *Politics in Western Europe: A Comparative Analysis.* New York: Holmes & Meier, 1972.

Bureaucracy

Aberbach, Joel D., Robert D. Putnam, and Bert A. Rockman. *Bureaucrats and Politicians in Western Democracies.* Cambridge, Mass.: Harvard University Press, 1981.

Crozier, Michel. *The Bureaucratic Phenomenon.* Chicago: University of Chicago Press, 1964.

Dogan, Mattei (ed.). *The Mandarins of Western Europe: The Political Role of Top Civil Servants.* New York: John Wiley & Sons, 1975.

Ferrel, Heady. *Public Administration: A Comparative Perspective.* Englewood Cliffs, N.J.: Prentice-Hall, 1966.

Galbraith, John Kenneth. *The New Industrial State.* Boston: Houghton Mifflin, 1967.

Gross, Bertram. *The Management of Organization.* New York: The Free Press, 1964.

Heclo, Hugh. *A Government of Strangers: Executive Policy in Washington.* Washington, D.C.: The Brookings Institution, 1977.

La Palombara, Joseph (ed.). *Bureaucracy and Political Development.* Princeton, N.J.: Princeton University Press, 1963.

Nadel, Mark V., and Francis Rourke. "Bureaucracies," in Fred I. Greenstein and Nelson W. Polsby, Eds., *Handbook of Political Science*, vol. 5. Reading, Mass.: Addison-Wesley, 1975, pp. 373–429.

On the Constitutional Order

Andrews, William G. *Constitutions and Constitutionalism.* Princeton, N.J.: Van Nostrand, 1961.

Bagehot, Walter. *The English Constitution.* Oxford: Oxford University Press, 1936. Originally published 1867.

Finer, Samuel E. *Five Constitutions: Contrasts and Comparisons.* London: Penguin Books, 1979.

Friedrich, Carl J. *Constitutional Government and Democracy: Theory and Practice in Europe and America.* 4th ed. Waltham, Mass.: Ginn & Blaisdell, 1968.

McIlwain, Charles. *Constitutionalism: Ancient and Modern.* Ithaca, N.Y.: Cornell University Press, 1947.

Spiro, Herbert. *Government by Constitution: The Political Systems of Democracy.* New York: Random House, 1959.

Wheare, Kenneth. *Modern Constitutions.* Oxford: Oxford University Press, 1966.

Federalism

Beer, Samuel, et al. *Federalism: Making the System Work.* Washington, D.C.: Center for National Policy, 1982.

Duchek, Ivo. *Comparative Federalism.* New York: Holt, Rinehart and Winston, 1970.

Friedrich, Carl J. *Trends of Federalism in Theory and Practice.* New York: Praeger, 1967.

King, Preston T. *Federalism and Federation.* Baltimore, Md.: Johns Hopkins University Press, 1983.

Riker, William. *Federalism: Origins, Operation, Significance.* Boston: Little, Brown, 1964.

Wheare, Kenneth. *Federal Governments.* Oxford: Oxford University Press, 1955.

On Judicial Review

Cappelletti, Mauro. *Judicial Review in the Contemporary World.* Indianapolis, Ind.: Bobbs-Merrill, 1971.

Chopper, Jesse H. *Judicial Review and the National Political Process.* Chicago: University of Chicago Press, 1980.

Levy, Leonard W. *Judicial Review and the Supreme Court.* New York: Harper & Row, 1967.

Shapiro, Martin. "Courts," in Fred I. Greenstein and Nelson W. Polsby, Eds., *Handbook of Political Science,* vol. 5. Reading, Mass.: Addison-Wesley, 1975, pp. 321–372.

3

Participation and Political Parties

Introduction

Government by the people has become government by consent of the people. In democratic regimes, the government acts on behalf of the people. It is a creature of the society, responding to societal forces and groups and, ultimately, is responsible to the source from which it derives its power: the people. But the democratic concept presupposes that the people organize in one form or another in order to exert their influence over the command structure. They participate on their own or are mobilized to participate. In democratic regimes, therefore, elaborate, institutionalized mechanisms for securing and reaffirming popular consent are established. Democratic regimes do not only require, as John Stuart Mill suggested, good judgment and restraint on the part of the people; they also require an active and interested public.

The electoral process is the main instrument through which most citizens in a democracy participate and exercise their influence. Periodic competition for public support between leaders and their opponents—in elections—encourages popular participation. Elections bring out tens and even hundreds of millions of voters, especially since most democracies have lowered the age of voting to eighteen. Even in small democracies the number of eligible voters may reach 3 to 5 million. In medium-sized countries (England, France, West Germany, Italy, Spain) it is around 32 to 38 million. In the United States, it is over 140 million.

The problem of bringing order out of the chaos of millions of individual wills and transforming them into recognizable electoral options is solved by having political parties. The voters emerge as collective entities and are viewed in terms of aggregates: Democrats, Republicans, Conservatives, Labourites, Gaullists, Socialists, Liberals, Communists, Agrarians, Greens, or Social Democrats. The voters become organized through a process of reconciliation and adjustment whereby individual interests and choices are boiled down to party formulas, pledges, and candidates. Parties simplify (some say they even determine) choice. But one thing is clear: Given the size of the electorate today, there could be no election and no choice without parties. Political parties provide the glue that holds both the electoral process and the representative institutions of the democratic regime together. Parties *identify, mobilize, articulate,* and *aggregate* societal interests and provide *choice* to the electorate.

Participation

Politics is not the major concern of citizens, not even in democratic regimes. Most people give priority to their personal concerns: family life, work and business, sports, entertainment and leisure, and most of all the satisfaction of everyday needs. Political participation consists of the various activities through which citizens communicate their socially relevant demands, interests, and expectations for the purpose of influencing the selection or the decisions of government officials.[1] These may include elected representatives or other officials of government.

Although there are many specific facets and dimensions to participation, leading researchers have identified four general types of activities. They are:

1. Individual citizen activity, initiated by the citizen (e.g., letter writing)
2. Cooperative or group activity (political clubs or associations)
3. Campaign activity
4. Voting

With all four of these activities we can measure the extent of participation easily. Clearly, men or women who usually vote and occasionally write to their representatives do not participate to the same extent as those who are constantly on the phone promoting candidates and issues and who are in constant communication with their representatives.

[1]We follow the excellent analysis of Sidney Verba, Norman H. Nie, and Jae-on Kim in *The Modes of Political Participation: A Cross-National Comparison* (Beverly Hills, Calif: Sage Publications, 1971). See also Sidney Verba and Norman H. Nie, *Political Participation in America* (New York: Harper & Row, 1972); and Norman Nie and Sidney Verba, "Political Participation," in Fred I. Greenstein and Nelson W. Polsby (eds.), *Handbook of Political Science*, vol. 4 (Reading, Mass.: Addison-Wesley, 1975), pp. 1–74

The most common method for measuring popular participation is the survey. A small sample of the population, if it is statistically representative, can faithfully reproduce the pattern of participation in the nation at large. It provides a profile in the following areas:

1. Efforts to persuade others how to vote
2. Active work for candidates
3. Attending political meetings or rallies
4. Contributing money to candidates or a political party
5. Membership in political clubs
6. Past voting record, usually for the last two national elections
7. Past voting record in local elections
8. Working with others on local policy matters
9. Forming a group to work on local problems
10. Activity and membership in political organizations
11. Communicating with local and national officials

Survey findings indicate that except for voting (which ranges from as low as 50 percent to as high as 95 percent), the percentage of participants is very low (from 8 to 30 percent) with regard to all other criteria. There is also no uniformity in participation and no clear correlation between one type of participatory activity or another. Some people write to their representatives every other week but do not belong to a political club; sometimes they may not even vote. The profile of the participant citizen is lopsided, and the conclusion one draws is that participation is low, sporadic, and unstructured.

Many authors have drawn gloomy conclusions from this situation. The people appear uninterested, uninformed, apathetic, or alienated. They do not seem to be interested in public affairs and put their private concerns before public ones. They accept the regime out of habit, inertia, apathy, or ignorance. Some people get aroused at election time, but this amounts to only once every two or four or five years; thereafter they lapse back into apathy. Many refuse to vote—abstainers range from 30 to 40 percent up to half of the eligible voters. How can there be democracy without massive participation? If only a few participate, the foundations of democracies must indeed be frail.[2]

A more cheerful view emerges if we consider participation in terms of two dimensions that are not frequently taken into account: *intensiveness* (as opposed to extensiveness) and *latency* (as opposed to actual participation). If we take this viewpoint, we will find that democratic regimes provide all the requirements for participation and often show a degree of participation that is not matched by any other political regime.

[2]Cf. V. O. Key, *The Responsible Electorate* (Cambridge, Mass.: Harvard University Press, 1966); and E. E. Schattschneider, *The Semi-Sovereign People* (New York: Holt, Rinehart and Winston, 1960).

Intensiveness

Intensive participation, often used synonymously with mobilization, refers to concentrated political activities initiated for the purpose of bringing about certain goals. They are related to issues considered very important by some people, even a small minority, even if for a relatively short period of time: nuclear energy, pollution and environmental issues, nuclear freeze, the deployment of American missiles in West Germany (for the Germans), the poll-tax imposed recently in Britain, unemployment (for almost all in Western Europe and the United States in the eighties), abortion versus the right to life, and so forth. Such activities are spontaneous. Organizers reach out to mobilize sympathizers or make converts. They often bypass the normal channels of political expression, i.e., the political parties or elections. The impact of such political activities may be far greater than voting percentages. It is like a flash in the darkness, but it is a flash that lights up and transforms the landscape of inertia and apathy.

Democratic regimes constantly experience such flashes of intense political activity and commitment for or against a given issue. The war in Algeria spurred the French into intensive participation for or against, just as Americans were aroused by the war in Vietnam. If we review the years since World War II, we will see a series of periodic flashes of intensive participation or mobilization in democratic regimes. In the United States, for example, the civil rights movement, the registration of blacks, the student demonstrations in the late sixties, the anti-Vietnam War demonstrations and the anti-draft movement, the environmentalist and more recently the nuclear freeze movements, and the pro- and anti-abortion movement are all landmarks of intensive activity about politics and political issues, mobilizing people for one particular purpose and inevitably inviting countermobilization.

Latency

The argument about intensiveness suggests that there is always a *potential* for political participation and involvement in democratic regimes. The public may show no interest and may appear apathetic, but it can show interest and can become active, because democratic regimes provide the structures and the institutions through which dormant interests can come to life. On the surface, democracies appear to leave the citizens alone with their problems and pursuits. Potentially, however, these same citizens may explode into activists, organizers, demonstrators, patriots, or revolutionaries. It is this *latency*, this potential participation, that constitutes a powerful restraint on officeholders lest they make decisions that will arouse citizens. This potential must be taken just as seriously as election returns (and usually is). The very possibility that a segment of the public (the elderly, the medicare recipients, the schoolteachers, the environmentalists, or others) will become aroused is a powerful check, so much so that policy makers may refuse to make some decisions for fear that the support they enjoy will dissolve or turn into active opposition. Thus, the anticipated reactions of the public to a given measure serve as guidelines and restraints on policy makers.

Can we measure intensiveness and latency? Only in terms of case studies that show how intensive participation is generated, how it spreads, how mobilizing it becomes, and how effective it turns out to be. Enough such cases over a relatively short period of time—twenty or thirty years—may show a degree and intensity of public involvement that neither voting nor surveys nor party membership reveal. The very prospect of intense participation amounting to mobilization is a consideration that officeholders must take into account in formulating policies.

Is participation a necessary condition of consent? Is nonparticipation, or low levels of participation, an indication of dissent and hostility toward the regime? Those who consider democratic regimes in terms of the participatory model of Athenian democracy will answer both questions affirmatively. In ancient Athens direct participation in the affairs of the city was deemed to be the essence of democracy. The people themselves made policy decisions and had a direct hand in running the government. For modern democracies, however, with tens and even hundreds of millions of citizens involved, the answer to both questions may well have to be negative.

Democratic regimes are based on the acceptance of (1) rules that maintain a set of values and (2) the institutions through which the government makes policy in the context of these fundamental values and rules. Nonparticipation is not always an indication of dissatisfaction or alienation, as is often argued. It may even indicate satisfaction. It may not be a sign of indifference or hostility; on the contrary, it may mean agreement. If those in command, elected and held responsible in periodic elections, respect the basic rules and act within them, the political regime is doing precisely what it is supposed to do: defend and protect the values its citizens hold dear. In this case, silence means consent. The fact that intensive participation emerges only when there are sharp differences about policy in a way favors our hypothesis that low levels of political participation may be a sign of satisfaction. Everyday participation and involvement, even if desirable, are not necessary conditions in democratic regimes. Readiness to participate and become active at any time, on the other hand, is sufficient.

Political Parties

The most important and most common vehicle of participation and representation is the political party. It is an association that *activates* and *mobilizes* the people; represents or *articulates* their interests; draws those interests together, or *aggregates* them, by providing for compromise among competing points of view; and becomes the proving ground for political leadership. The study of political parties relates to (1) their organization, their history and origins, and their ideologies and (2) the relationships parties have established among themselves and the functions and specific roles they perform. In the first case we study individual parties; in the second we examine the configuration of parties and their interaction within the democratic regime.[3]

Functions

All democratic parties perform the following functions, although not in the same way nor to the same degree:

1. They represent various societal groups and forces and organize and structure participation and representation.
2. They provide choices among competing candidates.
3. They advocate policies embodied in the party program, platform, or manifesto.
4. Democratic parties try to mobilize the citizenry and to aggregate interests and demands.
5. Most democratic parties aim at capturing and controlling the government; they are "government parties." But in a number of democratic regimes this is not possible because they can never gain the required majority; these are "parties of representation." It is only by forming coalitions with other parties that they are able to participate in the government or influence it directly.
6. Parties recruit men and women who are interested in politics and can rise to positions of leadership.
7. Democratic parties are supportive of the democratic regime; they not only draw from the principles of democracy but also legitimize it. By organizing the electorate to participate and to vote, they strengthen supports to the regime and induce loyalties.

Membership

Membership in democratic parties is voluntary and open to all. They are not *exclusionary* parties. The organization of the party allows free debate among its members. As a result, in most democratic parties there are

---

[3]One of the best analyses is Harry Eckstein, "Party Systems," in *Encyclopedia of the Social Sciences*, vol. XI (New York: Crowell, Collier & Macmillan, 1968), pp. 436–453.

recognizable factions that vie for the leadership. Decision making within the party (the formulation of the party program) takes place through open debate and voting by party congresses or conventions that meet regularly. Delegates to such congresses are elected by the rank-and-file party membership,and they in turn choose, by majority vote, the party leadership. One thing we hardly ever find in the congresses of democratic parties is a unanimous vote. Finally, members are free to leave the party or join another one.

Membership in democratic parties varies a great deal. In mass parties the membership may reach millions. The British Labour party, for example, has over 5 million members, and the Conservative Party has about 2 million. In other instances, as with American parties, actual membership is relatively small.

Leadership

As in all formal organizations, the leadership, the party officials, and the active organizers play the most important role. They initiate policy, they structure debate, and they have widespread influence on the decisions made by the membership. Although there is often oligarchic control by the leadership even in democratic parties, frequent revolts and defections confirm that internal democracy and pluralism also exist. In some instances, party rebels even manage to unseat the leadership and gain a controlling position in the party. This is what happened with the French Socialist party in the 1970s, the German Social Democrats in the 1980s, the British Labour Party in the 1970s, and both the Democrats and the Republicans in the United States between 1972 and 1980.

Discipline

How disciplined are democratic parties? We must answer this question in terms of voter discipline, member discipline, and the discipline of their elected representatives in the legislature. Little need be said about the first, since no organizational ties of any kind bind voters to a party. Voters are always free to vote for or against, to change their minds from one election to another. Over time, however, parties become institutionalized, and they develop a hard core of faithful and a periphery of sympathizers who vote the straight "party ticket" in every election. Major parties can always count, notwithstanding fluctuations, on a considerable share of the electorate's vote unless and until there are critical elections that cause a realignment of the basic patterns of party support.

Discipline within the party for party members varies from one party to another. As a rule, leftist parties, such as socialist and especially communist parties are more disciplined than others, although some conservative or right-wing parties have at times shown remarkable discipline. Members are expected to follow the directives of the leadership in the implementation of policy directives or nominations of candidates. The penalty for refusing to do so is often exclusion from the party.

The matter of discipline is particularly important when we come to the elected party members in the legislature, the party representatives. In parliamentary systems, where the political life of the prime minister and the cabinet depends on the support they get from the majority party, discipline has been tight and defections rare. The members of a party in Parliament vote for their leadership almost without exception; party splits are seldom seen. The most spectacular split in recent years occurred in Britain, when some members of the Labour party broke away and formed the Social-Democratic party. It is mostly the members of centrist parties, especially in France and Italy, who show the least internal cohesion.

Discipline in overall terms is a matter of centralized control and direction. The control of party funds, the organization of party activities between or just before elections, the preparation of documentation and educational services, the ability of the leadership to nominate candidates for various elections and give them support are all important elements in shoring up discipline. Most democratic parties have developed such institutionalized instruments of direction and control, including even the Democratic and Republican parties in the United States. Their effectiveness, however, has varied from one country to another, and from one party to another.

The Ideological Spectrum

Ideology is the set of beliefs, ideas, and policies advanced by the party and embraced by its members. In democratic regimes the range of ideological variations is virtually unlimited, and most democracies even allow parties that advocate the overthrow of democracy itself. The guarantees of freedom of speech and association entitle them to do so as long as they use persuasion and not force in bringing about their goals. In the election of 1973 the leader of a small revolutionary party in France urged the people to vote for him. "If we win," he pointed out, "it will be the last time you will be voting." They did not win!

Antiregime Parties

In democratic regimes we have *regime parties* and *antiregime parties*. In the first case there is wide agreement and approval of the political regime. It is accepted. Common values are shared by party members and the voters at large, and differences that divide parties relate to concrete policies. Antiregime parties, on the other hand, are characterized by their outright opposition to the regime. It is not accepted. When parties share common propositions about the society and the constitution, we have a consensual democratic regime. When parties divide sharply on fundamental issues, the regime is conflictual.

Ever since the emergence of democratic regimes there have been many antiregime movements, but it was only in the aftermath of World War I, particularly between 1920 and the beginning of World War II in 1939, that antiregime parties mushroomed in Europe and throughout the world to threaten and seriously subvert the democratic order. These were the communist parties that split from the socialists in 1919–1921 and the extremist right-wing organizations: the Fascists in Italy and the Nazis in Germany. Although they had different labels in different countries, they carried the same antidemocratic thrust throughout Europe and even in England and the United States. The communists revived the Marxist appeal for an armed uprising of the workers, for a revolution. Right-wing extremists advocated force, the destruction of democratic rights, and the creation of a new authoritarian political order. The East European democratic regimes established after World War I, caught between these two powerful antidemocratic movements, collapsed.

Today, the West European communist parties seem to be following the path the European socialists took at the end of the nineteenth century. They are eschewing revolution, abandoning the notion of class war, accepting parliamentary democracy and the institution of free elections, and recognizing individual and political rights. They have accepted the democratic rules of the game; they are willing to operate within democratic institutions and within the democratic order. This has been the case notably with the most powerful communist group in Europe, the Italian Communist party, as well as the Spanish and French Communist parties.

Parties of the Left, Center, and Right

Political parties greatly simplify the multitude of ideological points of view in the democratic electorate. It is impossible for all shades of an idea to become a party. If they did, representation would become fragmented, virtually atomized, and the selection of officeholders in the legislature or the executive would become impossible. Ideas, like interests, have to be compromised and accommodated so that comprehensive programmatic formulations can be made and political majorities formed. The greater the degree of compromise and accommodation necessary to forge an alliance, the less ideological the party that establishes the alliance becomes. In bringing together many different points of view, the party finds out what is acceptable to as many as possible and offensive to as few as possible. Nonetheless, the configuration of the party system in modern democratic regimes can still be plotted on the ideological map often referred to as left–center–right.[4]

The fundamental criterion that distinguishes parties along the ideological spectrum is the set of positions they take and the policies they advocate with respect to the role of the state in the production and distribution of goods. To the left, communist and socialist parties advocate, to varying degrees, nationalization of industry and other economic activities, national economic planning, and extensive redistribution of wealth through taxation, subsidies, and welfare spending. Their ultimate goal is to equalize or at least reduce inequalities in material conditions of life as much as possible by subordinating private incentives and private profit to collective needs. Socialist and communist parties appeal to those who appear to stand to benefit the most from such measures: workers, the unemployed, the aged, the underprivileged, the poor, and those groups in the population that appear to be in a permanent state of poverty and need, the so-called "underclass." The French Socialist party, the British Labour party, the Social Democrats in the Federal Republic of Germany and in the Scandinavian countries, and the socialist parties in the new democracies of the Mediterranean advocate these policies.

In the election for the European Parliament in June 1989, their combined strength, at least for the twelve members of the European Community (United Kingdom, Ireland, Belgium, Holland, Luxembourg, Federal Republic of Germany, France, Italy, Denmark, Spain, Portugal, and Greece), gave them a total of about 260 out of 518 seats. The socialist parties are equally strong in Sweden, Norway, Austria, New Zealand, and Australia. The absence of a strong socialist party in the United States is the exception among the developed democracies.

Not all socialist parties are alike, however. Some of them differ in critically important ways, both with regard to the speed of the reforms they advocate and the kind of socialism they plan to construct. The Labour party in England, after a long period of moderation, reasserted in the 1970s and until recently support for the expansion of socialism. The French socialists, on the other hand, after a period of drastic nationalizations and income redistribution upon assuming power in 1981 lost their enthusiasm for such changes, especially as their electoral support declined. The Scandinavian socialist parties have chosen an entirely different path, emphasizing workers' participation in management and ownership and income redistribution and equalization.

---

[4]Arendt Lijphart discusses the ideological spectrum of European parties in terms of socioeconomic, religious, cultural, ethnic, and foreign policy, and also what he calls "postindustrial criteria." See his "Parties, Ideologies and Programs," in David Butler, Howard Penniman, and Austin Ranney (eds.), *Democracy at the Polls* (Washington, D.C.: American Enterprise Institute, 1981), pp. 26–51.

Socialist parties differ on the kind of socialism they hope to construct. Few remain committed to the notion of bureaucratic-state direction of the economy. Today, even the communist parties have abandoned the Stalinist bureaucratic-statist model of national planning and state management. They are all searching for flexible mechanisms to align production to consumer choices and allow for associational and individual incentives. There has been a renewed emphasis on the market as a basis for organizing the economy, even in these regimes.

The same general observations can be made about the parties that fall on the right, mostly the conservative parties in Europe, North America, New Zealand, Canada, and Australia, and the Republicans (but also many of the Democrats) in the United States. While they have many differences, they are all characterized by a marked suspicion of the state and its role in economic and societal affairs. Most contemporary conservative parties are critical of the welfare state and the government spending that seemed to reflect the popular consensus in the developed Western democracies for almost three decades after the end of World War II. These parties generally appeal to the well-to-do, the middle classes, the propertied, and financial and industrial interests represented by powerful corporations, all of whom stand to benefit most from the withdrawal of state regulation of economic activity. The Conservative party in England, the Republicans (but, we repeat, many Democrats as well) in the United States, the neo-Gaullists and their allies in France, some of the Christian Democrats and conservatives in the Scandinavian countries, Canada, Australia, New Zealand, and the Mediterranean all follow the same approach.

Christian Democratic parties have had a history and an ideology that distinguishes them from most conservative parties. Heir to a strong Catholic intellectual tradition that throughout the nineteenth century stressed social solidarity and cooperation, they resurfaced in most of Europe after World War II. They favored social and egalitarian, sometimes downright socialist, policies that distinguished them also from centrists and liberals. Their view has been that the economy must be guided and regulated—the German Christian Democrats even speak of the "social market economy." Christian Democrats almost everywhere supported trade unions. They favored old-age insurance and pensions, family allowances, child support, health insurance programs. They appealed to *all* classes, stressing communitarian and interclass values. Most all of them became progessively secular and shed their religious identities and labels to appeal to all voters, irrespective of religion. In some instances, Christian Democratic parties and Protestant political organizations and parties merged. Christian Democrats took up also the cause of international cooperation and regional integration. They became the champions for the European Common Market.

Internationalism, social and communitarian considerations, emphasis upon moral and religious values, a progessive nondenominational orientation and a strong commitment to and involvement with workers' rights distinguished Christian Democrats everywhere from conservatives, centrists, or liberals.

In the early elections after World War II, Christian Democrats emerged in Europe as the only parties that could compete with the Left—particularly the communists—especially in Italy and France. Their voting strength in elections in the years between 1946 and 1960 averaged roughly 44 percent in Belgium, 46 percent in the Federal Republic of Germany, 45 percent in Austria, 43 percent in Italy, and 50 percent in Holland. In France the Christian Democrats, under the label of "Mouvement Populaire Républicain" (MRP), won between 1945 and 1951 (when many of their votes shifted to the Gaullists) 25 to 28 percent of the vote. Their strength in the most recent elections remains considerable: 27.5 percent in Belgium (1987), 35.3 percent in Holland (1989), 44.3 percent in FRG (1987), 41.3 percent in Austria (1986), and 34.3 percent in Italy (1989). In the election of March 18, 1990 in East Germany, Christian Democrats outdistanced all other parties, receiving 47 percent of the vote; they also showed significant strength in the Hungarian election of March–April 1990.

Disenchantment with socialism and economic planning is helping the Christian Democrats. They are parties that accept free enterprise and economic liberalism but with a social and human face. They continue to appeal to the social conscience and the moral values of many voters and to occupy a distinct place in the political landscape of European politics.

The center parties, often labeled liberals, take an eclectic stance and their programs are often a cross between the positions espoused by conservative and socialist parties. They pick and choose different propositions at different times and as a result appear to be the least ideological. The Liberals party in England (and most recently the alliance consisting of the old Liberal party and dissenters from the radical program of the Labour party), the Union of French Democracy in France, and the Free Democrats in the Federal Republic of Germany fit this pattern. So do most self-avowed liberal parties in virtually all contemporary democracies.

Parties constantly appear and disappear. New associations and groups committed to specific goals attempt to infiltrate existing parties or form their own. The most successful of these groups in recent years have been the so-called Greens. These are the parties born of the environmentalist, antinuclear, and disarmament movements. Some of them combine radical proposals for policy changes in these areas with open contempt for the existing institutions of democratic politics, a program that reflects a curious mixture of radical-leftist and populist ideology. The Greens in the Federal Republic of Germany managed to get over the minimum of 5 percent of the vote in the national election of 1983, entitling them to representation in the Bundestag. In 1987 they received 8.3 percent, while their strength has varied between 3 to 11 percent in various state elections. Their future, however, remains uncertain.

New groups and parties have also emerged at the extreme right. The National Front in France has averaged over 10 percent of the vote in local and national elections in the last decade, and its presidential candidate received a little over 14 percent on the first ballot in the election of 1988. In the Federal Republic of Germany, the Republican party, headed by a former Nazi petty-officer, received over 5 percent in local elections and 7.3 percent in the election for the European Parliament in June 1989. Extremist right-wing parties have mushroomed in Denmark and Norway as well. All of them have directed their campaign against foreign (mostly North African) immigrant workers, rejecting their participation in national politics and their claim to welfare benefits, and arguing for their return to their homelands.

The Catchall Party[5] Ever since the 1960s, most political parties of the industrially developed democratic regimes have been losing their ideological character. Because of the progressive structural differentiation and functional specialization of society, associated with the industrialization and modernization process and promoting the development of many social, professional, and occupational interest groups, the political parties, in order to secure electoral majorities, have become umbrella organizations appealing to a host of interests and points of view. They have evolved into "catchall" parties and in the process have begun to resemble each other in what they offer, like supermarkets that use different labels but in reality sell the same delicacies to all customers.

This phenomenon was attributed to the remarkable post-World War II economic growth that moderated the social and class distinctions that traditionally had provided the basis for party identification and the mobilization of mass support. Because of the growing differentiation of the working class into many layers and skills for which different incomes and gradually even different lifestyles developed, class was no longer synonymous with party attachments and voting. The remarkable social and physical mobility of individuals living in Western societies broke down regional attachments, and mobility also eroded sectional loyalties and contributed to the shaping of a single national electorate with similar political concerns, expectations, and demands. The growth

[5]The term "catchall" was used by Otto Kirchheimer, in "The Transformation of Western European Party Systems," in Joseph La Palombara and Myron Weiner (eds.), *Political Parties and Political Development* (Princeton, N.J.: Princeton University Press, 1968), pp. 177–200.

of the national media, especially television, also contributed mightily to the nationalization of politics: Neither parties nor candidates could tailor their appeals to particular groups without alienating others. The political parties accommodated themselves to these changes, so that differences between party platforms were no longer that great. The quest for victory at the polls and the gaining of governmental power became the only issue that actually divided such parties.

Catchall parties appeal to everybody. They become increasingly unable to represent particular points of view, political ideologies, and particular interests, or even to take sides. As a result, people have started to lose interest and identify less and less with their party. Political activity has begun to manifest itself either outside the political parties or through the formation of new ones. In many instances single-issue organizations, political clubs, direct action, and demonstrations have replaced the established political organizations and parties.

Party Systems

The term "party system" covers both the general rules and conditions under which interaction among political parties within a regime takes place and the patterns that have evolved over time.

Democratic parties compete for control of the government, to gain as many seats as possible in the legislature, or to select a president. Their victory depends on securing a majority (or, in a multiparty system, a plurality) of the vote. This dependence on periodic exercise of popular choice gives the voter a genuine opportunity to make a choice and to hold a party leadership or a candidate responsible at election time by voting against him or her. There are a number of factors that determine the manner in which political parties compete. Among the most important are:

1. The structure of representative government: whether it is presidential or parliamentary.
2. The social structure: How strong are the antagonisms between classes and religious or ethnic groups?
3. The electoral system and its rules for determining victory and apportioning representation.
4. The degree of agreement or disagreement between political parties on fundamental political values and institutions, which is often a matter of basic ideology.

The greater the disagreement among parties, the greater the threat to stability. Sharp class cleavages or deep-set ethnic and religious antagonisms account for a great, sometimes unbridgeable distance between parties. Competition may become confrontation. The stability of the government will be constantly in jeopardy because it will be difficult for competing parties to support a government or a president so legitimacy and performance will suffer. On the other hand, consensual parties are, as noted, those that share common orientations, goals, and tactics, so the distance between them is small. They appeal across classes and ethnic groups and become interclass parties. Consensual parties assume a broad national agreement and are most likely to develop in regimes where class, religious, and ethnic differences are not sharp. Sometimes, however, they manage to transcend even these differences and integrate disparate groups into their organizations. In such cases parties create political order and coherence out of disorder and conflict.

A number of differing patterns of political competition have developed over time. Let us examine some of these patterns.

Two-Party and Multiparty Systems

As the name would suggest, in a two-party system two major parties vie for control of the government in periodic elections. Strictly speaking, however, there is no democratic regime with only two parties. Rather, it is a system where all parties other than the major two have little strength and few members in the representative assembly. In the United States independent candidates who run for the presidency, including third-party candidates (Progressives, Socialists, Dixiecrats), influence the election of the president only by denying votes to one of the major parties (usually the Democrats) and thereby weakening its candidate. At the state and local level, these parties are sometimes more powerful and succeed in electing their candidates to local, state, and in rarer instances, even congressional office. The Liberal party in England, though receiving 5 to 10 percent of the vote in national elections (until 1970), had a very small representation in the House of Commons and little influence in the formation or the life of the cabinet, except when neither of the two major parties had a clear majority. West Germany, on the other hand, has been termed a "two and a half party" system. The two major parties were closely matched, and the Free Democrats averaged 7 to 12 percent of the vote and about 35 to 55 members in the parliament. One or the other of the two major parties, the Christian Democrats and the Social Democrats, allied with the Free Democrats to form a government. It is only recently that the environmentalists (the Greens) managed to gain representation in the legislature, with 27 candidates in 1983 and 42 in 1987. Most other European countries are "multiparty," with four or more major parties in close competition with one another and occasionally forming competing blocs.

Major, Minor, and Dominant Parties

Major parties are generally assured of a major share of the vote and occasionally attain a dominant position. A dominant party is one that manages (over the course of many elections) to gain a large share of the vote, even if it is not a majority. This was the case with the Gaullists in France, who between 1962 and 1981 received about 35 percent of the electoral vote; the Congress Party in India between 1947 and 1964 with over 50 percent of the vote; and the Christian Democrats in Italy, who have not fallen below 34 percent in a legislative election since 1946. Their electoral support assures them of a place in government, either on their own or at the head of a coalition. (See Table 3.1.) There are also many minor parties with a small membership and a small but steady share of the vote, something that distinguishes them from American "third parties." They do not expect, as a rule, to see their strength rise, and they have little, if any, influence on the formation of the government unless the major parties (two or three) are deadlocked. Their overall political relevance, on the other hand, may be quite significant. All third parties raise issues that may appeal to voters, and so the major parties have to give consideration to them and make compromises in proportion to the electoral strength such third parties show—even to the point of inviting their cooperation and participation in the cabinet.

Alternation

In many democracies, notably in England, the FRG, and increasingly France and the United States—at least for the presidential election— there is a pattern of alternation in the majority of a party or bloc of parties, which after a time turns it over to the opposition party or bloc of parties. Since World War II, the American presidency has been almost

TABLE 3.1 Dominance of the Christian Democrats: Italy [Legislative Elections]

Year	Percent of Vote
1948	48.5
1953	40.0
1958	42.4
1963	38.3
1968	39.1
1972	38.7
1976	38.7
1979	38.3
1982	37.4
1989	34.3

TABLE 3.2   Alternation in England (1945–1988)

	PARTY	PRIME MINISTER
1945	Labour	Attlee
1950	Labour	Attlee
1951	Conservative	Churchill
		Eden
1955	Conservative	Eden
		Macmillan
1959	Labour	Wilson
1964	Labour	Wilson
1966	Conservative	Heath
1970	Labour	Wilson
		Gallagher
1974	Labour	Gallagher
1979	Conservative	Thatcher
1983–1989	Conservative	Thatcher

Total: Labour	22 years
Conservative	23 years

evenly shared between Republicans and Democrats (although at present the Republicans appear to have secured a continuing incumbency). This is somewhat true in the Senate, though not true at all in the House of Representatives, where the Democrats have held a majority ever since 1946, with the exception of a total of six years. Tables 3.2 to 3.4 illustrate this phenomenon. Alternation, without being a *prerequisite* of democracy, is nonetheless a sign that the opposition is alive and well and capable of capturing the government. It is, as we noted earlier, a powerful constraint against officeholders.

TABLE 3.3   Alternation in the Federal Republic of Germany

Christian Democrats and Free Democrats	1949–1953
Christian Democrats and Free Democrats	1953–1957
Christian Democrats and Free Democrats	1957–1961
Christian Democrats and Free Democrats	1961–1965
Christian Democrats and Socialists	1965–1969
Socialists and Free Democrats	1969–1972
Socialists and Free Democrats	1972–1976
Socialists and Free Democrats	1976–1980
Socialists and Free Democrats	1980–1983
Christian Democrats and Free Democrats	1983–1990

Totals: Christian Democrats and Free Democrats	19 years
Socialists and Free Democrats	11 years
Christian Democrats and Socialists	4 years

TABLE 3.4   Alternation in the French Fifth Republic

LEGISLATURE
1958–1981	Gaullists and Centrists (allies)
1981–1986	Socialists
1986–1988	Centrists and Gaullists
1988–	Socialists

PRESIDENCY
1962–1981	Gaullists and Allies
1981–	Socialists

Deadlock

There is no good study of what may be called a deadlocked party system. It appears where over a considerable period of time the two major well-disciplined political parties are evenly matched without either of the two having a majority and without any hope of gaining one under the existing electoral system. Usually, one or more smaller parties hold the balance of seats in the legislature that could provide one of the two major parties with the needed majority to form a cabinet and govern. In other words, the vote of the smaller party or parties is indispensable for the formation of a majority. The best illustration of deadlock is found in Israel, where the two major parties have between them 110 out of 120 seats. The remaining seats are in the hands of four minor parties with one, two, or three seats each. It is literally impossible for either major party to reach the needed support level of sixty plus one; hence a continuing deadlock. The very process of governance under these circumstances becomes hostage to miniscule parties that ask for an exorbitant ransom. The deadlock cannot be broken unless the electoral system is changed, or unless a national crisis brings the two major parties together.

Parties of Representation, Parties of Government

In democratic party systems the most important difference is that between parties of representation and parties of government. Parties of representation usually represent well-defined segments of the electorate in terms of religious, ideological, sectional, ethnic, or class interests. They act and speak on behalf of clear-cut points of view and interests. They may be involved with material issues: the farmers, the shopkeepers, or small businesses. They may raise spiritual issues: the church, school prayers, or subsidies for Catholic schools. They may represent racial or ethnic interests (the Catalans or the Basques in Spain), or class interests, or simply deeply rooted ideological positions on the environment, nuclear proliferation, or war and peace. Parties of representation are primarily sectarian parties; they do not expect to gain a majority and form a government. They represent certain points of view.

In regimes where parties of representation are the rule, it is difficult for any single party to win a majority. The government consists of a coalition of the leaders of many parties. In forming a coalition, the emphasis is on the accommodation of conflicting interests and points of view. The formation of a coalition government, usually a cabinet, often resembles treaty making: an agreement that defines the common policies but rules out policy making on matters involving disagreements that cannot be resolved. When the parties that make up the coalition are disciplined, the coalition may last a long time; the treaty will be respected. This is the rule in the Scandinavian countries and Holland. When the parties are undisciplined, the coalition will not last; this was the case with the French Third and Fourth Republics (1871 to 1958) and has been the case in Italy since World War II and more recently in Portugal.

Parties of representation do not provide the conditions for the selection of a government or for a clear change of government at an election. In fact, alternation from one government backed by a given majority to another backed by a different majority is rare. The same parties represent the same variety of interests and ideologies, and every election brings about roughly the same party distribution in the legislature. The strength of the parties shows only incremental fluctuations. This kind of situation was particularly evident in France under the Fourth Republic and has obtained in Italy, Israel, Switzerland, some of the Scandinavian countries, and the Netherlands.

In contrast to parties of representation, parties of government are primarily concerned with organizing the electorate and appealing to it in order to gain a majority and form a government. Parties of government thus link their representative role to that of governance. As a rule, they are disciplined and coherent; they stand behind their leadership; they become truly national, appealing to all cross sections and classes; and they try to aggregate as many viewpoints and interests as possible. They reconcile interests, avoid internal conflicts, and eschew taking sharp ideological positions. They are pragmatic and they realize that they must reach a comprehensive synthesis in order to win a majority. The more they do so, the less the distance between them. They begin to appeal to the same groups, and in their quest of a majority they are particularly anxious not to leave out any minorities, since even a small percent of the vote may make the difference between victory or defeat. They are catchall parties.

Parties of government, as opposed to parties of representation, are able to form stable governments backed by a majority. They give the electorate a clear choice between competing leaders and basic governmental policies. This has generally been the case in Great Britain, West Germany, Canada, New Zealand, Australia, and (if we think of party alignments as "blocs") in France since 1958.

From "Representation" to "Governance"—The Case of France France under the Fifth Republic requires special attention. Until 1958 there were only parties of representation, which reflected sectional interests and ideological points of view. After 1962, however, the president was elected directly by the people, which changed the behavior of parties. Since the presidential election was limited to the two top candidates selected in a national primary, the political parties were forced to seek the widest support possible for their candidates or to align themselves behind one or the other primary winner. They were gradually transformed into parties of government, geared to the choice of a president. Even the Communist party was forced to align itself behind a candidate. Consequently, the party system was transformed. It gradually turned into a two-bloc system: the left and the right, with a dwindling center divided between the two. Because the stakes were high—the presidency and the cabinet—the parties became increasingly disciplined and highly distinct: The government party supported the president and the cabinet, while the other bloc found itself in opposition. Both parties also took on an increasingly national stance. They transcended sectarian, sectional, and even ideological points of view and instead tried to bring as many of them as possible under the same party roof. In 1981 the left-wing bloc ousted the center–right bloc to win the presidency and gain a Socialist majority in the legislature, which supported the president and his prime minister. In 1986 the center–right bloc won a slim majority in the legislature, and in 1989 the two blocs found themselves with about the same strength.

An Evaluation

Parties of representation or parties of government: Which system is "best?" Parties of government simplify and streamline the electoral process, because the public decides between two competing programs and leaderships. They also clarify the issue of responsibility. Election time becomes a day of reckoning for the party in office and gives the opposition a chance to unseat the existing regime. Parties of government truly nationalize the election by allowing the people at large to consider the issues put forth by the government. Such parties gather interests, combine them into policies, and press them upon the government. The great advantage of parties of government, therefore, is that they provide the means for the selection and the operation of a government, give it majority support, and allow the electorate to hold it responsible at election time.

Parties of representation reflect various opinions and differences, and they make it possible for these diverse views to be heard and debated in the legislature. Elections are not limited to a choice between two positions or two leadership teams but to the selection of candidates who express a variety of opinions and interests. Instead of allowing legislative proceedings to become a confrontation between the government majority and the opposition that aspires to replace it, parties of representation provide the conditions for a genuine debate on issues, problems, and policies.

It is only by joining the representative function with that of governance that the political parties can play the role they are cast to play: mobilizing interests, providing the necessary supports, and making it possible for the leadership to form a coherent and stable government. It is through this process that the citizenry can be involved in politics and hold the government responsible for its actions. Parties that are exclusively concerned with winning office may lose their representative character and alienate the electorate. Conversely, parties exclusively concerned with representation may fail to produce and sustain a government that will be able to make policy and resolve conflicts. It would seem, therefore, that the future of political parties in democratic regimes depends on achieving a mix between representation and governance.

Bibliography

On Participation
Almond, Gabriel, and Sidney Verba (eds.). *The Civic Culture Revisited.* Boston: Little, Brown, 1980.

Barnes, Samuel H., and Max Kaase (eds.). *Political Action: Mass Participation in Five Western Democracies.* Beverly Hills, Calif.: Sage Publications, 1979.

Dahl, Robert. *Polyarchy: Participation and Opposition.* New Haven, Conn.: Yale University Press, 1971.

Key, V. O. *The Responsible Electorate.* Cambridge, Mass.: Harvard University Press, 1966.

Milbrath, Lester W. *Political Participation: How and Why Do People Get Involved in Politics?* Chicago: Rand McNally, 1965.

Nie, Norman H., and Sidney Verba. "Political Participation," in Fred I. Greenstein and Nelson W. Polsby, Eds., *Handbook of Political Science,* vol. 4. Reading, Mass.: Addison-Wesley, 1975, pp. 1–75.

Schattschneider, E. E. *The Semi-Sovereign People.* New York: Holt, Rinehart and Winston, 1960.

Verba, Sidney, Norman H. Nie, and Jae-on Kim. *The Modes of Democratic Participation: A Cross-National Comparison.* Beverly Hills, Calif.: Sage Publications, 1971.

On Political Parties

Day, Alan J., and Henry W. Dagenhardt. *Political Parties in the World.* Detroit, Mich.: Gale Research Co., 1980.

Duverger, Maurice. *Political Parties.* New York: John Wiley & Sons, 1962.

Epstein, Leo N. *Political Parties in Western Democracies.* New Brunswick, N.J.: Transaction Press, 1980.

Janda, Kenneth. *A Conceptual Framework for the Comparative Analysis of Political Parties.* Beverly Hills, Calif.: Sage Publications, 1970.

La Palombara, Joseph, and Myron Weiner (eds.). *Political Parties and Political Development.* Princeton, N.J.: Princeton University Press, 1966.

Lawson, Kay. *A Comparative Study of Political Parties.* New York: St. Martin's Press, 1976.

Milner, A. J. *Elections and Political Stability.* Boston: Little, Brown, 1969.

Newmann, Sigmund (ed.). *Political Parties.* Chicago: University of Chicago Press, 1940.

Ostrogorski, M. *Democracy and the Organization of Political Parties.* 2 vols. New Brunswick, N.J.: Transaction Press, 1982.

Rose, Richard. *Do Parties Make a Difference?* 2nd ed. Chatham, N.J.: Chatham House, 1984.

Sartori, Giovanni. *Party and Party Systems.* Cambridge: Cambridge University Press, 1976.

4

Representation, Elections, and Voters

Introduction

In all modern democracies the notion of direct government by the people—the model of ancient Athens—has been replaced by representative government: legislative assemblies of freely elected representatives acting "on our behalf." John Locke, the great theorist of liberal democracy, spoke of the legislature as "the soul of the commonwealth," embodying and integrating the body politic and acting on its behalf. John Stuart Mill, the foremost liberal theorist of the nineteenth century, considered representative government as "the ideally best form of government," one in which "the sovereignty or supreme controlling power in the last resort is vested in the entire aggregate of the community and in which the whole people participate through their elected representative acting on behalf of the whole." But while endowing it with supreme controlling power, Mill considered the legislature ill-equipped to govern. "Instead of the function of governing for which it is radically unfit," he wrote in a well-known passage, "the proper office of a representative assembly is to watch and control the government . . . to throw the light of publicity on its acts; to compel a full exposition and justification of all of them which any one considers questionable; to censure them if found condemnable, and, if the men who compose the government abuse their trust, or fulfil it in a manner which conflicts with the deliberate sense of the nation, to expel them from office, and either expressly or virtually appoint their successors. . . ." The legislature, he argued, should not try to legislate or prepare the budget—it can only accept or reject legislative and spending or revenue measures prepared by the government. "All that is asked for is its consent and the sole power it possesses is that of refusal."[1]

John Stuart Mill clearly separated supreme power from governance. The legislature acting on behalf of the people had the ultimate power over the government, but it was the latter that governed; it made policy on all matters, including the budget, defense, and foreign policy. All the legislature was expected to do was to accept or reject a government and consent to or reject its measures, which often amount to the same thing.

Today in the greatest number of democracies the legislature remains the preeminent institution. Even though in some democratic regimes it has been overshadowed by a prime minister and cabinet or a president or a judiciary, it continues to play a comprehensive role in virtually all affairs of state and performs a great number of functions. These vary from one regime to another, but they can be grouped under two general categories:

1. Functions that relate to legislation as such and the enactment of the budget
2. Functions that are political; i.e., related to fundamental political issues that do not always require legislation[2]

Legislative Functions

Deliberation and Lawmaking

In theory, this is an all important function of the legislature. But as we noted with the British Parliament (and the same is true for most legislatures today), initiating legislation has become increasingly the prerogative of the executive, including the civil service. Deliberation has been reduced to a confrontation of the political parties and their leaders on general policy issues. The legislature does not have the time or the expertise to discuss highly complex measures involving technical, economic, social, and military problems. In virtually all legislative bodies, except the U.S. Congress, few important measures are initiated by the legislators, and among them only a small fraction become laws. Cabinet or presidential initiatives account for the great majority.

[1]John Stuart Mill, *Considerations on Representative Government* (New York: E. P. Dutton, 1970). Originally published 1867.
[2]On contemporary legislatures see Jean Blondel, *Comparative Legislatures* (Englewood Cliffs, N.J.: Prentice-Hall, 1973), and Gerhard Loewenberg and Samuel C. Patterson, *Comparing Legislatures* (Boston: Little, Brown, 1979).

Revenue and Expenses

The "power of the purse," the power to tax and to spend, lies at the heart of the origin and development of legislative assemblies not only in England but almost everywhere. Legislative assemblies deliberated and drafted the budget throughout the nineteenth century. But that was a period when the role of the state was limited to a few essential services: defense, foreign policy, the police, the post office. The budget today encompasses far more. It has become a complex instrument of economic policy involving investment, modernization, industrialization, reallocation of resources, health, education, transportation, and above all social welfare. In theory, all legislative assemblies still have the last word on the budget because they are the ones who are empowered to enact a budget. In practice, it is the executive branch (the president or the prime minister and cabinet) that develops the annual budget, which is then submitted to the legislative assemblies for passage. It is only the U.S. Congress that "makes" the budget, even though the initiative comes from the president. The Congress can amend it at will. In almost all other democracies restrictive rules prohibit the legislators from introducing amendments or initiating new taxes and new expenditures.

Investigations

Legislatures are free, within the limits and constraints deriving from the constitution or the internal distribution of political forces, to investigate every aspect of the polity or of government policy. The French National Assembly, in the aftermath of World War II, produced a monumental series of reports on the causes of the French military defeat. In Great Britain, royal commissions, initiated by the Parliament, produced reports that changed policies with regard to welfare, health, the civil service, the organization and recruitment of the armed forces, and other matters. In the United States, investigation is virtually "the name of the game," and there has been hardly any aspect of policy that has not been thoroughly investigated by congressional committees of inquiry. But investigation, aside from being a necessary condition for deliberation and legislation, is often used as a political instrument for control. How funds have been used by a given agency, how funds have been raised for electoral purposes by certain candidates, the qualifications of cabinet and other officers to be nominated, and the awarding of defense contracts are all topics that provide the opportunity for congressional committees to oversee the executive branch and become involved in policy making and policy decisions even where no legislation is required. In some instances, as in the Watergate and Irangate scandals, such congressional oversight has revealed serious weaknesses in the organization and operation of the republic and heightened public awareness of not only political but also moral questions.

Subordinate Legislation

With the coming of the welfare state and the intervention of the state in the economy, legislation has to deal increasingly with specific technical problems and discrete social and occupational categories. As a result, in almost all legislative assemblies there has been a tendency to draft laws, often referred to as "framework laws," that provide for a general statement of purpose and allow the administrative agencies of the executive to flesh out this legislation with more detailed regulations, ordinances, executive orders, orders in council, or decrees that remain within the guidelines of the framework law. This has produced a new body of law, called "administrative law," or "subordinate legislation."

The explosion of administrative or subordinate law in the modern state has robbed the legislature of control over what it has initiated. As a result, most legislatures are trying to regain that control through the establishment of select legislative committees to scrutinize all subordinate legislation and report to the legislature, often with the explicit recommendation for annulment. A similar technique is to give the legislature the right to veto executive legislation or specify that unless the legislature gives its approval within a given period of time, executive orders or presidential decisions will be automatically annulled. Despite these efforts, however, administrative law has gained overwhelming importance and the legislative assemblies have been unable to limit it or effectively supervise it.

Political Functions

The political role of representative assemblies lies primarily in the linkages they establish between the executive and the public, linkages that enhance its claims of direct control of the executive. Such control varies from one democracy to another, and different mechanisms have developed over time or have been explicitly written into democratic constitutions. We shall discuss the most important ones.

Control Over the Executive's Term

The executive (prime minister and cabinet) in all parliamentary democracies can be removed from office if the legislative assemblies vote against it. This may occur in a variety of ways. It may be by a vote of censure or nonconfidence. It may also result from the rejection by parliament of an important government bill. The government lost votes of confidence in England in 1979, in the Federal Republic of Germany in 1982, in France in 1962, and frequently in Italy and Portugal. Even in presidential regimes, where this ultimate weapon does not exist, the powers of the legislature over the appointment of top officials in the executive (in the United States, the consent of the Senate is required), over taxation and spending, and over treaties and related foreign policy (including defense), act as powerful constraints on the actions of the executive. Indeed, repeated failures by a president to win the confirmation of his nominees to high positions, repeated defeats of important legislative proposals, or refusals to ratify major foreign policy treaties and initiatives may rob a president of governing power just as effectively as a parliamentary vote of no confidence.

In the United States, Congress also has the ultimate and rarely used weapon of impeachment against the President, cabinet officers, and federal judges. Impeachment, provided for by the constitution, in contrast to a vote of no confidence, is a judicial procedure, used for violation of the law, not to resolve policy differences.

Debates

Nelson Polsby, in a perceptive essay on legislatures,[3] noted that some legislative assemblies are in fact forums (he calls them "arenas") where issues are debated, grievances aired, and policy positions outlined by the leaders of the major parties. Instead of legislating, these assemblies debate, and through a debate they present issues and mobilize the public. They are institutions of communication rather than decision. Polsby was drawing our attention to the political role of legislative assemblies, especially in parliamentary regimes with strong parties and strong party leadership, even in cases where legislation and the budget are virtually preempted by the executive. The debates offer the government an opportunity to present its overall policies, and they give the opposition a chance to voice its dissent. The purpose of the debates is to reach a wider public. The legislature thus becomes a forum, a political arena, that mobilizes and organizes opinion. Debate, however, is unlikely to affect the public and mobilize it unless the legislature consists of two organized parties, or stable coalitions of parties, so that opposing arguments can be presented clearly and cogently. Otherwise, the messages it sends to the public may become confusing, thereby alienating the public instead of mobilizing it.

[3]Nelson W. Polsby, "Legislatures," in Fred I. Greenstein and Nelson W. Polsby (eds.), *Handbook of Political Science*, vol. 5 (Reading, Mass., Addison-Wesley, 1975), pp. 257–310.

Electing the Head of State

Many legislatures participate in the election of the head of state, usually a president of a republic with limited tenure. Such was the case with the French National Assembly and Senate under the Fourth Republic, and it is today the case with the Greek legislature. It is virtually the case in Italy and the Federal Republic of Germany. This is clearly a political function, especially when the head of state is given some independent powers.

An Assessment

Despite many setbacks, despite the decline of legislative assemblies at the beginning of the twentieth century, and despite the suppression of many legislatures by authoritarian regimes and their total subordination by totalitarian ones, legislative assemblies have shown remarkable resiliency since World War II. They have reemerged in the Federal Republic of Germany, Japan, Italy, Greece, Spain, Portugal, France, Austria, and other countries that have experienced various forms of authoritarianism. They have even reemerged as significant political institutions in the post-totalitarian regimes of Eastern Europe and the Soviet Union. They continue to play an important role in England and some of the old Commonwealth countries: Canada, Australia, New Zealand, and India. However, they remain brittle in the new political regimes of the Third World, where neither time nor the depth of the existing cleavages have allowed them to gain some degree of acceptance.

Performance should be assessed in terms of the ability of legislatures to handle certain specific functions effectively, not necessarily all functions. Even more important, performance must be viewed in terms of adaptability; whether legislative assemblies can shift from one function to another as circumstances change and can develop new mechanisms to cope with new situations. Finally, they must be assessed in terms of their responsiveness to demands from the populace. If they have the multifunctionality and flexibility to confront new situations and respond to demands, then over time legislative institutions gain popular support and legitimacy.

Several legislative assemblies have gained a particular degree of recognition for the performance of some functions as opposed to others. The British Parliament is known much more as a forum for debate, airing grievances, and discussing issues than as a legislative body. It is a true arena. The major political parties confront each other in Parliament with an eye to the public and to mobilizing support in favor of certain policies and against others. The American Congress has gained respect for its investigatory powers, the major instrument through which it can check the enormous powers of the American presidency. The Scandinavian legislative assemblies have attained a judicious balance between control of the government and legislative independence. The French National Assembly is emerging from a long period of eclipse in which it was dominated by the Gaullist Presidency. It is now reasserting itself as a debating forum and has been particularly active in the enactment of economic reforms and decentralization. In a number of other European democracies the legislatures have reached a balance between their claim to legislate and their political role in controlling executive leadership.

Elections and Electoral Systems

An election can be considered democratic if the following conditions are fulfilled.[4]

1. Substantially the entire adult population has the right to vote and to run for office.
2. Elections take place regularly and within prescribed time limits.
3. No group in the adult population is denied the opportunity of forming a party and putting up candidates.
4. All the seats in the major legislative chamber can be contested and usually are.
5. Campaigns are conducted with reasonable fairness, in that neither law nor violence nor intimidation bars any of the candidates from presenting their views to the voters or prevents the voters from discussing them.
6. Votes are cast freely and secretly; they are counted and reported honestly; and the candidates who receive the proportions of the vote required by law are duly installed in office until their terms expire, at which time a new election is held.

An electoral system is the set of specific rules and regulations that govern the voting process. It governs the election of representatives to the legislature and, in presidential regimes, the election of the president. It has a direct impact on the composition of the legislature, the configuration of the party system, and the formation of a government. The electoral system determines, perhaps more than anything else, the tactics and strategy of political parties, and it has a direct impact on voters' choices. To qualify as democratic, an electoral system may not violate any of the conditions outlined above. Within these restrictions, however, there is a wide variety of electoral systems. In fact, no two democratic regimes have precisely the same electoral system.

[4]The criteria are set forth in David Butler, Howard Penniman, and Austin Ranney, Eds., *Democracy at the Polls* (Washington, D.C.: American Enterprise Institute, 1981), p. 3.

Electing the President

In most democratic regimes with a presidential or semi-presidential system, the goal of electing only a single candidate determines the electoral system. It is necessarily a majority or plurality system: The candidate with the highest number of votes is elected. Primaries are often held, either within the political parties or nationally (as in France and Portugal), to select the candidates; if there is a second round, it usually pits two candidates of the two major parties against each other, although third-party or independent candidates are free to run and often do. It is quite common for the American president, for example, to be elected by a mere plurality. This is not the case in France.

In the French electoral system, the first round of the electoral process is a national primary in which any number of candidates can run to qualify for election. If a candidate receives "fifty percent plus one" of the vote, that candidate is elected outright. If none receives this majority, a new election is held two weeks later between the two top candidates. In the election of 1974, the Gaullist-backed candidate won by 50.8 against 49.2 percent. In 1981 and again in 1988, the Socialist candidate won by 51.7 against 48.3 percent (1981) and 53.7 against 46.3 (1988) (see Table 4.1).

In all presidential elections, the candidate with the greatest number of votes wins. Many have argued that such a system is not fair to the electorate because it leaves a very sizable minority, sometimes half or depending upon the electoral system, even more unrepresented. But since the office of the presidency is in the hands of one person, there is no way, legally or politically, to elect one except by arithmetical majority. Once elected, however, the president is expected to represent the whole nation and act on its behalf. Even those who voted against the president accept the results of the election since they agreed in advance on the rules under which the choice would be made. It is only in a highly fragmented or divided society, when an ethnic, religious, or even ideological minority confronts a majority that the election of a president by a plurality, or even a majority, may cause serious conflicts.

Majoritarianism and Proportional Representation

In parliamentary systems the authority of the prime minister and cabinet, as well as their powers, derives directly from their having gained the majority in the legislature. Sometimes this majority is achieved through a victory by one party in an election, and sometimes it is achieved through a strong and stable coalition formed by several parties. Parties will therefore strive for an electoral majority and may even combine their strength in advance in order to get it.

TABLE 4.1 The French Presidential Election, (1988) (First and Second Round)

Registered	38,128.507
Abstentions	7,100.535 (18.62%)
Invalid	621.934 (2.0%)
Voting	31,027.972

FIRST BALLOT (PRIMARY)

François Mitterrand (Socialist)	10,367.220 (34.09%)
Jacques Chirac (RPR)	6,663.514 (19.94%)
Raymond Barre (UDF)	5,031.849 (16.54%)
Jean Marie Le Pen (National Front)	4,375.894 (14.39%)
Andre Lajoinie (Communist Party)	2,055.995 (6.76%)
Antoin Waechter (Ecologist)	1,149.642 (3.78%)
Pierre Juquin (Communist-Renovation)	639.084 (2.10%)
Arlette Leguillier (Socialist Left)	606.017 (1.99%)
Pierre Boussel (Extreme Left)	116.823 (0.38%)

Total: Left and Extreme Left	45.32%	
Center-Right and Extreme Right	50.87%	
"Ecologists" (Environmentalists)	3.78%	

SECOND BALLOT

Registered	38,168,869
Voting	32,085,071
Abstentions	6,083,798 (15.9%)
Mitterrand	16,704.279 (54.01%)
Chirac	14,218.970 (45.98%)

An alternative to majoritarianism is proportional representation, in which representation in the legislature is granted to parties in proportion to their respective voting strengths. A system of proportional representation encourages the establishment of narrowly defined political parties on the basis of various opinions, interests, ideologies, regionalisms, religious groups, ethnic minorities, and other bases of social division. It gives such groups a better chance of being represented in the legislature. Each vote, no matter where it is cast in the country, counts. Knowing this in advance, voters all over the country can organize themselves into political parties so that they will be able to cast enough ballots to elect even one of their candidates and thus have at least some voice in the legislature.

Perfect proportionality will tend to encourage the fragmentation of the electorate and of the representative institutions they create. If the process of fragmentation becomes extreme, the prospect of forming a stable government will become dim. Representation will be achieved at the expense of governance. This danger is the extreme opposite of that of the perfectly majoritarian system, in which one party, winning only a slim majority of the electorate, can nonetheless command all the seats in the legislature. In that case, a government is assured, but the representation of society will suffer. Representation or government—this is the question! In our earlier discussion on parties of representation and parties of government, we concluded that there should be a mix that gives a fair degree of representation to the people and enough authority and supports to the government so that it can function effectively. The electoral system must make room for both, and this is precisely what is often attempted. The potential impact of rules of representation on the outcome of an election is illustrated in Tables 4.2 and 4.3.

Majoritarianism: Qualifications

There are several methods by which the majoritarian principle (often referred to as the "first past the post" system) is *qualified*, or restricted, in democratic regimes in order to ensure representation.

Districting The country is divided into districts, each with about the same number of people and therefore, eligible voters. It is the winner in each district, by majority or plurality, who is elected. For example, the United Kingdom is divided into 635 constituencies; the United States has 435 districts for election to the House of Representatives; France is

TABLE 4.2   Electoral District: The Whole Country

PERFECT MAJORITARIAN SYSTEM (WINNER TAKES ALL OR "FIRST-PAST-THE-POST")			PERFECT PROPORTIONAL REPRESENTATION SYSTEM (WINNERS TAKE THEIR SHARE)
A			**A1**
PERCENTAGE OF POPULAR VOTE	LEGISLATURE: 400 SEATS		LEGISLATURE: 400 SEATS CORRESPONDING TO 50,000 VOTES PER SEAT
Party A 30	Winner: Party A = 400 seats	Party A	120 seats
B 23		B	92 seats
C 18		C	72 seats
D 9		D	36 seats
E 7		E	28 seats
F 5		F	20 seats
G 5		G	20 seats
H 1		H	4 seats
I 1		I	4 seats
J 1		J	4 seats
			400 seats

TABLE 4.3 Majoritarianism vs. Proportionality: A Concrete Illustration

The differences in the electoral outcomes between a majority and a proportional electoral system can be shown with reference to the British election of 1983. The second column indicates the distribution of seats under the present system, and the third column indicates what the distribution would have been under proportional representation.

PARTY	PERCENT OF POPULAR VOTE	NUMBER OF SEATS	UNDER PROPORTIONAL REPRESENTATION
Conservatives	42.4	397	260
Laborites	27.6	203	180
"Alliance"	25.4	19	165
Other	4.6	16	30
	100	635	635

divided into 577 districts. Territorial and regional subdivisions, with their peculiarities and different traditions or economic and occupational characteristics, provide for variations in party support from one constituency to another, and this makes it practically impossible for a single party to win a majority or a plurality in all the districts and capture all the seats in the legislature (see Table 4.4).

Primaries Primaries give many parties a chance to show their strength and allow voters to participate in the nomination of individual candidates as well as party leaders. Local and district primaries make it possible for local interests and movements to exert influence within a party. Even if new parties and groups fail to nominate their own candidates, they often succeed in gaining a foothold in a major party, broadening the party's program, and making it more representative.

Coalitions To mitigate the rigor of a majoritarian system, smaller parties may form electoral coalitions or agreements or pool their voting strength. Such a coalition appears to the public as one party, but their candidates are chosen from among the parties that make up the coalition. Thus candidates from different parties are listed under the same party ticket. In this manner smaller parties that had no chance may gain some representation. If no such coalition is formed, parties may run separately but may agree in advance to withdraw their candidates from some districts in order to support the candidate of another party, provided the other party reciprocates. If small parties manage to make such agreements, they may be able to overcome the obstacles of the system and gain some representation.

TABLE 4.4   Districting: 400 Electoral Districts (in squares) Electing 400 Representatives

A	A		B			B				C						A			
				D						C	C	C							
														E		E			
								A						G					
								B											
A								C		E							F		
A								D											
					F			E						D					
								F											
B								G				I							
B								H											
H		G						I	H						I				H
H								J											
					J						J						B		
			A														B		
			A														B		
									E										

French Majoritarianism   The British electoral system (also followed in New Zealand, Australia, India, and Canada), in which there are no primaries, has always been cited as a system that represses minority parties: The party candidate who passes the post first wins; all others disappear. The French electoral system that has been used since 1958 also penalizes minorities drastically, yet it also promotes the formation of coalitions. This system involves two stages. In the first stage, any number of candidates can run in the designated electoral districts. The candidate who wins 50 percent plus one is the winner. Only some 70 to 130 deputies are elected in this manner on the first ballot, leaving about 365 to 425 seats undecided. Within a week a second balloting takes place in all the undecided districts. Only candidates that were supported by more than 12.5 percent of the registered voters in the electoral district on the first ballot are allowed by law to run again. This virtually eliminates all small and even middle-sized party candidates, since 12.5 percent of the registered voters amounts to well over 20 percent of the votes cast. Thus only the candidates of three or four of the major parties can run again, but in fact only two run. The major parties and their candidates make reciprocal agreements in advance to pool their votes on the second ballot. In almost all districts the second ballot becomes what the French call a "duel" between candidates of two rival party blocs. (See Table 4.5.)

TABLE 4.5 French Majoritarian System (Legislative Election—An Illustrative Example)

ELECTORAL DISTRICT X REGISTERED VOTES 120,000*

	D1 PRIMARY (FIRST BALLOT)	D2 RUNOFF (SECOND BALLOT)
1. Communist: Binet	15,000 (withdraws in favor of 2)	Trinet 50,700
2. Socialist: Trinet	23,000	
3. Revolutionary/Trotskyite: Finet*	1,200 (withdraws in favor of 2)	vs.
4. Radical: Quinet*	13,000 (withdraws in silence)	Traboulet 53,000 ELECTED
5. Union of French Democracy: Traboulet	21,000	Traboulet received his own votes, plus those of the Gaullists, plus the votes of the extreme right, plus at least two-thirds of the radicals and fractions of others.
6. Gaullist: Cassoulet	19,000 (withdraws in favor of 5)	
7. Environmentalist: Le Foret*	3,000 (withdraws in favor of 2)	
8. Europeanist: Bardoulet*	1,500 (withdraws in silence)	
9. Extreme right: Barbaroux*	5,000 (withdraws in favor of 5)	Two thousand voters who abstained on the first ballot voted in the second.
Total Vote = 101,700		Total vote: 103,700 thousand

Note: There are 577 seats in the National Assembly. They correspond to 577 electoral districts that vary in size and population and hence in the number of registered voters.

*Candidates 3, 4, 7, 8, and 9 do not receive the requisite 12.5 percent of the registered votes and do not qualify for the runoff; candidates 1, 2, 5, and 6 do.

At this stage, the voter is forced to choose between two party candidates, and the parties are forced to form blocs. In this manner, parties of representation are gradually transformed into parties of government. The coalitions or blocs that are formed give a modicum of representation to smaller parties and a maximum of support and authority to the government.

Proportional Representation: Qualifications

Proportional representation is widely used in most European countries: West Germany (a modified form), Belgium, Luxembourg, Switzerland, Holland, Italy, Austria, Finland, the Scandinavian countries, and the Southern Mediterranean countries (Spain, Portugal, Italy, and Greece). It is also being adopted by the emerging democracies of Eastern Europe. All these countries have been and remain multiparty systems, and in most of them the government relies on party coalitions to secure majority support in parliament. But in virtually all of them the electoral system used favors the stronger parties.

Districting In almost all countries with proportional representation, districting is also used. Candidates in a district are elected if they win a number of votes amounting to the quotient of the district's voters divided by the number of seats allotted to it. (Seats are allotted according to the number of residents in each district.) Thus, if the total vote in a district allotted three seats is 100,000, any candidate who received at least 33,334 votes would be elected. Usually, a number of electoral districts make up an electoral region, and there may be five or six electoral districts in each electoral region. All excess votes, i.e., all votes that are in excess of the required minimum for winning a seat or below the minimum for a losing one in any given district, are added up for the whole electoral region and redistributed among party candidates in accordance with their strength. There is usually a third and last distribution, where all votes that were not counted in all the electoral regions are added up and party candidates are chosen accordingly.

Exclusions In proportional representation systems, every vote counts. This distinguishes them from majoritarian systems that effectively discard the votes of even a large minority. Yet there are proportional representation systems that exclude minorities. In West Germany, for instance, unless a party receives 5 percent of the national vote, it is not represented at all; its votes are lost. This system is calculated to discourage small parties and splinter groups. In other countries, unless a party receives 10, 15, or 17 percent of the national vote, it has no right to the second and third distributions. Thus, many of these systems, while stressing representativeness, try to avert the fragmentation of the electorate by making it possible for a party to win an absolute majority of the seats in the legislature even if it receives less than a majority of the vote. In many of these countries a popular vote of 43 to 45 percent assures a party of such an absolute majority in the legislature.

Representativeness and Governance

The qualifications of majoritarian or proportional principles of representation try to effect a balance between representativeness and government support. They attempt to reconcile the democratic principles of fair and equal representation of as many points of view as possible with the needs of stable and effective government. Consent and command have to be linked. It would be foolhardy to say that modern democracies have managed to accomplish this with complete success. In England and the United States minorities remain grossly underrepresented. In France coalitional politics do attenuate, but only to a degree, the inequalities in representation, especially of minorities and ideological groups. In many democracies sizable fractions of the electorate frequently find themselves without a voice. If they remain excluded from the appropriate vehicle of expression (the legislature) they will seek to make themselves heard elsewhere. They may move to confrontational politics or resort to violence. On the other hand, a regime that gives a voice to all in proportion to numerical strength, no matter how slight, may deprive a society of the opportunity to attenuate differences and seek compromise. Without such compromise there can be no strong plurality or majority to support a government and its policies. Everyone will hear his or her own voice until no voice can be heard, and there will be no policy and no viable government.

The qualifications we have outlined both to majoritarianism and proportional representation attempt to avoid these extremes and structure and organize consent and support without stifling dissent on the one hand or paralyzing governance on the other.

Voter Alignments: Parties and Society

As we have seen, parties reflect and in turn organize various social forces. They try to be both representative and aggregative. There are several important factors, social and otherwise, that structure an individual's attachment to and vote for a party; in other words, his or her partisanship. Some of them include social determinants such as class, occupation, religion, regionalism, ethnicity, race, language, income, and education. Others relate to broader considerations: traditions, specific historical circumstances, particular short-term issues, the state of the economy, war and peace, and sometimes even the integrity, personality, and leadership qualities of candidates themselves.

It is virtually impossible to do more than suggest some descriptive generalizations on how people vote in elections and why they vote for one party or another. While the social determinants mentioned above can be clearly spelled out, they have to be qualified in a number of ways because there is no *single* social determinant that accounts for partisanship. There are only *clusters* of determinants that can account for it, and the clustering in one country rarely duplicates that in another. Moreover, there are parties whose voter support does not seem to correlate clearly with *any* set of social determinants. As Richard Rose suggests, "Because parties may unite support on several grounds [or none] party systems must be perceived in terms of a multidimensional space." It is even possible, he adds, "to have a no-dimension party system, i.e., one in which [parties] can [not] be placed on a social dimension because they are heterogeneous . . . in terms of major social characteristics."[5] In fact, there is a degree of heterogeneity in all parties. In a democracy it is almost impossible for a party to be exclusively and solely identified with any single social characteristic, not even class, language, ethnicity, or race. Practically all parties are multidimensional.

The most significant dimensions in identifying political parties are 1) class, (2) religion, (3) ethnicity, and (4) region. Party programs rationalize the position of the voters in terms of particular groups from whom the party seeks to derive its major support. There have been religious parties, farmers' parties, middle-class parties, working-class parties, ethnic, linguistic, and racial parties, and parties directly sponsored by business groups. Class has always been considered a key factor, but nowhere is there a full identification between a given class and a political party; at best, there is only a rough correlation. In fact, all political parties straddle social classes, particularly those in Canada and the United States. In other countries, such as England, France, and Italy, however, the correlation between the working classes and left-wing parties (the Labour Party in Britain and the Socialists and Communists in France and Italy) is clearly marked. It is only with ethnic parties, and especially when ethnicity coincides with language, religion, and territory, that identification is overwhelming: the Flemings and Walloons in Belgium, the French Québecois in Canada, and the many ethnic or nationality groups in multi-ethnic Yugoslavia, Czechoslovakia, and the Soviet Union have established their own political parties.

Class

Working-class identification with left-wing parties remained powerful until World War II. Since the war, modernization has undermined the political coherence of the working class. What was in fact the most

[5]Richard Rose, Ed., *Electoral Behavior: A Comparative Study* (New York: The Free Press, 1974), p. 19.

homogeneous and self-conscious group in industrial societies in the nineteenth century is today fragmented in terms of occupation, income, and lifestyle. With the waning of the homogeneity of the workers, the correlation between left-wing parties and workers has declined. Socialist and communist parties that used to appeal to an undifferentiated mass of workers now have to straddle class and appeal to other social and economic groups for votes and support.

As a result, the partisanship and the votes of the workers go to various parties. In England, as much as 30 percent of the working class votes Conservative. In France, an even greater percentage of workers supported DeGaulle and continue to vote for conservative and centrist parties. In the United States during the last thirty years, the working class has generally divided its vote for president between the Republican and Democratic candidates.

Religion, Race, and Ethnicity

In some countries, Belgium, Holland, or Canada, for example, partisanship based on religion is strong. In others, such as France, where 90 percent of the population is Catholic, the major distinction is between those who attend church regularly and those who attend intermittently, or are agnostics. It is an important factor, since the believers tend to vote for the conservative parties while the lukewarm Catholics and agnostics vote for the center, the socialists, and even the communists. In the election of 1981, however, the socialists captured many Catholic votes, only to lose many of them since then. In England, the religious factor reinforces class: nonconformist groups that are mostly working class or lower middle class vote for Labour, while Anglicans and Episcopalians vote for the Liberal or the Conservative party. In the United States, Caltholics voted overwhelmingly for the Democratic party for decades. Recently, however, there has been a marked realignment of the Catholic vote in the direction of the Repubican party. Economic and social factors account for it, since many of the second and third generation Catholics have improved their economic status and living standards, and they now vote their "pocketbooks."

Race plays a major role in American politics. On the national level, Blacks increasingly identify themselves with the Democratic party. Ninety percent of the Black electorate voted for the Democratic candidate in the 1984 presidential election, and 88 percent in the 1988 election. Throughout Eastern Europe and the Soviet Union, the mobilization of ethnic identities in opposition to the old, authoritarian communist regimes has strengthened political groups and parties seeking to establish autonomous democratic regimes in their ethnic homelands. Lithuanian, Latvian, Estonian, Ukrainian, and other ethnically based parties seeking to establish autonomous, democratic regimes in their respective parts of what is now the Soviet Union have recently won impressive electoral victories, and gained sufficient power to challenge the continuation of the existing order. In Yugoslavia, the Slovenian democratic opposition has won control of the Slovenian regional government. And in Czechoslovakia, the Slovak democratic movement seeks to alter the imbalance it perceives in the distribution of power between Czechs and Slovaks. While in these cases the politicization and mobilization of ethnic identity has strengthened the drive toward democracy in the local territory, it has also produced the mobilization of other identities among the other peoples of these multi-ethnic states, and made the transition to a democratic order more complex. For, unlike claims based on material interests, competing claims based on affective power of ethnic identity are very difficult to compromise. As the recent experience of Canada and Quebec suggests, the peaceful resolution of such claims may require a redefinition or even dissolution of these multi-ethnic states.

Regionalism

Regionalism denotes common political attitudes and orientations that stem from the economic and cultural concerns of people in a particular region. It may be, and it usually is, associated with levels of economic underdevelopment or ethnic and linguistic characteristics that form the basis of an incipient separatist movement. If a region is predominantly inhabited by people sharing a religious denomination and if historic, ethnic, and national factors have perpetuated a sense of autonomy and independence among them, then it is likely that the great majority of the people will affiliate themselves with a party that espouses their cause. The French-speaking Québecois in Canada and the Flemings and the Walloons in Belgium are good examples, as are the Lithuanians in the Soviet Union and the Slovenes in Yugoslavia. But significantly enough, regionalism in these cases is enhanced by class, as well as by occupational and linguistic factors. It is a combination of many determinants: religion *plus* class *plus* regionalism *plus* language *plus* economic conditions. It is always such a special kind of clustering that accounts for regional voting. A single factor does not suffice; we need a number of them that are linked, and we cannot tell which link is the strongest.

Cross-cutting Loyalties

One of the characteristics of socioeconomic modernization and political development has been the weakening of attachments that relate directly to class, region, ethnicity, language, religion, or occupation. Society as a whole has become characterized by an increasing number of highly particularized interests and attitudes. One individual is increasingly likely to straddle many attachments and loyalties and will therefore be unable to attach himself exclusively to one of them. Individuals who fit into a number of socioeconomic categories (i.e., into many determinants that shape their attitudes) may eventually transcend them all. By belonging or being attached to many categories, they may end up belonging to none!

The existence of diverse social forces, as well as groups that have multiple and often contradictory or cross-cutting loyalties, gives individuals more freedom to vote their preferences and shape their partisanship. Independent voters, those with no partisanships, vote for their choice regardless of party, often shifting from one party to another. Their decisions and choices are made on the basis of other considerations and factors. What are they?

Judgment, Issues, and Leadership

Besides the theory that social determinants determine partisanship and voting, there is also a theory of voluntarism, whereby people exercise their own independent judgment. It is a thesis supported by the recent decline in party membership, the weakening of partisan attachments, the growth of independent voters, and the rapid rise and fall of some political parties. Consider, for example, the following developments: the drop of about 15 percent in the votes for the Labour party in the British election of 1983 and the corresponding rise of the Alliance (comprised of Social Democrats and Liberals), and again the resurgence of the Labour party in the late eighties; the decline by at least 10 percent of votes for the French Communists and the rise of the Socialists by about 11 percent in the French legislative elections of June 1981 and 1988; the emergence of powerful right-wing extremist groups in France and elsewhere between 1986 and 1990. Most striking of all is the emergence of a dual pattern of support in the United States: for the Republicans at the presidential level and for the Democrats at the congressional and local levels. None of these changes can be attributed solely to changes in social structure and determinants. The proposition that issues and leaders make an important difference in how people vote, perhaps even more important than class or income, and the thesis that they exercise their own judgment should be seriously entertained.

The catchall party, which we discussed earlier, was without any doubt a stimulus to the independence of voters. By definition it was a party that was multidimensional: it tried to get the vote by cutting across class, occupation, ethnicity, religion, and regional attachments. In so doing, it gradually moved people from their social moorings (their determinants). The catchall party, in trying to appeal to so many social groups, did not provide an adequate center of loyalty and partisanship. The voters found themselves increasingly on their own and free to espouse issues and support leaders as they saw fit. Choice became subject to personal judgment rather than organizational pressure. Particular policy concerns of the moment became more important than long-range policy considerations. The importance of the personality of the candidate overwhelmed the issues, as candidates came to be judged by the mass media in terms of empathy, charisma, "leadership" qualities, trustworthiness, and honesty.

Leadership traits have played a crucial role in most of the recent elections in Western Europe and the United States. Party leaders have detached themselves from their party organizations and have appealed directly to the people. They have attempted to convert elections into personal plebiscites.

Bibliography

Legislatures
Blondel, Jean. *Comparative Legislatures.* Englewood Cliffs, N.J.: Prentice-Hall, 1973.

Crick, Bernard. *The Reform of Parliament.* 2d ed. London: Weidenfeld & Nicolson, 1968.

Hirsh, Herbert, and M. Donald Hancock. *Comparative Legislative Systems.* New York: The Free Press, 1971.

Jennings, Ivor. *Parliament.* London: Macmillan, 1940.

Kornberg, Alan (ed.). *Legislatures in Comparative Perspective.* New York: David McKay, 1973.

Loewenberg, Gerhard, and Samuel C. Patterson. *Comparing Legislatures.* Boston: Little, Brown, 1979.

Loewenberg, Gerhard (ed.). *Modern Parliaments: Change or Decline?* Chicago: University of Chicago Press, 1971.

Mill, John Stuart. *Considerations on Representative Government.* South Bend, Ind.: Gateway Editions, 1962.

Pitkin, Hannah. *The Concept of Representation.* Berkeley and Los Angeles: University of California Press, 1972.

Wheare, Kenneth. *Legislatures.* Oxford: Oxford University Press, 1963.

On Elections
Bogdanor, V., and David Butler (eds.). *Democracy and Elections: Electoral Systems and Their Political Consequence.* New York: Cambridge University Press, 1983.

Butler, David, Howard Penniman, and Austin Ranney (eds.). *Democracy at the Polls: A Comparative Study of Competitive National Elections.* Washington, D.C.: American Enterprise Institute, 1981.

Carstairs, Andrew M. *A Short History of Electoral Systems in Western Europe.* London: George Allen & Unwin, 1980.

Dalton, R. J., S. C. Flanagan, and P. A. Beck. *Electoral Change in Advanced Industrial Democracies: Realignment or Dealignment.* Princeton, N.J: Princeton University Press, 1984.

Kavanagh, Dennis. The British General Election of 1987. New York, N.Y.: Macmillan, 1988.

Penniman, Howard (ed.). "At the Polls." Washington, D.C.: American Enterprise Institute. 1983.

Rae, D. W. *The Political Consequences of Electoral Laws.* New Haven, Conn.: Yale University Press, 1967.

Sallnow, John, and Anna John. *An Electoral Atlas of Europe, 1968–1981.* Stoneham, Mass.: Butterworth's, 1982.

5

Interests and Rights

Introduction

Democratic regimes provide guarantees of the broadest possible freedoms: individual freedoms, rights of association and expression, and freedom for interests to organize and manifest themselves. We shall first discuss interests and interest configuration, and then we shall turn to a discussion of individual rights.

Interest Configuration

The civil society enjoys almost full autonomy from the state. Interests— interest groups and interest associations—constantly strive for maximum benefits and constantly pressure the government for favors, concessions, help, and even direct or indirect material supports. Interests are so many and variegated that it would be impossible to give a detailed account of them. Generally speaking, however, there are three generic types of interest groups: *material, spiritual,* and *promotional.*

    Material interest organizations are primarily concerned with the preservation and the advancement of material benefits, even if they couch them in idealistic terms. General Motors, trade unions, the American Medical Association, the Trade Union Congress in England, the Jeunes Patrons in France, various Chambers of Commerce, and the many business and professional associations belong to this category. *Spiritual interests* are primarily religious, philanthropic, and educational.

But there are also material considerations linked with these lofty vocations. Would not universities and their supporters protest if contributions were to lose their status as tax exemptions? Would not churches protest the application of a property tax to their holdings? *Promotional interests* advocate causes that do not seem to be directly linked to material interests; for example, environmentalists, right-to-life advocates, or reform groups (i.e., to reform the tax structure or the civil service or local government). Yet if you scratch the surface of such groups, you will find material interests and concerns underneath. Finally, various agencies of the state often act like pressure groups in order to maintain their autonomy and satisfy their constituencies. The military, for example, is widely recognized as a powerful political "lobby" in both domestic and foreign affairs.

Interests in different democratic regimes are configured in many different ways. But there are also important similarities.

The first and foremost similarity is the fact that there is *freedom* in a democracy. Interests are *allowed* to organize and propagate their claims and points of view independent of the state. Fraternal associations, veterans of various wars, snake worshippers and sun worshippers, margarine and butter producers, tobacco growers and nonsmokers, homosexuals and polygamists, working mothers and unemployed husbands, private schools and colleges, businessmen, farmers, manufacturers, spinsters and school teachers, feminists and male chauvinists, divorced women and alimony payers, the young, the aging, and the aged—name any occupation, any predicament, any cause, any situation, any loyalty, and you will find an organization, an association, a lobby, a club, or a fraternal association representing it.

Second, the interest configuration in democratic regimes shows a great *diversity*. Interest groups mirror the manifold societal forces, and their very multiplicity attests to the vitality of the societal forces.

Third, interest associations are formed *spontaneously*, and they are constantly mushrooming. They spring from the societal soil. They express common concerns and predicaments, which they hope to promote or alleviate. There is a great degree of creativity in this process, providing change or at least keeping the door open for change.

Fourth, individual participation in interest organizations is *voluntary* and interest organizations are *independent* from one another.

Finally, interest group activity serves as a means for the identification and *recruitment* of future leaders. It provides a training ground for them. Interest groups also add additional dimension to participation in the political process. People who are disenchanted by political parties and government officials find their group to be a center of loyalty and a vehicle of participation that inevitably will bring them to grips with policies and policy makers.

Strength and Tactics

Interest groups and associations rely on many sources for their strength: membership, ideology, organization, material resources, and the particular skills of their members.

Membership In any group, one source of strength lies simply in numbers. How many members does it have? The larger the membership, the greater the potential strength.

Ideology While the basic beliefs of an association are important, the intensity of these beliefs is even more important. The extent and the degree to which members identify with the overall purposes of the group and how deeply they are involved in it are of critical significance. They provide for common action.

Organization A group with a large and diversified membership may be unable to get its members mobilized and active. Trade unions in many industrialized societies find themselves in this predicament today. On the other hand, a small interest group with a small, well-organized membership that strongly believes its ideology can be very effective.

Material Resources and Skills Solid financial backing is obviously a major source of strength. So are the particular professional skills of the members. Small associations whose members have special knowledge and can perform important and sensitive jobs—computer programming or air-traffic control, for instance—have greater impact and influence than groups with members who are numerous but lacking in skills. This is the major reason why the process of modernization, and the creation of highly differentiated and specialized occupations, also tends to produce a great variety of new and influential interests.

Modes of Action Interest groups in democracies share common modes of action. We list some of the most important.

Information and Propaganda. The means used to influence public opinion are the mass media: press, radio, and television. Many interest groups have their own newspapers, and some control radio and television stations through which they inform and often help shape public opinion.

Political Organization. Interest groups try to influence elections by actively throwing support and resources behind certain candidates and against others. They mobilize the electorate and provide, within legal limits, direct financial help to candidates. Sometimes even more important is the fact that organized interests, especially trade unions, are able to mobilize human resources—people—to perform the mundane tasks associated with political campaigning. If elected, the candidates who received this support are expected to defend and promote the interests that helped them get into office. The impact of the Moral Majority or the National Rifle Association in the United States on the election of senators and congressmen in the seventies and eighties cannot be underestimated. The American Association of Retired Persons (AARP), which actively represents the interests of Senior Citizens, is one of the most influential political lobbying groups in American politics. Similarly, the impact of the nuclear freeze movement and the environmentalist lobby cannot be ignored. As for trade unions, business associations, and religious associations, their direct weight in elections continues to be significant almost everywhere.

In trying to persuade everybody about the validity of their claims, all interest groups use lobbying tactics; i.e., putting direct pressure on legislators and public officials. With dominant interest groups the tactics may prove successful, and efforts are being made to use public funds to underwrite electoral campaign costs in order to safeguard the independence of elected officials.

Access

Interest groups not only want to shape or influence public opinion, but also they want to get candidates sympathetic to their views elected, or at least avert the election of candidates with opposing points of view. In their attempt to gain access to policy making, interest groups interact with all four major components of the command structure: the legislature, the executive branch (cabinet or presidential), the bureaucracy, and the political parties.

Interests and Political Parties Four types of relationships between interest groups and political parties can be envisaged: *separation, affiliation* and *collaboration*, and *fusion*.

Separation. Separation characterizes interest groups that claim to be apolitical. They give or withhold their support from a political party depending on where a party stands with regard to their interests and their demands. They may also shift support from one party to another depending on the positions the parties take. They usually reward their friends, whoever they may be, and punish their enemies.

Affiliation and Collaboration. Major interests may align themselves behind one or another political party through collaboration rather than support. This typically has been the case with trade unions and socialist parties in Western Europe and Great Britain. Sometimes collaboration can lead to affiliation: trade union members, for example, have automatically become members of the Socialist party, as in the British Labour party. Collaboration with the Democratic party through the endorsement and direct support of Democratic candidates has been a predominant tactic of American trade union leadership since 1932. French and Italian unions have collaborated with the Socialist and the Communist parties. Similarly, a number of religious and conservative parties in Europe, especially in the Netherlands and Belgium, continue to be supported by and to collaborate with the Catholic church.

Political parties, while welcoming support and collaboration, are generally apprehensive of affiliation, particularly in two-party regimes. The parties want to extend their appeal beyond single, particularistic interests and avoid any identification that might alienate some voters. They prefer supports and discreet collaboration. In multiparty regimes, however, where no single party is likely to win a majority, a party that identifies with a particular interest group may mobilize its members and consolidate its voting strength. This is even more so in regimes that have a proportional-representation electoral system. When a party becomes the voice for one powerful interest or a cluster of a few interests, it can count on its votes at election time. In majority and plurality electoral systems, close collaboration and especially affiliation are avoided. Where they do exist, there is constant friction between the political party and the particular interest groups affiliated with it.

Fusion. Fusion between an interest association and a party is rare for the same reasons that inspire caution in establishing collaboration. Although religious movements have frequently come close to fusing with a given political party, they have never actually done so. The Popular Republican party (MRP) that emerged in France after World War II was led and organized by progressive and liberal Catholic Action leaders, but it became a lay organization that appealed to Catholics and non-Catholics alike. Indeed, some of its younger leaders at the time have now joined the Socialist party. Similarly, the Catholic party of Germany that became the Christian Democratic Union after World War II abandoned many of its ties with the Church. The same may become the case with the Italian Christian Democrats.

Trade unions have sought to establish not only the collaborative ties with political parties outlined above, but also outright fusion, notably with communist and socialist parties. This was the case between the General Confederation of Labor (CGT) in France and the Communist party, as well as the Confederation of Democratic Labor (CGTD) and the Socialist party. It has also been the case with British and Swedish trade unions and the Labour and Social Democratic parties. The same pattern was followed between the National Confederation of Labor and the Communist party in Italy and between the trade unions and either communists or socialists in Spain and Portugal.

There is real fusion when an interest group aggressively captures an existing political party or itself becomes one. Environmentalists, professional groups, and extremist movements from the right and left have often followed one or the other of these paths. One of the most spectacular movements of this kind was the formation of the Union of French Fraternity in the mid-1950s, a political movement representing the interests of small manufacturers, artisans, shopkeepers, and small farmers. Similarly, the Greens in West Germany emerged as a party to represent the demands of environmentalist groups. We have also seen specialized parties favoring tax cuts, prohibition, tariff reforms, or environmental concerns, which have been spawned by interest groups to serve their purposes. But most such parties develop an independent organization and purpose and detach themselves from the interest that gave birth to them in order to survive.

Interests and the Legislature Major decisions about allocation of resources, welfare programs, and taxation are formally adopted by the legislature. The legislative process is the component of the command decision-making process most open and accessible to pressure groups. Interests are concerned about the legislative agenda in order to make themselves heard about impending legislative measures. Frequently there are identifiable groups of lawmakers within a legislature, sometimes cutting across party lines, that are particularly responsive to well-known interests, even to the extent of speaking on their behalf, and they can be relied on to advance the claims of these interests. Legislators are approached directly by interest representatives, or lobbyists. Legislative committees are given information by interest spokesmen, who are asked to testify before legislative committees. When legislators themselves initiate legislation, the drafts are often prepared with the assistance of representatives of interest organizations.

The impact of interests on legislators, directly or indirectly or in committees, depends to a great degree on the organization of the legislative process. In cases where legislation is initiated by a government that heads a strong and disciplined party, interest representatives must influence the government itself while it is still formulating its policies, an often difficult task. However, in cases where a legislature consists of a number of political parties, interests that gain access to party leaders may be more effective. Generally speaking, the effectiveness of interest groups in the legislature correlates inversely with the coherence of the legislative process; that is, with the ability of the executive to control and coordinate it.

Interests and the Executive   Only major interests with a national organization can and successfully do influence the executive branch directly.
They can use personal and direct contacts with cabinet members, with
the advisers of the various ministers, or with the prime minister or the
president. In some cases, such interests may "colonize" a department or
a ministry responsible for the administration of policy on matters that
concern them.

    The civil service is constantly being exposed to pressure. Since civil
servants implement legislation and have considerable discretion in doing so, interest group spokesmen provide information, advice, research
papers, studies, and so forth. They establish direct personal contacts
with civil servants and develop a consultative relationship pattern.
Moreover, interest groups have other means to reinforce their positions.
They can always provide job opportunities to government officials,
military or civilian, when these officials resign or retire.

    A number of forces account for the institutionalization of coopera-
tion between interest groups and the agencies of the state. Trade unions
came to be accepted as workers became more numerous and their
potential impact on the political order more powerful. Industrial organization and the outlook of business firms in general also began to change.
The family firm gave place to managerial and bureaucratic organizations
operating on the basis of well-established and agreed-upon rules.
Paternalism yielded to highly organized forms of management. After
World War II interest representation in all democracies was in a state of
rapid expansion and ferment. It could no longer be ignored or contained.

Corporatism

The first stage in the legitimization of interests begins when state agencies try to secure information from them—through royal commissions,
special commissions of inquiry, or investigating committees staffed by
civil servants. Facts ferreted out from the professional organizations by
such commissions inform policy makers. The second stage comes with
the creation of advisory boards consisting of representatives from various interests who participate, even in an advisory capacity, in policy
making. The difference between information-gathering groups and
advisory boards is that the latter are granted a representative role: they
can speak "authoritatively." The practice of soliciting information and
seeking advice from professional organizations strengthens them. It
elevates them to a position of expertise and qualifies them as government consultants. Inasmuch as interest organizations develop their own
staffs and experts, often recruiting them from universities and top managerial personnel, their claim of expertise injects an element of objectiv-

ity and pragmatism in the dialogue between professional organizations and state agencies. The third stage amounts to the granting of deliberative and policy-making functions to representatives of various interests. This is the stage of corporatism, which is present to various degrees in all contemporary democracies.

Charles S. Maier defines corporatism as "a partial devolution of public policy-making and enforcement on organized private interests."[1] It is the joining of public agencies and private interest groups in the making and implementing of government policy. In its early institutionalization it brings various interests in key economic activities into an organization or "corporation" that encompasses all those who participate in the same economic activity. The conflicting interests of the participants are reconciled, and concomitantly, the various corporations are represented in a council or chamber where various economic, industrial, labor, and other interests are discussed and some policies are made. The rationale behind corporatist arrangements is that class conflicts will be muted and that, through the presence and intervention of the state, the collective and public interest will prevail.

Corporatist institutions developed in Italy under the Fascists; in Vichy France, during the short period of that regime's existence (1941–1944); in Portugal under the dictatorship of Salazar and his successor, Marcello Caetano (1931–1973); and also in Spain, Austria, and elsewhere. As is evident from this list, corporatism was first developed in nondemocratic regimes. The state retained a controlling voice over the corporations, often overriding the interests that were represented.

Corporatist practices reemerged after World War II, however, and are very much in evidence in democratic regimes today. In democracies that have instituted economic planning, the major guidelines of the economic plan are drafted by assemblies or councils that represent various interests. In regimes that have nationalized industrial and other sectors of the economy, the directors of industries and other enterprises are advised by councils elected by the major interest organizations involved. In democracies where there is neither nationalization nor economic planning, many regulatory decisions affecting the economy are made through direct cooperation between government agencies and interests, often bypassing the parties and even the legislature. Sam Beer has called such practices "collectivist,"[2] and they are very much in evidence in England, Italy, Austria, Belgium, France, and to a lesser degree, even in the United States. In the Scandinavian countries, many major social and economic policies are fashioned through negotiations

---

[1]Suzanne Berger, Ed., *Organizing Interests in Western Europe: Pluralism, Corporatism and the Transformation of Politics* (New York: Cambridge University Press, 1981), p. 49.
[2]Samuel H. Beer, *British Politics in the Collectivist Age* (New York: Random House, 1965), and *Britain Against Itself: The Political Contradictions of Collectivism* (New York: W. W. Norton, 1982).

between the representatives of interests and the governmental agencies. We may then speak of the emergence of "democratic" or "societal" corporatism as opposed to "state" or "authoritarian" corporatism.[3]

Democratic Corporatism

Democratic corporatism shares some similarities with democratic pluralism: (1) the formation of interest and *professional* organizations is spontaneous; (2) the dialogue among them and between them and the state is voluntary; and (3) interest associations remain autonomous in their relationship to public authorities, even when special policy-making functions are given to them. But there are some significant differences. In democratic corporatism—especially in the Scandinavian countries— interests are organized vertically and include all members of a given economic activity. Professional organizations tend to become monopolistic; that is, common interests shared by individuals in the same profession can be defended or promoted only within the representative organization. As a result, professional organizations are closed: Individuals and member organizations can neither leave without jeopardizing their professional standing nor join unless they have such standing. But above all, professional organizations develop institutionalized and legally binding links with the state agencies, and they consequently become semi-public agencies, acting on behalf of the state. Corporatist practices impose structure, hierarchy, and binding ties between the members and their organizations and between the representative organizations and the state. In so doing, they undermine individual and associational freedoms.

The cases of democratic corporatism are plentiful and they do not appear only in labor–management relationships. In the United States, the National Recovery Act of 1934 provided instances when industrial policies regarding employment and collective bargaining could be made by private industry. In Italy, as Schonfield points out, the idea of a "balanced and responsible economic group with quasi-sovereign power administering itself" continues to hold wide currency. Trade unions in the Netherlands show "restraint" in dealing with the state in order to preserve jobs. In Sweden the interest groups are strongly organized and "their habit of bargaining with the government [is] well established." In fact the process of government in Sweden is "an extended dialogue between experts drawn from a variety" of representative interest associations. West German national business and professional associations

---

[3]This corresponds to the distinction made by many French authors between *corporatisme d'etat* and *corporatisme d'associations*. See also Philippe C. Schmitter and Gerhard Lehmbruch, (eds.), *Trends Toward Corporatist Intermediation* (Beverly Hills, Calif.: Sage Publications, 1979).

have been viewed "as the guardians of the long-term interests of the nation's industries." This is not so in France, however, where they have been identified by the left and, during World War II, by the Gaullists as hostile to the national interest and responsible for France's collapse in the 1930s. Yet even in France, on a number of occasions business interests have acted together with trade unions in determining wages, employment, and social policies, and they have reached collective agreements that became binding on both business and labor.[4] Public policy outcomes, especially in education and agricultural policies, have been shaped and often implemented by their professional organizations.

In summary, interests and interest representation, including corporatist practices, have gained acceptance in democratic regimes. Interest representation has become institutionalized, which gives groups greater weight and strength, but may also undermine their autonomy and freedoms. Corporatism in its broadest terms may be viewed as the long overdue realization that interests, like ideas and political parties, constitute an important factor in the organization of consent. They can speak out through qualified spokesmen and participate in the formulation and implementation of policy. In this sense the question raised by Philippe C. Schmitter, about whether the twentieth century was "still the century of corporatism," must be answered in the affirmative,[5] even for many contemporary democratic regimes.

Nationalization

While neocorporatist practices bring together the private and public sectors in deliberation, consultation, and decision making, nationalization divests private organizations and the interests associated with them of their property and freedom of decision. The state assumes the direct ownership and operation of major industries, compensates the owners for their property, and manages them on behalf of the public. The mode of management may vary: It may be statist and bureaucratic, directed and controlled by state agencies, or it may provide the management with autonomy. In some instances, management can make its own decisions on investment, growth, production, employment, and wage policies, and it can even set itself up as a profit-making company. In

---

[4]See the discussions in Andrew Schonfield, *Modern Capitalism: The Changing Balance of Public and Private Powers* (New York: Oxford University Press, 1965); in Suzanne Berger, Ed., *Organizing Interests in Western Europe;* and in Philippe C. Schmitter and Gerhard Lembruch, (eds.), *Trends in Corporatist Intermediation.* (Beverly Hills, Calif.: Sage Publications, 1979).
[5]Philippe C. Schmitter, "Still the Century of Corporatism?" in Philippe C. Schmitter and Gerhard Lembruch (eds.), *Trends in Corporatist Intermediation.* (Beverly Hills, Calif.: Sage Publications, 1979), pp. 7–52.

other instances, however, management operates in terms of the public policy guidelines set forth by the government.

Britain and France have been two of the democracies with the most extensive nationalizations. In Britain the major effort was made from 1945 to 1951 under the first Labour government. The Bank of England, coal production, air transportation, electricity, gas, land transportation, and iron and steel were nationalized. In 1967 the British Steel Corporation took over all steel-producing firms, which accounted for a total production of about 27 million tons of steel, and nationalizations were extended to the North Sea oil, atomic energy, and the partial nationalization of Rolls Royce and Leyland automobile production. The British economy has, however, undergone denationalization, or *privatization*, under the Conservative goverment of Prime Minister Margaret Thatcher in the 1980s.

In France there were two waves of nationalizations. The first occurred in the postwar period, between 1945 and 1948. It involved partial or comprehensive nationalization of coal, Renault (automobiles), aircraft production and air transportation, railroads, atomic energy, electricity, gas, insurance companies, and of course the Bank of France. The second wave came between 1981 and 1982 under the Socialist government elected in June 1981. Virtually all banks were nationalized, and through the nationalization of eleven major industrial conglomerates the state became the biggest producer of aluminum, metals, steel, iron, coal, textiles, chemicals, pharmaceuticals, glass, construction materials, cement, air conditioners, electrical equipment, telecommunications, furniture, kitchen utensils, armaments, and computers.

Approximately 1,250,000 additional employees were transferred into the nationalized sector. When added to the first nationalized sector—and if we include the post office, which handles mail, telephone, and telegraphs—at least 30 percent of the gainfully employed worked directly for state-owned and state-operated industrial enterprises, businesses, and services. As for industrial production, the state owns and controls at least 40 percent of the total. But, as in Great Britain, there has been a strong reaction against nationalization, and in 1986 and 1987 a number of banks and industrial firms were privatized; i.e., returned to the private sector.

By contrast, in Sweden, except for the telephone and postal services, nationalizations are limited: A good part of civil aviation and the railroads, about half of gas, electricity, coal, and oil, only a small part of banking, and the greater part of steel are directly controlled and operated by public bodies. In the Federal Republic of Germany, Canada, and the United States, private ownership and management still remain the dominant form of economic organization.

Conclusion

Whether in the form of consultation and cooperation, or in line with the neocorporatist practices we mentioned, a structured and institutionalized participation of interests with governmental agencies in policy making is in place in all industrialized democracies. A symbiosis exists between the political and the interest universes. They penetrate each other and they vie with each other for influence, control, and decision-making authority. But neither has the last word, or even the upper hand. It is at best a constant dialogue and a give-and-take; at worst, a constant war where victors and losers alternate. It had been taken for granted that in democracies the societal forces, and notably the economic forces, would have the upper hand; but with the advent of state regulation and controls, public spending and the welfare state, as well as defense spending and outright nationalizations of the economy, the balance has tipped in the direction of the state and its agencies. This is so despite the recent reaction against government regulation and welfare spending. On the other hand, it had been also taken for granted that in authoritarian and especially communist regimes the state could arbitrarily and authoritatively take over all private property and organize production and distribution, thus replacing the market. The interest universe was to be "absorbed" by and into the state. However, recent events throughout Eastern Europe and in the Soviet Union, which we shall discuss in some detail in Part Four of the book, clearly show a resurgence of societal forces and of the economy. Unable to provide the impetus and flexibility in the economy, the authoritarian state and its agencies are withdrawing increasingly from the economic sector. Throughout Eastern Europe interests are beginning to mushroom, professional organizations are on the rise, and the state finds itself in retreat. They may all be moving back . . . to where industrialized democracies had moved forward throughout the twentieth century!

Individual Rights

Even if individuals are not kingmakers, they are the kingpins of democracy, at least in theory. They all "have a life to live," and they are entitled to live it according to both their whims and their innermost beliefs. According to democratic theory (if not always practice), power, secular or transcendental, stops at the individual's door. His or her conscience cannot be invaded; his or her volition and judgment cannot be forced.

At the very bright dawn of democracy in Athens, around 430 B.C., Pericles proclaimed that the individual had both a public and a private life and that the latter was to be respected and protected.[6] Christianity sharpened this claim: some things belonged to Caesar and others to God. The Reformation opened the gates to religious pluralism, which ultimately led to a clearer distinction between churches and state. Under the impact of liberalism, especially in the nineteenth century, economic and personal freedoms were added to religious ones.

To the rights against the state and equality of all before the law new claims were added, which deepened and broadened the substance of individual rights. Since they included material services that were to be provided to all people by the community as well as by the government, the emphasis gradually shifted from equality before the law to equal conditions for all. Individual liberties, defined at first by eliminating some of the state's awesome powers, have been redefined often in terms of what obligations the state owes to its people and what services it must perform for them. In most democracies today, after long and bitter conflicts and sacrifices on the part of so many, the government and its agencies have become the major purveyors of the services without which individual rights cannot exist.

While assertions of individual freedoms were often proclaimed in the past, the institutionalization of such freedoms in the form of procedures and structures that protect and guarantee them and punish their violation is a relatively recent phenomenon. "We have also granted to all free men of our kingdom," proclaimed King John of England in 1215 in the *Magna Carta*, "all liberties written below: . . . no free man shall be taken or imprisoned or . . . outlawed or exiled or in any way destroyed . . . except by the legal judgment of his peers or by the law of the land; . . . to no one we shall deny or postpone right or justice." Almost four centuries later, in 1628, when it was clear that the liberties promised had not been respected, both "lords and commons" petitioned the king to reaffirm them. This was the Petition of Right, condemning the king for imprisoning and sentencing individuals without due process of law and the consent of Parliament, for taxing indiscriminately, and for exiling citizens. Finally, in 1689 the Parliament affirmed in the Bill of Rights "that the pretended power of Suspending laws, or the execution of laws, by Regal authority, without consent of Parliament, is illegal."[7]

It was a century later that these affirmations found a mighty echo across the Atlantic with the Declaration of Independence and the Constitution of the United States. England's colonies in America made the same complaints against the king: imposing taxes without consent of the

---

[6]From the Funeral Oration, as rendered by Thucydides in *The Peloponnesian War*, edited by Terry Wick (New York: Modern Library College Series/Random House, 1982).
[7]For the major English constitutional documents see R. K. Gooch, *Source Book on the Government of England* (New York: Van Nostrand, 1939).

people's representatives; depriving persons of trial by jury; abolishing some of "our most valuable laws"; and "suspending our Legislature." The signers of the Declaration stated that all people are endowed with inalienable rights to "life, liberty, and the pursuit of happiness" and that it is the government's obligation to ensure that these rights are preserved. They also asserted that the powers invested in the government could be given only through the consent of the governed. Later, when the Constitution was adopted, individual rights were protected against encroachment in the ten amendments known as the "Bill of Rights," which provide the foundations of personal liberty in America.

The cause for individual rights and freedoms grew all over Europe after the French Revolution (1789). The Declaration of the Rights of Man and the Citizen issued in 1789 proclaimed, like the Declaration of Independence, the inalienable rights of individuals.

Following the liberation of Europe from Nazi occupation, the same reaffirmation of individual freedoms was made throughout the whole of Western Europe. Spain and Portugal followed in the 1970s. Democratic constitutions adopted as part of the postwar decolonization of the Third World also affirmed individual freedoms. A comprehensive statement of individual rights was prepared and proclaimed by the United Nations in its Declaration on Human Rights (1948), which included the following provisions:

> . . . All human beings are born free and equal in dignity and rights. . . .
>
> No one shall be subjected to arbitrary arrest, detention, or exile. Everyone charged with a penal offence has the right to be presumed innocent until proved guilty.
>
> No one shall be subjected to torture or to cruel, inhuman, or degrading treatment or punishment.
>
> Everyone has the right to leave any country, including his own, and to return to his country.
>
> No one shall be arbitrarily deprived of his property.
>
> Everyone has the right to freedom of thought, conscience and religion. . . .
>
> Everyone has the right to freedom of peaceful assembly and association.
>
> Everyone has the right to take part in the government of his country, directly or through freely chosen representatives.
>
> Everyone, as a member of society, has the right to social security. . . .
>
> Everyone has the right to work. . . .
>
> Everyone has the right to a standard of living adequate for the health and well-being of himself and of his family. . . .

> Motherhood and childhood are entitled to special care
> and assistance. . . .
> Everyone has the right to education. . . .[8]

From Individual to Social Rights and Entitlements

The major landmarks in the development of rights are merely the signposts of constant political struggle in an ever-widening arena. From the Petition of Right to the Universal Declaration of Human Rights, the substance of rights has been deepened and broadened, but only because of political organization, struggle, and often outright violence, confrontation, and the sacrifice of human lives.

The right to vote in most democracies has been extended to all who have reached the age of eighteen. Every effort is being made to see to it that the principle of "one person one vote" is adhered to; the right to register to vote has been added to the right to vote, with all attendant protections and safeguards. Similarly, in many democracies individual rights have been strengthened against unwarranted arrest or detention, and the presumption of innocence until proven guilty, protection against unlawful searches and seizures, and the right of defendants to be assisted by counsel if they cannot afford one have all been guaranteed. The right of asylum for individuals fleeing political persecution is also recognized—a sad reminder that many political regimes do not allow free expression of ideas and do not tolerate dissent. In substance, however, the transition from individual to human rights is due to the incorporation of new economic and social rights into the fabric of individual and civil rights.

The Welfare State

The major instrument for ensuring social and economic rights is the welfare state—the complex of state organizations and public agencies that provide services and payments that support the well-being of the population. Although originally conceived of as privileges, the various forms of publicly funded support characteristic of the modern welfare state have come to be understood as social and economic rights and "entitlements." They benefit not only the poor and underprivileged but the middle and even upper middle classes as well.

---

[8]The United Nations Declaration on Human Rights (1948), in B. H. Weston, R. A. Falk, and A. d'Amato, *Basic Documents on International Law and World Order* (St. Paul, Minn.: West Publishing Co., 1980), pp. 161–164.

To provide for social services and maintain incomes above the poverty level, the state simply extracts, through taxation, a growing percentage of the gross national product (goods and services produced) and redistributes a sizable portion of it in the form of services and cash or cash-equivalent payments. The magnitude of entitlements is staggering. In most advanced democracies, as much as 35 to 45 percent of the total gross national product is taken by the state to be redistributed in this way. In overall terms the state accounts for 40 to 55 percent of total expenditures!

Major Social Services[9] In all contemporary democracies the growth of social and economic rights calls for a series of choices, and this is what social policy is all about. Which services should be provided for everybody? What groups merit special attention? What is the definition of poverty, and what, if anything, should be done for the poor? The list is long, but by and large most democratic regimes have followed a similar route in establishing priority choices. Children and their education were first to receive public support and, with ever-expanding requirements for schooling, the amount of public expenditures also grew. Support for postsecondary education was added in some countries, the United States being the first to do so through the establishment of public universities.

Support for the aged came next, with emphasis on pensions. In the United States, social security began as a form of insurance for the aged and has evolved into extensive public support for medical services and other expenses. In many countries the age limit for retirement is set at sixty for women and sixty-two for men.

The third step came with legislation requiring the state to provide employment or cover the unemployed through special benefits (unemployment insurance). It is presently financed through compulsory contributions and public funds, but public subsidies have grown steadily. In Europe after World War II, a comprehensive scheme was developed, which provided for uniform payments and minimum income levels. In the United States, since the Social Security Act of 1935, an ever-expanding number of employees have been included, contributions have been raised steadily, and benefits have increased. In 1983, however, this trend slowed down everywhere, as mounting public debt imposed greater fiscal restraint on governments.

Health care was originally provided as a form of charity by private and religious organizations to those who could not afford to pay for it on their own. But since World War II, it has been increasingly assumed by

[9]Our discussion on social and economic rights and social legislation draws a good deal from Arnold Heidenheimer, Hugh Heclo, and Carolyn Adams, *Comparative Public Policy,* 3d ed. (New York: St. Martin's Press, 1987).

the state, either through insurance programs or through direct payments and services. Germany was the first country to develop a nationwide health program even before the turn of the century. England followed, and in 1948 it introduced a most comprehensive medical care program: it nationalized all health services and hospitals and incorporated almost all the doctors into the National Health Service. Health care became free, a matter of right. In Sweden a health insurance plan is mandatory, and every citizen receives health care free of charge. In France medical expenses are covered through a system that combines insurance paid for by individuals with direct payments from the employer and the state. In the United States it is only after age sixty-five that citizens become directly covered through the Medicare and Medicaid programs. Employers' and individuals' contributions provide coverage for most—while government-funded Medicaid covers others.

Although education, health, retirement, and unemployment coverage do provide some safeguards against catastrophic costs, the so-called "safety net" referred to by those who seek to hold the line on or even reduce such benefits is full of holes. Despite this supplementary income, there are millions who find themselves without adequate income. They are the poor.

It is to plug these holes and support the poor that income-maintenance and public assistance programs have been developed. They aim at raising minimal income levels to tolerable ones. Minimum wages have become a matter of public policy, and most democratic regimes have set a floor below which wages cannot fall. But with a family to support, a minimum wage is often inadequate. Tax exemptions, direct payments, rent allowances, food subsidies, aid to dependent children, day-care centers for working mothers, school lunch programs, maternity benefits, and all sorts of other services are provided in an effort to maintain the quality of life of the poor. Although these programs also vary from one country to another, they are almost always available, at least for a given time. However, their purpose is to provide a family with a minimum standard of existence, not to equalize income. They reduce the distance between the rich and the poor only marginally and, in practical terms, negligibly.

Conclusion

Virtually all democracies show the same trends with regard to interests and human rights. Whether through regulation, nationalizations, or corporatist practices, economic interests have assumed a more public character. Organized interests speak for the public, but the public asserts its voice, goals, and policies through the state and its agencies. There has been a growing symbiosis between the interest universe and the public sector to the extent that in each and every case private considerations must be rationalized in terms of overriding public themes. Democracies have moved away from the early propositions of liberalism and economic individualism to impose social and public imperatives. Liberal democracies have been transformed almost everywhere into social democracies. The material and economic requirements that now define the notion of individual rights has strengthened this trend everywhere. The welfare state and the supports given to individuals by the state accentuate the social dimensions of public policy and delineate the new functions and role of the democratic state. To the early battle cry of individual rights against the awesome powers of the state, a new vision and sometimes a new reality are emerging that point to the needs of social solidarity and interdependence within the state.

Individual *civil*, *political*, and *economic* rights provide the tripod on which human rights rest. They reinforce one another in providing freedoms and satisfying material wants, giving all of us the means to fulfill ourselves. Democracies and democratic regimes should be measured in terms of the implementation of these rights.

Bibliography

Berger, Suzanne (ed.). *Organizing Interests in Western Europe: Pluralism, Corporatism and the Transformation of Politics*. New York: Cambridge University Press, 1981.

Groth, Alexander, and Wade L. Larry (eds.). *Comparative Resource Allocation: Politics, Performance and Policy Priorities*. Beverly Hills, Calif.: Sage Yearbooks, vol. 13, 1984.

Hayward, E. S., and B. P. Berki (eds.). *Society in Contemporary Europe*. New York: St. Martin's Press, 1979.

Heidenheimer, Arnold, Hugh Heclo, and Carolyn Adams. *Comparative Public Policy*, 3d ed. New York: St. Martin's Press, 1987.

Miliband, Ralph. *The State and Capitalist Society: An Analysis of Western Systems and Power*. New York: Basic Books, 1969.

Schmitter, Philippe C., and Gerhard Lehmbruch (eds.). *Trends in Corporatist Intermediation*. Beverly Hills, Calif.: Sage Publications, 1979.

Schonfield, Andrew. *Modern Capitalism: The Changing Balance of Public and Private Power*. New York: Oxford University Press, 1965.

Wilensky, Harold. *The Welfare State and Equality*. Berkeley: University of California Press, 1974.

Part Three

Authoritarianism

Introduction

The essence of authoritarianism is unchallengeable power. It is the oldest form of government, dating back to ancient tyrants, despots, and the Roman Empire. "What pleases the Prince has the force of law" was the famous maxim that consecrated the power of the Roman emperor. It grew and blossomed in the Western monarchies of France, England, and Spain, where the monarchs claimed absolute power and prerogative and ruled by hereditary and divine right. In Eastern Europe, and especially in Russia and the Ottoman Empire, the power of the Tsar or the Sultan remained absolute until the end of the nineteenth century. It was the staple form of government virtually throughout the world—in the Chinese empire, in Japan, among the tribal kingdoms of Africa, in the Aztec rule in Latin America. Authoritarian regimes remain widespread to this day, despite the process of democratization in the 1970s and 1980s.

While it is relatively easy to distinguish authoritarian regimes from democracies, it is not so easy to devise categories of analysis that differentiate authoritarian regimes from one another. This is especially true of one particular form of authoritarianism—the totalitarian regime.

Two Basic Types of Authoritarianism

It is only by linking elites, levels of modernization, the political culture, and the underlying societal forces that we can make a clear distinction between the two basic types of authoritarianism and indicate the particular characteristics of the totalitarian regime. One type of authoritarian regime is *conservative:* The political elites and the regime they shape or support are committed to the maintenance of the prevailing societal forces, most notably its class structure. Conservative authoritarianism is therefore *defensive*, in that the political leadership attempts to maintain the status quo against new forces pressing for change. Such an authoritarian regime attempts to stifle change. In its commitment to the existing and traditional forces within the society, it turns inward, becomes increasingly attached to the past (rather than to the future), and shies away from modernization, including technological change. Its political ideology (when it promotes an ideology) exalts national tradition and order. It shuns participatory mechanisms and individual freedoms and, of course, open elections. Spain under Franco, Portugal under Salazar, the Tsarist regime before the Bolshevik revolution, and more recently, some military dictatorships in Latin America and the rule of the military junta in Greece were, by and large, conservative forms of authoritarianism.

The second type of authoritarianism is *radical*. It is *transformist* and *mobilizing*. It calls for change, sometimes even radical change in the social structure. It is associated with the emergence of new groups and new classes that wish to replace the status quo. One of the earliest manifestations of this kind of authoritarianism was the regime in Turkey established by Kemal Ataturk in 1924. The Sultan and religious leaders were dethroned and a modernizing, emerging middle class undertook efforts to transform a backward society, even going so far as to change the script used in schools and impose Western styles of clothing in place of traditional dress. The rapid modernization of Soviet society under Stalin, begun in earnest in 1928, corresponded to the same type of radical, transformist authoritarianism. Some military and other regimes in Latin America and Africa may be included in this category, as well as what was until recently the one-party regime in Mexico.

The characteristics that allow us to distinguish between the two types of authoritarianism—conservative and radical—are the attitudes and ideology of the ruling elite. In conservative regimes, the elite (political and socioeconomic) is bent upon the maintenance of the existing privileged order. In transformist regimes, the elite begins to follow the logic of modernization. It does so either because it has undergone an internal change while still in power, as was the case in the last years of Franco's rule in Spain, or because it is being threatened with the loss of power by alternative modernizing elites. The transformist elite reaches out to seek supports and in so doing mobilizes the people and develops participatory mechanisms. It seeks political legitimation through popular participation and consent.

It is this second type of authoritarianism that is often indistinguishable from totalitarian regimes like the Nazi and Fascist dictatorships and the communist regimes of the Soviet Union, China, and Eastern Europe.

The differences between totalitarian and transformist authoritarian regimes lie principally in the degree and intensity of mobilization, the degree and extensiveness of the penetration of society by the state and the ruling elite, and the intensity and pervasiveness of the official ideology. But all regimes, even totalitarian regimes, must meet the critical test of performance, whether economic or (as with the Nazis, Fascists, and Stalinists) military. They also have to cope with new groups spawned by the process of modernization itself, which begin to demand genuine participation in decision making.

The following table, to which we shall return, gives a synoptic view of the two basic types of authoritarianism and its totalitarian variant:

	VERY STRONG	STRONG	MODERATE
Penetration of society Mobilization Ideology Ruling party Participation	Totalitarian	Radical	Conservative

Instabilities and Conflict

Authoritarianism in all its forms is inherently unstable. There is ongoing conflict among competing political elites—some holding on to power, others attempting to gain it. There is also conflict between political elites (those who exercise power and control) and socioeconomic elites. This is the conflict between state and society characteristic of these regimes. Where the political elite is conservative, legitimates its rule through traditional values and institutions, and makes no attempt to modernize society, conflict will tend to be lowest. Conflict is far greater where a modernizing, transformist elite forces changes upon recalcitrant societal forces: landowners, religious groups, and powerful economic actors, to name just a few of the privileged groups whose status may be threatened by changes in the economy, in education, and in social policies likely to be pursued by such an elite. This conflict between state and society produces instability. Its outcome is uncertain and depends on the relative strengths of the modernizing elite and the social forces that refuse to accept change.

Conflict is at least as great and may even become greater in those regimes in which conservative elites are resistant to changes generated by societal forces from below. Intellectuals, worker groups, peasants' cooperatives, students, and other social groups affected by the social consequences of the modernization process to become socially mobilized and begin to address demands for change to the political elite and its allies. Where the elite attempts to repress these new groups and their demands, the latter often attempt to gain power by force. In contrast to the "revolution from above" wrought by an elite that is more modernized than its society, it is "revolution from below" that results when a society becomes more modernized than its ruling elite.

Many of the Latin American military regimes now going through the process of transition from authoritarianism to more democratic forms, as well as the Communist regimes of the Soviet Union and Eastern Europe, can be described as authoritarian regimes in which the conflict between conservative elites and modernizing societies finally produced political instability. Where a modernizing elite is able to secure power and link forces with modernizing societal forces and groups, instability can lead to liberalization and democratization. Just who the modernizing elites and the modernizing societal groups are depends upon the particular country. In the Soviet Union, the modernizing elite is emerging both from within the ruling Communist party elite and from the intellectual, technical, and scientific elites produced by the modernization process. In Poland, in contrast, the most powerful force for change emerged from the working class, in the form of the Solidarity movement that effectively overthrew the conservative Communist elite and has now taken over the government. Sometimes traditional social forces such as religion and nationalism support the modernization of the regime, as in Poland. Sometimes, as in the multinational Soviet state, these forces are themselves split.

This relationship between elites, society, and the stability of the authoritarian regime is summarized in the following table:

	SOCIETY	
ELITES	Non-Modernizing	Modernizing
Conservative	Stability	Instability
Modernizing	Instability	Transitional

In the following chapters we discuss the varieties of authoritarian regimes and their characteristics, including the special category of totalitarian regimes. We focus on stable regimes, but suggest the sources of instability within them. We reserve discussion of the coming together of a modernizing elite and the modernizing sectors of society, which ushers in a period of flux with various forces jockeying for position, until the final chapter. There, we discuss the features of political transition in both democratic and authoritarian regimes.

6

Authoritarian Regimes

Background Factors

Before we examine the characteristics of authoritarian regimes, let us briefly discuss some of the social, economic, and political factors that have given rise to such regimes.

Elite Decisions

One of the most common explanations of and justifications for authoritarianism is reflected in the Latin maxim "*Salus Populi Suprema Lex Esto*". Roughly translated, this means "the security of the people [or state] is the supreme law." A newly established regime is always fragile. Its ruling elites are often not sure of its acceptance by the leaders of other states, especially their immediate neighbors. When a ruling elite perceives other states as potentially aggressive, or when actual aggression occurs, they are likely to strengthen their control by turning to authoritarian practices. But even in established regimes elites turn to authoritarian means in response to internal strife or when a small but extremely committed minority tries to subvert the existing legal order, as when a revolutionary party attempts to organize the violent overthrow of the regime.

To meet such situations, all political regimes, even democratic ones, provide for authoritarian devices. In the Roman Republic, constitutional provisions existed for what may be called a "temporary dictatorship": when there was a grave crisis, the established institutions were set aside and a temporary dictator stepped in with full powers, but with the understanding that within a given period of time he would step down. We have noted similar crisis arrangements in contemporary democracies: Article 16 of the constitution of the Fifth French Republic gives the president ample powers to deal with a crisis; the President of the United States, as Commander-in-Chief, can invoke sweeping powers, as when Lincoln blockaded the Southern ports at the outset of the Civil War, or when Roosevelt confined hundreds of thousands of Japanese-Americans in detention camps after the Japanese attack on Pearl Harbor. In almost all contemporary regimes there are special provisions for the exercise of emergency power.

The conditions established for resort to these emergency powers represent implicit justifications for authoritarianism. They are designed to give the government the means to act "quickly," "effectively," "for the public interest," and to "save the nation," using means that by implication democratic governments are normally excluded from using. In the United States, Congress gave President Roosevelt sweeping powers during the Great Depression. "When the house is on fire, we call the fire department," said one congressman. He was speaking the same language that the Romans spoke when they would invite an illustrious figure to become a temporary dictator and put their affairs in order. The salvation of the state is the supreme law. But this maxim, if carried too far (and it often is), may bring about the end of democratic government. This, in fact, is the way many of the authoritarian regimes of Latin America came into being.

Political Culture

Political culture can be defined as the general pattern of values and beliefs that guide political behavior in a given society—in short, the political norms of the society.[1] The elements of political culture that gave rise to modern democratic regimes are difficult, if not impossible, to establish rapidly or through conscious effort. They include but are not limited to the establishment of law as both a limitation on state power and the standard for resolving individual and group conflicts; the spontaneous formation of interest groups and associations and their autonomy from the state; tolerance for conflicting values, even when such basic ones as religious belief are concerned; respect for individual rights; the development of individual entrepreneurial values; and the creation of a liberal capitalist order. In short, the political culture of democracy revolves, as we discussed earlier, around the balance between state and society.

[1]For a series of essays on diverse political cultures, see Lucian W. Pye and Sidney Verba, Eds., *Political Culture and Political Development* (Princeton, N.J.: Princeton University Press, 1965).

Political cultures vary, of course, even among democratic regimes. But, when some close approximation of these values prevails, it is exceedingly difficult for a political elite to assume infallibility and impose orthodoxy, concentrate absolute power in its own hands, or force the richness and multiplicity of social life and individual endeavors into a single mold. There is no reason, however, to expect or to assume that these values, which became institutionalized in Western Europe and Britain over a period of centuries, can develop elsewhere quickly or, for that matter, at all. Their successful transfer to the United States can be explained in large part by the fact that early American social and political culture was a "fragment" of the same culture that gave rise to democracy in Britain.[2]

Authoritarian regimes have developed in countries where there is a highly unbalanced relationship between the state and society. In some cases the state and its agencies overpower society by playing a dominant role in the economy, in employment, or in organizing and controlling other societal activities and associations, including religious ones. As a result, the civil society remains weak and unorganized, and social forces consist of powerful but isolated individuals instead of groups and classes. Where the middle classes remain weak and are unable to form associational, representative parties or networks that limit the state, liberal political institutions are unable to sink roots. Restraints on state penetration are few and weak, because the state tends to incorporate institutions rather than secure their consent. The state itself—that is, the ruling elite—formulates the public interest rather than allow its synthesis from among a number of conflicting demands and interests.

In short, when societal groups are unable, through political instrumentalities (e.g., interest groups and associations, trade unions, cooperatives, elections, political parties, and other political organizations and institutions) or through extrapolitical or parapolitical activities (e.g., lobbying, participation in policy deliberations, demonstrations, marches, and campaigning in the media), to acquire influence and power in decision making, the foundations for authoritarianism are already present. When the ruling classes refuse to compromise and share power, they will invariably impose authoritarian solutions.

Modernization

The argument is often made that authoritarian regimes emerge at times of rapid economic development. Modernization unsettles the traditional patterns of economic and social life. It pushes society to high levels of industrialization. It prompts migrations from the countryside into the

---

[2]See Louis Hartz, *The Liberal Tradition in America* (New York: Harcourt Brace Jovanovich, 1955), and Hartz et al., *The Founding of New Societies* (New York: Harcourt Brace & World, 1964).

cities, promotes rapid social modernization, exposes the population to mass communications, and heightens the expectations and demands of the people. It is also a process that intensifies social strife and, according to this argument, authoritarian measures are often needed to quell it.

The opposite argument, however, is also made. Authoritarian regimes (in this case, radical "transformist" regimes) are established, in this view, in order to bring about modernization. A new political elite emerges and seeks to promote the rapid modernization of society by imposing certain patterns of development. They establish control over the configuration of interests, induce mobilization around modernizing goals, and attempt to destroy the traditional elites that oppose change.

The marriage of authoritarian rule and a commitment to modernization is, we repeat, characteristic of many Third World countries, some of the Latin American regimes, and of course, the communist totalitarian regimes. The sweeping economic changes imposed on the Soviet Union by Stalin in the 1920s and 1930s were clearly designed to industrialize the country as fast as possible. This commitment provided much of the impetus for the tightening of authoritarian controls and reinforcing mobilization through the Communist party. Even in this extreme case, however, the authoritarian/totalitarian outcome was shaped primarily by the conscious political actions of the elite, especially the would-be leader.

The association between modernization and the onset of authoritarianism is, however, internally contradictory. Modernization carried beyond a certain point may lead to the erosion of authoritarian rule. Paradoxically, the very modernization process such regimes were established to implement in Latin America, southern and eastern Europe, China, the Soviet Union, and elsewhere seem to have sown the seeds of their own demise.

With these background factors in mind, we now turn to the general features of the totalitarian regime.

General Features of Authoritarian Regimes

The Organization of Command

In an authoritarian regime the organization of command is characterized by the concentration of power in a limited political elite. The particular composition of the elite—conservative or radical—is, as we have noted, an important basis for distinguishing between "types" of authoritarian regimes.

The "representation" of certain social groups and the kinds of groups represented in the ruling elite are equally important. The link between elites and social groups in authoritarian regimes is not based on responsibility and accountability. The state and groups associated with or coopted by it therefore enjoy a great deal of autonomy.

The state/society distinction is only partially blurred in many authoritarian regimes. Autonomous groups are permitted to exist, especially those that antedate the regime itself, such as the Church and the many politically active but primarily economic groups and organizations characteristic of precapitalist or capitalist economies. Indeed, the retention by most authoritarian regimes of a capitalist market economy based on private ownership is a major factor in the preservation of a certain degree of pluralism in these regimes.

Modernizing authoritarian regimes undertake the mobilization of the population, but sustained, extensive mobilization efforts are particularly characteristic of totalitarian regimes. In fact, modern authoritarian regimes are mostly characterized by efforts to *demobilize* the population, to render it apathetic to the distributions of power and influence and goods and values.

Consistent with the absence of mobilization, authoritarian regimes do not attempt to impose an official, comprehensive ideology on the populace. Authoritarian regimes either do not have an ideology or are unable to link their political organization to an ideology to give it vitality and supports. Their most characteristic appeals have been nationalism, "order," professionalism, or modernization. Except for nationalism, these are not "ideas that grip the masses," as Marx characterized an ideology; they do not mobilize the people.

The Organization of Interests and Consent

Authoritarian leaderships confront two contradictory tasks: on the one hand, they are committed to suppressing conflict and opposition; on the other, they must secure at least some popular compliance, if not consent. In order to achieve both these goals, authoritarian leaderships generally attempt to improve regime performance, and thereby generate at least instrumental support, by emphasizing decisional efficacy and civic order. They emphasize the satisfaction of the material demands and the values of those groups *included* in the regime at the expense of those *excluded*. For the masses, participation is limited to those forms that contribute to efficacy and order.

Corporatist formulas for the organization and representation of interests have been used by some authoritarian regimes as a device both to establish political control and to secure some participation and supports. The state organizes certain interests and associations, allows them representation, and gives them policy-making power on matters that concern them. Interests are organized into corporations on the basis of common or related economic activities and operations. Hundreds of such corporations may be established, representing and encompassing not only production and related enterprises but also social, professional, and cultural activities. Members elect their representatives, who in turn elect a national council to deliberate and decide on matters like production, wages, prices, and investment. In this way, extensive incorporation of socially autonomous groups is achieved.

In some authoritarian regimes the whole corporatist edifice is integrated under the state, which is the ultimate arbiter of the decisions made as well as the ultimate guarantor of the organization of the society. As the ultimate arbiter, the state can intervene to settle unresolved disputes and also harmonize and control various economic activities. In some cases, the state may control the various socioeconomic sectors through a dominant political party, such as the Institutional Revolutionary Party of Mexico. The corporatist structure thus allows an authoritarian leadership to provide institutional channels for the integration of various interests and their participation in carefully delimited areas of policy making. And it avoids the conflict and challenges to elite power inherent in the aggregation and articulation of interests through competitive party politics. It allows an authoritarian state to broaden its supports by structuring the participation of new interests into the corporatist network, thereby achieving adaptability and maintaining responsiveness. And by restricting participation to organized interests based on economic functions, corporatist authoritarian leaderships also exclude class, ethnic, religious, or other interests from the political process.

Corporatism in Action

One of the longest-lasting examples of institutionalized authoritarian corporatism has been that of Mexico since 1937. The Mexican regime has been characterized by the partial inclusion of interests in the corporatist organization of participation and consent. Control remains almost completely in the hands of a single party, the Institutional Revolutionary Party (Partido Revolucionario Institucional, or PRI).[3] The PRI is referred to as a dominant party because other, smaller parties have been tolerated and are allowed to participate in elections. But their combined strength has never exceeded 20 to 25 percent of the electorate. For more than forty years, until the 1989 elections, the PRI controlled the election of the national legislature and the nomination and election of the president, the state governors, and state legislatures. In 1989, however, the opposition united around a charismatic figure and mounted a credible challenge to the PRI candidate. The 1989 elections may signal the beginning of a transitional period for the Mexican regime.

[3]On Mexican corporatism and the role of the party, see David Levy and Gabriel Szekely, *Mexico: Paradoxes of Society and Change* (Boulder, Colo.: Westview Press, 1983).

At present, however, the PRI remains firmly in control of a powerful authoritarian system. It has an official membership of over 7 million. Affiliation with the PRI is structured by socioeconomic sector. There is an agrarian sector, a labor sector, and a "popular" sector. The agrarian sector includes the *Confederacion Nacional Campesina* with over 2.5 million members; the labor sector includes industrial workers of many unions (railroad workers, mining and metal workers, telephone workers, motion-picture workers, and others) and has a total membership of about 2 million. The majority of workers and peasants are thus excluded from the PRI. The third, popular sector encompasses a diverse collection of primarily middle-class groups, such as civil service unions, teachers, cooperatives, small farmers and merchants, professionals, intellectuals, artisans, women's organizations, youth organizations, and some independent organizations. The popular sector has a total membership of a little over 2 million.

The Catholic church, the military, and organized business groups in industry, banking, and trade—like the majority of laborers and peasants—are not incorporated into the party. They act independently of the party and constitute a countervailing force to the ruling PRI leadership. Thus, the Mexican regime is only semi-corporatist in nature.

The party was founded in 1929 to bring local and provincial notables—the *caciques*—into a single organization that would provide a forum for reconciliation of regional and local conflicts and a more organized channel for dispensing patronage. Under President Cardenas (1930–1940), however, the party became more revolutionary in character. He turned the party against the local bosses and opened it to the people, especially the peasants and the workers. The party was to become the channel for mass participation and the mobilization of support for a program of genuine land distribution and economic reform. The goal was to penetrate deep into society and energize the masses with a revolutionary, socialist, and democratic ideology that would mobilize them, thwart the business community and the landowners, and neutralize the Church and the military.

The PRI leadership recruited and encouraged the participation of members of new social groups, including skilled workers, professionals, and technical personnel. These new elites helped to promote economic and social modernization and supplied the personnel for an expanding state bureaucracy. Thus, the PRI organized societal interests and secured their consent through semi-corporatist arrangements. But it has also legitimized its rule through the electoral process.

Periodic elections renew the PRI's mobilization function and compel it to pay attention to those aspects of regime performance that affect electoral support. Thus, exclusion of the masses from the semi-corporatist arrangements for interest representation is counterbalanced by the real sensitivity of the PRI to the impact of its actions on mass

electoral behavior. Mass discontent arising out of poor regime performance has been translated into an electoral challenge to the PRI's political monopoly, and we may be seeing the possible onset of a political
transition in Mexico.

Forms of Authoritarianism

In discussing the most common forms of authoritarian regimes, we will
continue to focus on basic structural characteristics: the organization of
command, the organization of supports and consent, and the organization and configuration of interests and rights. But the features of each
regime are shaped by the specific historical circumstances of its origins:
by particular events, by the restraints imposed by economic conditions,
by the nature of the social forces confronting it, by the personal psychology and political choices of individual leaders, and by the international
environment. All these factors and others combine to produce the particular profiles of such regimes and account for the differences among
them.

Using the organization of command as a basis for differentiating
regimes, four major types of authoritarian regimes can be identified:
tyrannies, dynastic regimes, military regimes, and *single-party regimes.*

Tyrannies

Regardless of how or why tyrants acquire power, they wield it personally and absolutely. Aristotle gave us what is probably the best
portrait of a tyrant, and the ancient Greeks were just as familiar with
tyranny as we are with military dictatorship. The tyrant seized political
power pretty much as a modern-day gangster seizes a household or
even a whole community. But his rule (in those days it had to be a "he")
was coterminous with the power he could muster to keep the household, village, small city, city-state, or even a whole people or many
peoples under subjection and in his service. The purpose of rulership
was selfish: to extract as much as possible for personal enjoyment and
ego glorification. Dionysius (the tyrant of Syracuse, 432–367 B.C.),
Aristotle tells us, "in the space of five years collected all the private
property of his subjects into his own coffers."

In a few lines, Aristotle gives us the characteristics of tyranny that
political scientists have been rediscovering ever since. A tyrant pre-
serves his power by

> the "lopping off" of outstanding men, and the removal of
> men of spirit . . . the forbidding of common meals, clubs,
> education, and anything . . . likely to produce the two quali-
> ties of mutual confidence and a high spirit. A second measure

is to prohibit societies for cultural purposes, and any gathering of a similar character: in a word, the adoption of every means for making every subject as much of a stranger as is possible to every other. (Mutual acquaintance always tends to create mutual confidence.) A third . . . is . . . to give the ruler a peep-hole into the actions of his subjects, and to inure them to humility by a habit of daily slavery. . . . A fourth line . . . is that of endeavoring to get regular information about every man's sayings and doings. This entails a secret police. . . . [A]nother line of policy is to sow mutual distrust and to foster discord between friend and friend. . . . Finally, a policy pursued by tyrants is that of impoverishing their subjects . . . to keep them so busy in earning a daily pittance that they have no time for plotting.[4]

In summary, Aristotle sets forth three rules for "successful" tyrants: "break the spirit of their subjects," "breed mutual distrust," and "make their subjects incapable of action." Consent is to become obedience. And there is no attempt to legitimize the tyrant's rule through participation.

Since tyrannies are intensely personal regimes, they are not easily amenable to institutionalization. As a result, their major weakness lies in the organization of command. No tyrant by himself can be strong enough to keep everyone under subjection. He has to organize a guard and the only way he can gain and hold its loyalty is to share some of the perquisites of power with its members. And once a guard is organized the tyrant becomes beholden to it.[5] He has to create a rudimentary set of rules and procedures for the distribution of benefits to his associates, which limits his own power. To implement these rules, he must delegate some of his power to his associates, giving rise to the constant fear that such delegation will spawn subordinate power fiefs from which a conspiracy against him may be organized.

If the power of the tyrant survives, and if his guard controls the means of coercion, tyranny represents the most "successful"—and the most extreme—type of authoritarian regime. In it, power has no restraints, can be exercised arbitrarily and even whimsically, subordinates every interest and every individual, is based on intimidation and fear, and allows no political freedoms or civil rights. The individual is less than a subject; he is literally, as Aristotle suggested, a slave. His life and possessions are completely at the mercy of his master.

---

[4]*The Politics of Aristotle*, Book V, chapter XI, ss 4–8. Edited and translated by Ernest Barker (New York: Oxford University Press, 1962), pp. 244–245.
[5]Robert Jackson and Carl Rosberg, in a discussion of tyrannies in Africa, point out that "the key to tyranny is the relations between the tyrant and his mercenaries without whom tyranny is impossible," in *Personal Rule in Black Africa: Princes, Autocrats, Prophets, Tyrants* (Berkeley: University of California Press, 1982), p. 235.

Modern tyrannies (fortunately, declining in number) have organizations that are far more complex than the classic prototype. The instruments of coercion are carefully developed, through the police and the army, to include prevention, repression, surveillance, and intimidation. But whatever the whims of the tyrant, services have to be provided: transportation, public health, training of the young, and above all, domestic and national security. Without them his power may become nil. In some cases, the army is organized as an extension of the tyrant's personal guard, a private gendarmerie. In other cases, his guard consists of relatives or, more likely, political associates whose intense personal allegiance has been secured through a combination of threats and rewards. The tyrant is thus flanked by indispensable organizations, including of course the army and the secret police, which begin to develop their own practices and acquire a certain autonomy.

The Case of the Dominican Republic: A Profile of Tyranny

Both in Latin America and, since World War II, in Africa and Eastern Europe, a number of tyrannies developed—Batista in Cuba, Somoza in Nicaragua, "Papa Doc" Duvalier in Haiti, Emperor Bokassa in Central Africa, Idi Amin Dada in Uganda, and Nicolae Ceausescu in Romania. But few have come so close to the Aristotelian model as the regime of "General" Trujillo in the Dominican Republic (1930–1961).

"Trujillo's was a highly personal dictatorship in which power was not shared even among a small clique, but was concentrated in the hands of one man."[6] Trujillo's career began in the ranks of the armed forces, which were established and trained by the United States during their long occupation of the island from 1916 to 1926. He gradually rose to the highest posts and reached a position that gave him control over appointments and assignments. But he did not take power by a military coup. He was "elected" president in 1930. It was a campaign in which his squads terrorized the countryside and forced the liberals to withdraw.

Once in office he organized his own personal government. The military remained the pillar of his regime, and they grew in numbers and waxed in wealth. At the very top of the officers' hierarchy were the tyrant's cronies, but as with Dionysius, Trujillo suspected them. They were shifted from post to post, special police organizations spied on them, and some disappeared. Since the governmental structure was highly centralized in the hands of Trujillo, all local autonomies were

[6]Howard Wiarda, *Dictatorship and Development: The Method of Control in Trujillo's Dominican Republic* (Gainesville, Fla.: University of Florida Press, 1968), p. 26. We are greatly indebted to the author for the sketch we give here, although we tend to emphasize the tyrannical aspects of Trujillo's regime rather than its development.

abolished and the bureaucracy grew. Unlike many tyrants, Trujillo established a party, the Dominican Party, forcing almost everybody to "belong." It was primarily an instrument of propaganda, which organized demonstrations, festivals, holidays, and special events to bring out the people. At election time, the party was expected to bring out the vote, one way or another. The police also grew in numbers, and its presence was felt everywhere. After Trujillo's enemies had been silenced, especially among the traditional elites, potential enemies were sought out, such as those who refused to show their outright support, remained passive, or "talked with strangers." The police utilized all instruments of intimidation and terror, including torture, and thousands lost their lives. Professional associations were destroyed and, in some cases, new ones were established by Trujillo.

Yet what was perhaps the most singular trait in Trujillo's tyranny was his overwhelming control of the small island's economy. Like Dionysius he amassed enormous personal wealth at the expense of his subjects, gradually dispossessed them of their property, and became the biggest capitalist on the island. He owned the two newspapers, controlled the national bank, was the biggest owner of sugar plantations, the biggest importer and exporter, the owner of the greatest part of the island's arable land, the owner of the shipyards, the dockyards, and two shipping lines, the major manufacturer of cigarettes, the biggest cattle rancher and cattle raiser, the sole distributor of pasteurized milk, the biggest meat producer and exporter, and last but not least the owner of gambling casinos and whorehouses. It was difficult to distinguish the economy from Trujillo. Some 50 percent of the gainfully employed worked for him, and their livelihood depended on his will as expressed in the form of laws he himself drew up.

While the control of the economy was a device to acquire greater wealth for himself, his family members, and some of his immediate counselors and friends, it was also the surest instrument of political domination. Trujillo used his wealth and control over the economy to increase his power, and the citizenry was reduced to a state of abject dependency. In sum, "the state functioned as the legal servant of Trujillo's agricultural, industrial and commercial enterprises, the armed forces as its security guards, the national territory as its field of operation and exploration, and the populace as its labor force, producer and consumer."[7]

There was one center of power, or at least of potential opposition, that Trujillo did not try to invade, restructure, or reduce: the Catholic church. There was no need to. The Church remained his staunchest ally in return for the many benefits and privileges he bestowed upon it. New churches were built, and special benefits and subsidies were provided

---

[7]Wiarda, op. cit., p. 81.

for the church and the churchmen. Above all, a concordat was signed between the state (i.e., Trujillo) and the Church, which declared that the Catholic religion was to be the religion of the state. Only religious marriages were recognized, divorce remained outlawed, the Church was given the freedom to establish schools, and needless to say, there was no interference with ceremonies and rituals. The Church had indeed reached a position "of splendor," according to one cleric. Being rich and apparently autonomous, it lavished praise on its benefactor. It was only in the last years of Trujillo's reign that frictions developed, and then the Church used its autonomy to criticize.

Although overtly Trujillo's control was total and absolute, it never became totalitarian in substance or intent. First, the ideology was kept to the level of rationalization and justification for the rule of the tyrant: It was used to extol order and obedience. Second, the ideology was used to idolize the leader rather than mobilize the public. Fear rather than involvement characterized the public's behavior, and the majority of the people, mostly peasantry, remained atomized and apathetic. The organizations that Trujillo had set up, including the army and the police, were devoid of strong ideological attachments, or even loyalties, to Trujillo. What bound them together was no purpose other than self-interest in its most naked form. It led to corruption and the never-ending effort to satisfy an increasing number of material wants. Trujillo's wealth simply whetted the appetites of his subordinates, and economic resources were drained away from the people to satisfy the interests of the tyrant and his ruling entourage.

Trujillo met the fate that he feared, the fate that tyrants who are unable to translate their power into authority usually meet. He was assassinated. But even before his demise, the regime that he had put together began to unravel. The army, the police, the party, the middle classes, and foreign powers, including the United States and the Organization of American States, turned against him. The Church too began to reconsider its unholy alliance with the tyrant. The instruments of intimidation and control that Trujillo had set up, each operating independently of the others to carry out his will, now began to move independently of each other and against him. It is irrelevant from where the shot that killed him came.

Dynastic Regimes

There are few dynastic monarchies in existence today. Saudi Arabia, some of the Emirate states, and the Sultanate of Brunei are examples. What distinguishes them from such other monarchies as those in Britain or Scandinavia is that the monarchs, or members of the royal family, actually govern. What distinguishes them from tyrannies is that they come to power and use it according to certain well-established rules.

Power is generally shared by the monarch's family (as is wealth). It is a familial as well as patrimonial form of government. For example, the Sultan of Brunei, after acquiring independence for his tiny sultanate in the northern part of Borneo in 1984, appointed members of his family to various governmental posts. His father became secretary of defense, his brother took care of foreign affairs, and so on. The same is true in Saudi Arabia. The wealth of the kingdom is indistinguishable from the personal wealth of the monarch; he can dispose of it at will. Unlike tyrants, dynastic monarchs do not have to take it by force. It is theirs by divine law, custom, and inheritance.

In contrast to tyrannies, the power of the king is tempered by immemorial customs, conventions, understandings, and religious canons, which establish the subjection of the people to the monarch but also put restraints on arbitrary rule. Dynastic rule, in other words, is legitimized by tradition. Subjection therefore does not result from the overt application of force; it is accepted by the vast majority of the population simply as "the way it always has been." Tradition binds not only the people but the dynastic monarch as well. The prescription among Moslems against the use of alcohol, for example, must apply to rulers and ruled alike, as must the rules limiting the public roles of women. Traditional limits on the behavior of the ruler take the place of guaranteeing rights to the populace. Considerable discretion, however, exists for the ruler when his will is contradicted or in the case of political dissent. Such discretion derives not only from the absolute power of the monarch but from the tradition itself—it is a necessary ingredient for the preservation of dynastic rule.

The legitimization of these regimes through tradition distinguishes them from all other authoritarian regimes. The leaders of military or single-party regimes—even if they are able to establish personal tyranny in a totalitarian order—cannot pass their power on to their descendants. For example, despite concerted efforts by Nicolae Ceausescu, the aging dictator of the totalitarian regime in communist Romania, to share his power with his wife and prepare his son eventually to succeed, these efforts failed to avert his violent overthrow and execution.

The most conspicuous characteristic of absolutist dynastic regimes is the lack of representative institutions. There are no political parties, not even a single ruling party. Consent is derived from tradition, not from the institutionalized expression of popular will. There is little effort to organize interests, and there are no associations dealing with political issues. Nor is there a free press or free speech. Some contemporary dynastic monarchies, however, do enjoy a major source of support in place of that derived from the organization of consent: the generous distribution of goods derived from their enormous oil wealth. This wealth has been used to provide free health services, advanced technical education, retirement benefits, transportation, and leisure and entertainment to their entire though relatively small populations on a scale unknown in other parts of the world. Hence, traditional obedience is reinforced by the satisfactions derived from material well-being, even affluence.

As long as a fair balance is maintained between wealth that can be distributed and traditionalism that nurtures deference, and as long as there are no international forces that upset it, such a regime can endure. But a change in traditional values, or the emergence of new values associated with social modernization, or a sudden fall in oil income, may very well destroy the source that gives these dynastic rulers their supports. For rulers whose regimes enjoy no such wealth, the changes wrought by social modernization, international communication, and economic development represent even greater challenges to the preservation of their claims to rule.

Military Regimes

A great deal of attention has been paid in the past to various forms of military intervention and military regimes. In ancient Rome, the emperors established a special bodyguard, known as the praetorian guard, to protect them and carry out their orders. It eventually became a powerful political force that made and unmade emperors and had a highly destabilizing influence over the course of the Roman Empire. Armies that intervene in politics in the contemporary era and states in which army intervention occurs are thus called "praetorian" armies and "praetorian" states.

Amos Perlmutter defines praetorian states as those "in which the army has the potential to dominate the political system."[8] However, for this concept to be useful in our analysis we must also add the "disposition" to dominate. The potential to dominate is present in almost all armies, but the disposition to do so is not.

To survey the praetorian armies, states, coups d'etat, and military regimes since the end of World War II is to recount the experience of almost two-thirds of the nation-states of our world. It is also a survey that will have to be rewritten and brought up to date every year as military dictatorships constantly give place to civilian rule, and vice versa. In his classic study of the role of the military in politics, Eric Nordlinger notes that the study of military authoritarian governments "is the study of one of the most common, and thus characteristic, aspects of non-Western politics."[9] In fact, it is everywhere the most common form of contemporary authoritarianism.

[8]Amos Perlmutter, *Egypt: The Praetorian State* (New Brunswick, N.J.: Transcription Books, 1974), p. 4.
[9]Eric Nordlinger, *Soldiers and Politics: Military Coups and Governments* (Englewood Cliffs, N.J.: Prentice-Hall, 1977), p. 6.

Why Armies Intervene

If we can give the reasons why armies have *not* intervened in some countries, we might generalize more easily about the reasons why they *do* in so many others. There seem to be two major reasons why the armed forces do *not* intervene. The first is the existence of a strong and genuine affinity between the officer corps, the governing elite, and the public at large about the political norms, values, and institutions of the political regime. The acceptance of civilian rule and its institutions is internalized in the officer corps. Military intervention is considered improper and unacceptable by everybody concerned: the government, the people and, most important, the officers themselves.

This condition can be present in democratic and authoritarian regimes alike. Despite extraordinary crisis conditions, for example, the Yugoslav army has refrained from intervening in the Yugoslav authoritarian regime. The Soviet army, too, appears not to be inclined to challenge civilian rule in the Soviet regime, even in periods when the civilian leadership has been unstable. Not all communist armies refrain from such intervention. The most obvious case of intervention by a communist army is, of course, the imposition of military rule in Poland. Despite the failure of an earlier attempt to carry out a coup, elements of the Romanian army played a key role in the overthrow of Ceausescu.

The second reason that armed forces do not intervene appears to be the prospect of failure. Where the prospect of mobilization by social forces strong enough to resist military control is great enough, this is likely to raise doubts among military leaders about their ability to achieve whatever specific policy goals they hope to advance by intervening, even to maintain civic order. The prospect of such mobilization against military rule is highest where civilian governance is deeply rooted and legitimated.

These conditions are, of course, more likely to obtain in long-surviving, well-institutionalized political societies. The ruling elites in newer, less well-institutionalized regimes have not yet organized command structures that are adaptable and responsive or that penetrate society sufficiently to ensure the implementation of policy. The participatory mechanisms that link those in the command structure with the people are inadequate. The organization of interests and consent is insufficient to mediate conflicts and translate interests and demands into policy, so that the regime is unable to produce enough benefits to generate sufficient instrumental support to serve as a basis of regime legitimacy.

Actual intervention may take place under a number of different circumstances, which include the following.

Crisis   There is a breakdown in the orderly process of community life in a locality, region, or the whole nation. Such a breakdown can be caused by an earthquake, civil disobedience, famine, or of course, the threat of an enemy attack. It can also be caused by the breakdown of the economy. Third World, Latin American, and East European debts have engendered social unrest and political crisis. In cases where military regimes were already in place, these crises stimulated the onset of a transition to democracy. But newly established democracies in Brazil and Argentina, confronting huge debts, rampant inflation, and economic crisis face the almost daily threat of military intervention. In Poland, economic crisis produced social unrest and contributed to the birth of the Solidarity labor movement. Faced with economic crisis and the paralysis of the political leadership, the military leadership moved to take indirect control over the country and eventually established direct control through martial law.

Crisis may also be engendered by the failure of an existing regime to perform. The inability of a civilian leadership to deal with the problems confronting the county may prompt intervention, especially in less developed countries where the professional military officer corps is a repository for highly skilled technical and administrative elites. Frequently, military officers receive advanced training in developed countries and become agents of modernization at home. They are sometimes impatient with incompetent political elites and unmoved by traditional bases of authority. Such a disproportion between civilian and military elites vastly increases the probability of intervention in response to crisis.

Conflict Over the Distribution of Goods The army is a corporate entity entitled to privileges, rewards, and special attention. Even in democratic regimes the proposition that the army is neutral and will stay so is based on the assumption that it receives proper and often privileged consideration. In societies that are poor, however, resources are scarce to begin with, and there are just not enough resources to satisfy the expectations of the military. The result is an unhappy army, which can very quickly develop a disposition to intervene.

Counterrevolution In many cases the military intervenes to protect the existing social and economic *status quo*, especially when the *status quo* has satisfied military interests. Social protests and revolutionary ideologies and movements endanger the ruling elite. Any threat to an elite that satisfies military interests spells danger to the military as well.

Military Heroics In times of war or its aftermath, the adoration heaped upon a victorious military hero increases the temptation for him and his associates to impose military-style, and therefore authoritarian, rule on the civilian population. The Roman generals fresh from victory vied with each other to become emperors. Napoleon actually did become an emperor. Had the British been forced to relinquish their control of the Falkland Islands, General Galtieri, then the president of Argentina, and the rest of the military junta ruling Argentina would certainly have strengthened popular support for and perhaps even legitimized military rule, instead of having had to face disgrace, a court martial, and the end of military rule in the wake of ignominious defeat. Even well-established democracies are not immune to the seductive power of military heroes. General Dwight D. Eisenhower, the American general who served as Supreme Allied Commander in Europe during World War II, returned to civilian life in the United States to be wooed by both political parties to be nominated as their candidate for President, for his attractiveness to the American people was almost irresistible.

Breakdown in Succession   Armies intervene when there are no clear and legitimized procedures to replace a ruler after his death. Even under such circumstances, however, civilian contenders for power must be unable to agree on a successor before the military intervenes. If one of the conditions outlined above is also present, military intervention is almost certain. In the absence of such conditions, the military may inherit the political leadership by default.

Forms of Military Rule

A military regime can assume a variety of forms. As Eric Nordlinger points out, "Many [military] coups entail immediate and fundamental changes in regime structure. . . .[The officers] establish an authoritarian regime that is closed to popular participation and competition. In doing so, they destroy or alter those structural features of the previous regimes that do not accord with their own preferences."[10] Every time the military intervenes it restructures the government. There are therefore different forms of praetorianism, each of which has its own characteristics. Nordlinger identifies three different roles assumed by the military when it intervenes: "guardians," "moderators," and "rulers."[11] We identify two basic forms of military rule—direct and indirect—which subsume the roles attributed to the military by Nordlinger.

Direct Military Rule   Direct military rule involves the assumption by the military itself of direct responsibility for the administration of civilian society. The military chain of command replaces the civilian organization of command. Orders and decisions are made by military officers assuming leadership of the country and are passed down the line for implementation and execution through the military chain of command.

[10]Nordlinger, *Soldiers and Politics*, p. 7.
[11]*Ibid.*, p. 11.

The army in effect becomes the government. Civilian officials are often dismissed, and many civilian institutions are dismantled or superseded by military ones. There is naturally an internal functional division in military governance. A collegial body of top military officers—usually referred to by foreign observers as a "junta"—makes the major political decisions. High-ranking officers also take over ministerial positions in the state bureaucracies and high positions in the executive branch of government. Actual management and administration are entrusted to the lower military echelons.

This is the purest form, or "ideal type," of military governance, which can be found virtually nowhere. Turkey between 1980 and 1983, Greece between 1967 and 1974, Chile after 1973, and Poland under martial law in 1981 and 1982 have come close. In reality, even when there is direct military governance, civilians are also involved. The civil service and local administrations continue to be manned by civilians. While military courts assume and exercise ultimate jurisdiction, the civilian courts are allowed to administer at least civil justice, leaving the military to deal with the penal code. Civilian experts are asked to participate and deliberate with the military at the highest levels in the cabinet. Military organizations themselves are simply not large enough and do not command enough administrative talent and experience to take over all the mundane tasks of government.

Military regimes must also attempt to preserve some degree of legitimacy. Often, they attempt to achieve this by presenting their rule as a temporary expedient, an emergency measure pending the organization of a more competent, more legitimate, civilian leadership. Thus if the regime that was replaced by the military had a civilian as chief of state, a president or hereditary monarch, the military may sometimes be inclined to keep him in office (as long as he remains compliant) as a symbolic manifestation of the military's commitment to restoring civilian rule. The military junta in Greece (1967–1974), for example, allowed the king to keep his throne until his attempts to oppose the junta— including an abortive military countercoup—brought about his removal. On the other hand, where the office of a civilian president is constitutionally powerful, as in some Latin American and African regimes, military intervention has frequently been followed by the dismissal, the arrest, or sometimes the assassination of a civilian president and a takeover by a military leader.

Figure 6.1 briefly shows the organization of the command structure in a military regime. The generals leave their barracks to become statesmen. But in so doing, they imbue the regime with their own alleged virtues: organization, hierarchy, command and obedience, discipline, punctuality, and efficiency. They eliminate participatory mechanisms such as legislatures, parties, and political associations, because they see little need to organize consent. They do away with competitive politics

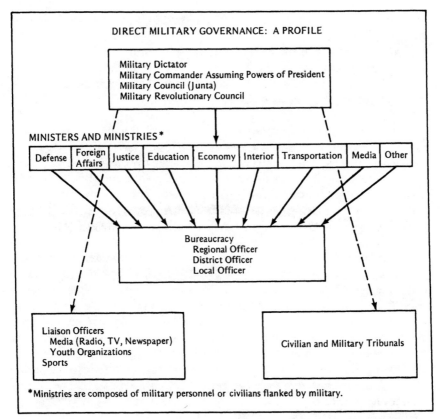

FIGURE 6.1

and all instrumentalities of representation in order to reduce complex issues to simple, clear-cut issues. As General Pinochet of Chile said in an interview, "Everything is either black or white."[12]

Naturally, the major pillar of military rule is force, or the implicit threat of force, without any limits on its use or scope. The military and the civilian police coordinate their efforts to seek out and destroy dissenters. Suspects are exiled, imprisoned, tortured, or even killed. Preventive measures are taken in the form of arrests or summary executions. Disobedience of the commands of the military is often considered treasonous and dealt with accordingly. The purpose of such violence is to intimidate the population into obedience and eventual withdrawal from political involvement quite as much as it is to root out any actual disobedience.

Indirect Military Rule   Indirect military rule differs from direct military rule in that civilian political institutions are permitted to survive and

[12]*The New York Times*, August 6, 1984.

function. Even if only a facade, civilian government retains a degree of legitimacy, and its procedures are respected. In a formerly democratic regime, these may even include limited civil and political rights and some participation, representation, and even the continuation of limited political competition. There are three different types of indirect military rule: *control, arbitration,* and *veto.*

Control.   Under a system of *military control,* the military remains in the barracks, but the civilian government is subject to political direction from the generals. Their instructions may range over the whole gamut of policy issues: foreign and defense issues, domestic social policies, and problems of the economy. The civilian government may even amount to little more than a facade to provide the military with a scapegoat for its errors or failures. Such regimes may be called "cryptomilitary."

Arbitration.   Under a system of *military arbitration,* the military also remains in the barracks, but civilian officeholders undertake their own policy initiatives. In a formerly democratic regime, parties advance their own political programs, and there are representative government and competitive politics. But when conflicts or disputes pit not only political parties and leaders but also separate units of the command structure (e.g., a monarch and his parliament, a president of a republic and his prime minister, a prime minister and his parliament) against one another, the military resolves the problem and endorses one policy, one civilian leader, or one political party over the others. Arbitration by the military often leads to direct rule. It has existed not only in some Latin American and African regimes, but also in communist Poland. Arbitration to settle a government-succession crisis has at times occurred even in democratic regimes. An effort was made to exercise it in France in 1958, when the French generals in Algeria tried to intervene in the formation of a civilian government. Some even argue that military arbitration was a central characteristic of the political order in the Soviet Union after the death of Stalin.

Veto.   The *military veto* is the mildest form of indirect rule. Civilian government operates normally in this case. In a democratic regime, the organizations of command, consent, interests, and rights are in full operation. Even competitive politics in the form of parties and open (and often free) elections take place and civil rights exist. There are certain policy matters, however, for which the consent of the military is required before any action can be taken.

In conclusion, we should note that it is not always easy to identify the varieties and variations of indirect military rule. There are many shades and degrees of indirect rule: It can range from support for a given government, to military intervention in selected policy areas, to selective military arbitration only when the civilian political leaders and the interests they speak for seem to be deadlocked, to the open preferences given by the military for some political parties and leaders as opposed to others. All these arrangements, however, correspond to various degrees of authoritarianism. As we move from direct to indirect military rule we also move from strict authoritarianism to varying degrees of controlled pluralism where there are representative and party institutions, political participation, competitive elections, and political and civil rights. The army becomes one of the players. But its weight is ever-present even if not always seen, and in the last analysis, the parameters of political freedom and competition are set by the army. When we move from authoritarian to democratic regimes, the military no longer exercises such dominant control over the political order. But because of the political importance of its mission, its appeal to the populace, and the considerable economic power it wields, the military remains an important element in the organization of command, remains a part of the organization of consent, and is one of the more influential interests even in democratic regimes.

Bureaucratic Authoritarianism

Bureaucratic authoritarianism is a special form of military regime in which the ruling coalition is dominated by the military but also includes civilian bureaucrats or "technocrats." This coalition seizes control of the government and determines which other groups are to be allowed to participate. In order to exclude groups from participating, these regimes undertake the demobilization of the population. But they also resort to outright coercion and violent repression of real and suspected opponents. The bureaucratic-authoritarian-regime "type" was developed on the basis of Latin American experience in the 1960s and 1970s. Brazil, Argentina, Chile, and Uruguay all fell under bureaucratic authoritarian regimes. Contrary to the view widespread in the 1960s that higher levels of development are associated with the emergence of democratic regimes, bureaucratic authoritarian regimes were established in Latin American states that had reached higher rather than lower levels of social and economic development.

The emergence of bureaucratic authoritarian regimes was initially often attributed to international economic conditions that placed these countries in a condition of "dependency" on the more highly developed industrialized countries. The authoritarian leaderships were seen as "modernizers" seeking to improve their economic power in the world economy. But reconsideration of these regimes has yielded an explanation of their emergence that focuses more on the concrete preferences and choices of elites. Their emergence is explained in terms of the choices of military elites, civilian technocrats, and economic leaders who became impatient with political conflict and economic difficulties caused by the politicization of the population. This politicization is a by-product of the industrialization process and especially the social mobilization of the population associated with the development process. Because political and economic conflict "gets in the way" of further economic development, military, bureaucratic, technocratic, and economic elites conspire to exclude the population from the policy-making process by imposing authoritarian constraints on participation and interest representation. By the time these alliances seize control, however, the higher levels of development of these regimes have already produced higher levels of political consciousness and political demands in the population. These necessitate higher levels of coercion in order to impose and maintain the authoritarian political order. As a result, these regimes resort to increasing levels of violence against their own people, including kidnappings ("disappearances"), torture, and the outright murder of innocent civilians.

Single-Party Authoritarian Regimes

The creation of a dominant or single authoritarian party provides an organizational basis for securing much broader popular support than is possible in a military-led regime. The authoritarian single party is, however, only one of the institutions such a regime may establish or allow to survive from the preauthoritarian era in order to organize societal interests and secure popular consent for its rule. It coexists with other institutions such as the military, the Church, economic groups and associations, professional groups, and even the institutions of government. It is just one of the many pillars on which the regime rests. This was the case in Franco's Spain, where the single party, the *Falange,* was in constant competition for support with other organizations and institutions. It never gained a completely dominant position. Even in Mexico, where the PRI is dominant, the necessity of renewing mass electoral support periodically compels the ruling elite to seek compromises with and the support of groups and organizations outside the party.

The single authoritarian party is in a constant state of flux; it goes through periods of ebb and flow. It may grow in complexity as it establishes ancillary social organizations, penetrates society more fully, and improves its adaptability and responsiveness. When the regime increases its popular appeal, membership increases, and the party itself becomes a nearly dominant political force. At other times the same party may begin to atrophy as the government, the military, the Church, or another organization or cluster of organizations begins to overshadow it.

In many authoritarian regimes the single party has shown clear signs of erosion and decline. All societies that go through rapid and radical changes tend eventually to revert to "normalcy." Emphasis in the ruling elite gradually shifts to performance and efficiency, to the satisfaction of everyday needs, and to ensuring obedience and compliance rather than participation. As a result, the elite and its most capable cadres shift their attention and effort to the task of government and administration rather than party building, and the authoritarian party is denied vital human resources. In virtually the whole of Africa, for example, authoritarian parties went into decline as the mobilizational phase of development gave way to regime consolidation. Henry Bienen summarizes the experience of African political parties this way:

> as the victorious parties formed governments, they lost functional relevance and coherence. The growth of state agencies proceeded, and party functions atrophied. The party became largely an agency of the government bureaucracy or, at the expense of its rank and file, in certain cases it became a mere extension of the personality of a strong president or prime minister.[13]

In general, single parties in authoritarian regimes have failed to institutionalize themselves. They have retained their centrality only where the most extreme form of authoritarian rule—totalitarianism— has been established. And the totalitarian party remains powerful only as long as the regime emphasizes the mobilizational and ideological functions and seeks to penetrate and subordinate society completely. With the weakening of communist ideology, to which we shall presently turn, it is quite likely that the totalitarian party will also weaken even where it still holds sway—in Cuba, China, Ethiopia, Albania, and elsewhere.

A Footnote on Iran—the Party of the Faithful   The Iranian revolution of 1979 was directed against the secular authoritarian regime of the Shah. It was led by religious elites who reasserted the old values of Islam. They wanted to cleanse the society of Western influences, and promised to penalize the rich and make resources available to the poor. They wanted to reestablish the brotherhood of Moslems, with particular appeal to the Shiite Moslems both in Iran and elsewhere. More than a decade after the Revolution and despite the death of its spiritual and actual leader, the Ayatollah Khomeini, the religious elite remains in full control of the "Islamic Republic." The Shiite Moslem clergymen control

---

[13]Henry Bienen, "One Party Systems in Africa," in Samuel P. Huntington and Clement Moore (eds.), *Authoritarian Politics in Modern Societies* (New York: Basic Books, 1970) pp. 99–100.

an overwhelming majority in parliament through their single party, the Islamic Republican party. They spearhead and guide a vast network of clergymen who exercise direct influence and control over the local mosques, approximately 15,000 of them. (The mosque has become for all practical purposes the equivalent of the vocal authoritarian party organization and its ancillary social organizations.) In the name of religion, the clergy carries out political propaganda and performs political roles. They act as if they were grand juries, deciding on whom to prosecute and very often deciding the reasons; they distribute benefits and favors; they hand out ration cards for scarce goods. They are the building blocks of the political power of the ayatollahs.

Thus Iran, in the name of religious fundamentalism, nationalism, and anti-Westernism, has become a single-party authoritarian regime. It is a regime that constantly evokes traditional values and is addressed to the vindication of past values. It is a regime that eschews the concepts of enlightenment, rationality, science, and the institutions and practices of liberalism, where power is legitimized in religious terms. It is a regime that is dedicated to the elimination of all infidels, especially the state of Israel. It is also a regime that, after unifying the society around the basic myths it proposes, now wants to impose its ideology and political practices abroad—particularly among the Shiite Moslems who are spread throughout the region. It is dedicated to Islam. In terms of leadership, the organization of the single party, the conformity the regime has attempted to exact, the religious mythology that it has elevated into an official ideology, and the mobilization and use of force, the Iranian regime is truly totalitarian.

The clergy has recruited and organized a paramilitary force, the Revolutionary Guards, about 150,000 strong. They are the eyes and ears of the clergy, the dogs that sniff out treason and silence opposition. Whenever the spiritual arm of the clergy cannot assure conformity, the secular arm they forged is called upon to enforce it through intimidation and assassination. The party and the Revolutionary Guards permeate the society. They control family life, impose religious conformity, appeal to the young to join the army for both material and heavenly rewards, and punish those who fail to volunteer. They also deal out swift justice to anyone who violates religious taboos.

Over and above the party, the mosques, the Revolutionary Guards, and the Parliament, there are three institutions that stand supreme. The first is the Supreme Religious Guide. The second is the Assembly of Experts (eighty-three clergymen), which was established in 1983 to decide Khomeini's succession. The third is the Council of Guardians, a very small group of clerics (with scholarly reputations) who go over legislation, government decrees, and orders to check their conformity with the religious faith. They are, in a sense, the highest court.

Finally, there is the army. Purged of all pro-American or pro-Western elements, it is now manned with converts and new recruits and serves faithfully the religious–political leadership. Unable to win the war against Iraq, the army maintains nonetheless its position and prestige. It is and probably will remain an obedient instrument of the Islamic revolution that it hopes will extend beyond the borders of Iran. In the meantime, dissenters and critics have been eliminated at home, and those who live abroad have been the victims of terrorist attacks and threats. Salmon Rushdie is in hiding somewhere in England, sentenced to death for blasphemy for his book *The Satanic Verses*, that parodied some religious observances.

While the contours of the Iranian regime are fairly clear, one should not conclude from this sketch that it has gained stability and legitimacy. It faces fundamental problems. First is the problem of leadership. The post-Khomeini leadership appears internally divided over domestic and, especially, foreign policy issues. The second problem is whether the present leadership can satisfy the lower middle-class groups and the farmers who provide it with supports. Promises made are hard to fulfill in the deteriorating economic situation caused in part by the long war with Iraq. Nationalism and religious fanaticism can provide mobilization and supports for only a given period of time, but concern with material satisfactions will soon take precedence. The regime will have to meet the ultimate test of performance—the ability to provide goods and services—that we discuss in Chapter 9.

Bibliography

Bienen, Henry. *Kenya: The Parties of Participation and Control.* Princeton, N.J.: Princeton University Press, 1974.

———. *Tanzania: Party Transformation and Economic Development.* Princeton, N.J.: Princeton University Press, 1970.

———. (ed.). *The Military Intervenes: Case Studies in Political Development.* New York: Russell Sage Foundation, 1968.

———. (ed.). *The Military and Modernization.* New York: Lieber-Atherton Press, 1971.

Bill, James A., and Carl Leiden. *Politics in the Middle East.* 2d ed. Boston: Little, Brown, 1984.

Booth, John A. *The End of the Beginning: The Nicaraguan Revolution.* Boulder, Colo.: Westview Press, 1982.

Clements, Frank. *Saudie Arabia.* Santa Barbara, Calif.: American Bibliographical Center/Clio Press, 1979.

Clogg, Richard, and George Yannopoulos (eds.). *Greece Under Military Rule.* New York: Basic Books, 1972.

Coe, Michael D. *Mexico.* 2d ed. New York: Praeger, 1977.

Collier, David (ed.). *The New Authoritarianism in Latin America.* Princeton, N.J.: Princeton University Press, 1979.

Devlin, John F. *Syria: Modern State in an Ancient Land.* Boulder, Colo.: Westview Press, 1983.

Dickenson, John P. *Brazil.* Boulder, Colo.: Westview Press, 1978.

Elbow, Martin I. *French Corporatist Theory 1781–1948.* New York: Columbia University Press, 1953.

Elliott, David L. *Thailand: Origins of Military Rule.* London: Zeal Press, 1980.

Feit, Edward. *The Armed Bureaucrats: Military–Administrative Regimes and Political Development.* Boston: Houghton Mifflin, 1973.

Findlay, Allan M., Anne M. Findlay, and Richard Lawless. *Tunisia.* Santa Barbara, Calif: American Bibliographical Center/Clio Press, 1982.

Finer, Sam E. *The Man on Horseback: The Role of the Military in Politics.* New York: Praeger, 1962.

Flynn, Peter. *Brazil: A Political Analysis.* Boulder, Colo.: Westview Press, 1978.

Gonzales, Casanova. *Democracy in Mexico.* New York: Oxford University Press, 1970.

Green, Jerrold D. *Revolution in Iran: The Politics of Countermobilization.* New York: Praeger, 1982.

Hodges, Donald C., and Ross Gandy. *Mexico 1910–1982: Reform or Revolution?* Westport, Conn.: L. Hill, 1983.

Huntington, Samuel, and Clement Moore (eds.). *Authoritarian Politics in Modern Society.* New York: Basic Books, 1970.

Jackson, Robert A., and Carl Rosberg. *Personal Rule in Black Africa: Princes, Autocrats, Prophets, Tyrants.* Berkeley: University of California, 1982.

Janowitz, Morris. *On Military Intervention.* Rotterdam, The Netherlands: Rotterdam University Press, 1971.

Lord Kinross. *Ataturk: A Biography of Mustafa Kemal, Father of Modern Turkey.* New York: William Morris and Co., 1965.

Kay, Hugh. *Salazar and Modern Portugal.* New York: E. P. Dutton, 1970.

La Palombara, Joseph, and Myron Weiner (eds.). *Political Parties and Political Development.* Princeton, N.J.: Princeton University Press, 1966.

Lasswell, Harold, and Daniel Lerner (eds.). *World Revolutionary Elites: Studies in Coercive Ideological Movements.* Boston: M.I.T. Press, 1966.

Latin American Studies Association Forum, vol. XV, no. 2, Arturo Velenzuela, "Pinochet in Chile," (pp. 11–15) and "The Political Crisis of the Pinochet Regime," (pp. 17–20).

Levy, Daniel, and Gabriel Szekely. *Mexico: Paradoxes of Stability and Change.* Boulder, Colo.: Westview, 1983.

Linz, Juan. "Totalitarianism and Authoritarianism," in Fred I. Green-
stein and Nelson W. Polsby, eds., *Handbook of Political Science*, vol. 3.
Reading, Mass.: Addison-Wesley, 1975.
Lipset, S. M., and A. Solar (eds.). *Elites in Latin America*. New York:
Oxford University Press, 1973.
Lowenthal, Abraham F. (ed.). *Armies and Politics in Latin America*. New
York: Holmes and Meier Publications, 1976.
Lowenthal, Abraham (ed.). *The Peruvian Experiment: Continuity and
Change under Military Rule*. Princeton, N.J.: Princeton University
Press, 1976.
Needler, Martin C. *Political Systems in Latin America*. New York: Reinholt
and Co., 1970.
Nordlinger, Eric. *Soldiers in Politics: Military Coups and Government*. En-
glewood Cliifs, N.J.: Prentice-Hall, 1977.
O'Donnell, Guillermo A. *Modernization and Bureaucratic Authoritarianism:
Studies in South American Politics*. Berkeley: Institute of International
Studies, University of California, 1973.
Payne, Stanley. *The Falange: A History of Spanish Fascism*. Palo Alto,
Calif.: Stanford University Press, 1961.
Paxton, Robert O. *Vichy France: Old Guard and New Order, 1940–1944*.
New York: Columbia University Press, 1972.
Perlmutter, Amos. *Egypt: The Praetorian State*. New Brunswick, N.J.:
Transaction Books, 1974.
———. *The Military and Politics in Modern Times*. New Haven: Yale
University Press, 1977.
———. *Modern Authoritarianism: A Comparative Institutional Analysis*.
New Haven: Yale University Press, 1981.
Perlmutter, Amos. *Modern Authoritarianism*. New Haven, Conn.: Yale
University Press, 1981.
Schoultz, Lars. *The Populist Challenge: Argentine Electoral Behavior in the
Postwar Era*. Chapel Hill, N.C.: University of North Carolina Press,
1983.
Shaw, John A., and David E. Long. *Saudi Arabia's Modernization: The
Impact of Change on Stability*. New York: Praeger, 1982.
Stein, Steve. *Populism in Peru*. Madison, Wisc.: University of Wisconsin
Press, 1980.
Stepan, Alfred (ed.). *Authoritarian Brazil: Origins, Policies and Future*.
New Haven: Yale University Press, 1973.
Stepan, Alfred. *The State and Society: Peru in Comparative Perspective*.
Princeton, N.J.: Princeton University Press, 1978.
Strauss, Leo. *On Tyranny*. Ithaca: Cornell University Press, 1975.
Wesson, Robert G. *Brazil in Transition*. New York: Praeger, 1983.
Wiarda, Howard J. *Corporatism and Development: The Portuguese Experi-
ence*. Amherst: University of Massachusetts Press, 1977.

———. *Corporatism and National Development in Latin America.* Boulder, Colo.: Westview, 1981.

Wiarda, Howard, and Harvey Kline. *Latin American Politics and Development.* 2d ed. Boulder, Colo.: Westview Press, 1985.

Wittfogel, Karl. *A Comparative Study of Total Power.* New Haven, Conn.: Yale University Press, 1957.

Zinn, Ricardo. *Argentina: A Nation at the Crossroads of Myth and Reality.* New York: R. Speller, 1979.

7

Totalitarian Regimes

Introduction

Totalitarian regimes share many of the characteristics common to all authoritarian regimes: political power is concentrated and the command structure is not subject to limitations and rules of responsibility; the leadership manipulates and controls consent, using police and other mechanisms of coercion to ensure compliance; it controls the various media of communication to limit demands; it dominates and controls the configuration of interests; and it pays scant attention to individual rights—few guarantees are extended to the individual, who remains at the mercy of the ruling elite. But there are also important differences that distinguish totalitarian regimes.

Intellectual Origins

Those familiar with Hobbes's *Leviathan* and Rousseau's *Social Contract* can trace authoritarianism to the former and totalitarianism to the latter. Hobbes argued for the absolute authority of the state over the people in order to guarantee them security in their persons and their property and to allow them to pursue their interests in peace. Rousseau, in contrast, argued for direct governance by the people based on what we now call popular participation and mobilization, and he proclaimed that the people in their collective capacity were infallible and absolute. Hobbes's call for the establishment of order and security under the control of the state provides the intellectual origins of authoritarianism, while Rousseau's claims for popular sovereignty and the infallibility of the people provides us with the intellectual background to totalitarianism. These origins account, to an important degree, for the different political vocabularies of these regimes.

Totalitarian regimes employ the vocabulary and terminology of democracy, frequently using variations of such concepts as the "sovereignty of the people," the "representation of the people," "individual rights," "representative assemblies," and "responsibility and accountability to the people." They establish many of the formal institutions of consent, such as elections, referendums, parliamentary government, and especially the political party. They encourage the organization of interests through the political party and other social organizations which become the vehicles of mass mobilization. In form, totalitarian regimes may appear democratic, but in substance they are structured to facilitate the unlimited exercise of power by the totalitarian leader and his lieutenants.

State and Society

In totalitarian regimes, the state penetrates and virtually absorbs societal forces. New institutions are created in order to bring all societal forces under the unchallengeable control of the ruling elite. They do so by penetrating interests and associations; destroying some, reshaping those that remain, and creating new ones. Totalitarian penetration and control extends to the economy, education and culture, religion, and even the family itself. Although authoritarian regimes also impose controls and restrictions, they hardly even attempt to reshape and restructure society in this way. Interests and associations, even if they are subordinated to the authoritarian state, often maintain their autonomy and separateness, most notably churches and economic enterprises. Authoritarian regimes are satisfied with control rather than penetration. As a result, in sharp contrast to totalitarian regimes, they allow for what Juan Linz has called a "limited pluralism" of social forces.[1]

We have defined mobilization as the intensification of participation. It is the process by which a regime brings as many citizens as possible into active involvement in public life. Mobilization has two functions in the totalitarian regime. First, it creates supports for the leader and others in the command structure. Since it is so extensive it begins with the schools and is continued through a number of associations and organizations set up by the ruling elite. As in other regimes, the chief mobilizing agency in a totalitarian regime is the political party. In totalitarian regimes, there is only a single party, consisting of the ruling elite and other elites. It is portrayed as a vanguard that speaks for

[1] Juan J. Linz, "Totalitarian and Authoritarian Regimes," in Fred I. Greenstein and Nelson W. Polsby (eds.), *Handbook of Political Science*, vol. 3 (Reading, Mass.: Addison-Wesley, 1975), pp. 175–411.

the masses. It is the vehicle through which the elite provides the cues for popular thought and action and authoritatively interprets the official ideology. Its members penetrate every social activity in an effort to see to it that all act in conformity with regime goals and policies. No citizen is left out, and all are encouraged or coerced to participate, but under carefully controlled conditions. In this manner the party appears to be a powerful link between the regime and the people, creating the image and sometimes the reality of regime responsiveness.

The second function of mobilization is developmental: It serves as an instrument for marshalling resources for social and economic modernization. To speed both development and the social revolution to which they were committed, the Communist totalitarian regimes of the Soviet Union, China, and Eastern Europe subjected all material and human resources to mobilization in support of the establishment of centrally planned economies under direct state control.

It is the centrality of mass mobilization that distinguishes totalitarian regimes. It is not sought by dictators, autocrats, tyrants, military juntas, or bureaucrats. Their emphasis is on the authority of the state, which implies and invites obedience, not participation. There was, for example, little mobilization under the Franco regime in Spain from 1936 to 1975, under the military–bureaucratic authoritarian regimes in Latin America, or in Portugal from 1931 to 1968. These regimes did not seek popular involvement; they avoided it.

Ideology

The essence of the totalitarian regime is its ideology. It offers a set of overarching propositions about society and human nature in which the existing order of things is to be radically overhauled. It is geared to the refashioning of society, family life, education, culture, and of course, politics. The totalitarian ideology is thus comprehensive in nature, and its proponents claim singular authority for it, to the exclusion of all other beliefs. It is the marriage of such a totalist ideology to a monopoly of power that creates what might be called the totalitarian imperative: The drive to establish complete control over all activity, to enforce social conformity based on the ideology, and to prevent the emergence of competing ideas and beliefs.

Totalitarian elites tend to be highly ideological in the goals they posit. They are often utopian and transcendental and often radically different from the values and goals of the society they seek to control and modify. The official ideology is a highly mobilizing one: It calls for both action and sacrifice, and it is formulated exclusively by the political leadership. Most authoritarian regimes, in contrast, do not develop the same all-encompassing official ideology. Some of them are committed to pragmatic goals: reviving the economy, doing away with foreign competition, averting civil war, or maintaining law and order. They ask for acquiescence rather than individual devotion and adherence; they do not try to turn the citizen into a believer. Obedience is defined in terms of the absence of any overt resistance to the state. Within this limit, citizens are free to operate within their established associations, groups, or other societal institutions, including their churches. They can develop their own parochial loyalties as long as they do not undermine obedience to those who command.

The totalitarian elite attempts, through its efforts to mobilize the population, impose its ideology, and organize consent, to develop a broad popular consensus around regime values and goals; a consensus similar to that which exists in genuinely democratic regimes. As we have already noted, authoritarian regimes do not strive for consensus. They are satisfied with acquiescence, even apathy. They equate stable government with obedience, with the absence of overt opposition. Authoritarian regimes simply do not want the citizenry to externalize thoughts that run counter to the political status quo. Totalitarian regimes, on the other hand, want the individual citizen to internalize the values they promote.

Background to Totalitarianism

The rise of totalitarian regimes is a phenomenon associated with a particular historical period: the era from the 1930s to the 1950s. All the major totalitarian regimes were established during this period of international economic crisis and world war: the Stalinist regime in the Soviet Union, Nazi Germany, and Fascist Italy in the years before World War II, and the communist states of Eastern Europe and China in the postwar years. Both the Nazi and the Fascist regimes were destroyed by the war. But Stalinist totalitarianism survived it and was spread by force to Eastern Europe, by revolution to China and other countries. The establishment of totalitarian regimes was made possible by the onset of internal crisis in the antecedent regime, by the dominant political culture of the regime, or by outright conquest by another totalitarian power.

Internal Crisis

The existence of a political group committed to a revolutionary, totalist ideology, is by itself insufficient to establish a totalitarian regime. That ideology must offer an attractive basis for the mobilization of mass support, or at least the support of key elite groups. Revolutionary ideologies appear to be most attractive under conditions of internal crisis. The breakdown of democratic regime performance, caused by the destruction of the social fabric resulting from defeat in war and the deprivations imposed on the population by the international economic depression and crisis of the 1920s and 1930s, helped account for the rise of Nazism; the political threat to the survival of the authoritarian Soviet regime posed by the erosion of penetration and control and the rise of domestic opposition in the 1920s help explain the appeal of Stalin's efforts to mobilize support for the imposition of a totalitarian order.

Political Culture

Deliberate attempts to establish a totalitarian order must generate affective support if the regime is to achieve legitimacy and become institutionalized. Affective support is easiest to generate when totalitarian values coincide with values in the population. In the absence of a militarist, statist, Prussian tradition, of unfulfulled nationalist ambitions, of middle class fears of Communism and reduction to proletarian status, and of widespread attraction to racist theories of human relations, it is unlikely that Nazism could have mobilized popular support in Germany.[2] Similarly, the appeal of totalitarian responses to policy dilemmas was strengthened in the Soviet Union by the existence of a centuries-long historical legacy of autocracy and a Russian revolutionary tradition that was antiliberal and disinclined to democratic procedure or compromise. And it was reinforced by a Bolshevik culture of submission to the authority of "the party." These conditions provided fertile ground upon which the totalitarian leader could exploit the tragic mistakes of his opponents.

External Conquest

Some totalitarian regimes are established not as the result of internal circumstances, but as the result of external conquest. The postwar totalitarian regimes of East Germany, Poland, Hungary, Bulgaria, and Romania, for example, were established as the result of the occupation of these countries by the Soviet Red Army in the later stages of World War II and their political domination by the Soviet Union, then itself still a Stalinist, totalitarian regime. The dependency of these regimes on Soviet political and military support has meant that the onset of political changes in the Soviet Union, and especially the withdrawal of Soviet military backing, very quickly undermined these regimes.

General Features of Totalitarianism

The totalitarian regime is characterized by adoption of a *totalist ideology* as the official state ideology, whose propagation by the ruling elite requires the exclusion of all other belief systems. Its implementation, therefore, requires the carrying out of an assault on all organizations and

---

[2]On the appeals of Nazism, see W. S. Allen, *The Nazi Seizure of Power: The Experience of a Single German Town* (Chicago: Quadrangle Books, 1965).

institutions, such as independent political parties and organized religions, that propagate their own belief systems. In other words, the ideology requires the carrying out of a total social revolution.

The *ruling elite* that directs this revolution is highly centralized and homogeneous, or unidimensional, in composition. It wields its power through a hierarchically organized, authoritarian, elite organization of command that penetrates society completely. And it wields its power without constraint. It is not accountable to any group or institution. It perpetuates itself by recruitment through cooptation, with emphasis on vertical mobility through the ranks of the organization of command, rather than horizontal mobility from outside the ranks. The totalitarian elite exercises monopolistic control over the organization of social interests, including the military and the economy. It relegates preexisting social groups and institutions to subordinate status or annihilates them completely through widespread use of coercion and even mass terror. In their place, the totalitarian regime establishes a whole host of new organizations and institutions. (See Table 7.1.)

To achieve its goals, the totalitarian ruling elite directs the *total mobilization of society*. It creates multiple opportunities for the participation of the masses in activities and organizations under the direct, institutionalized control of the organization of command. And it employs coercion to ensure that such participation takes place. The totalitarian elite reinforces the effects of mass participation through mass propaganda designed to elicit support for the regime.

The *coercion* employed by totalitarian regimes is distinguished from that employed by other authoritarian regimes by its scale, motivation, and targets. It is also distinguished by process, timing, and the moral self-righteousness of its public justification. The scale of violence, coercion, and terror in the totalitarian regime is far greater than that in other authoritarian regimes. It is motivated not just by the effort to intimidate but by the attempt to mobilize the population. Terror serves the totalitarian regime as an instrument of penetration, which is why it unfolds in the early stages of regime creation and consolidation. The targets of the terror are not just individuals and their families, or even small groups. They are whole categories of society, including at times even the totalitarian elite itself.

TABLE 7.1 Characteristics of Elites in
Totalitarian Regimes

Monopolistic
One-dimensional (political conformity)
Vertical (dominance of the political elite)
Exclusive
Integrative

Usually, the totalitarian *organization of command* takes the form of a single political party, to which all other organizations and institutions are subordinated. But the state organization may supplant the party in this role. With the establishment of a totalitarian tyranny, a hybrid police-state apparatus may emerge. Whatever its makeup, the totalitarian organization of command is employed for the purpose of implementing the precepts of the official ideology. At the same time, however, the content of the ideology itself is subject to redefinition by the ruling elite. Thus the ideology can be shaped to the preferences and needs of the totalitarian elite or leader, and does not constrain regime actions in the way that traditions or cultural values constrain authoritarian regimes.

The *totalitarian party* functions as a true political party in the period before the assumption of power. It is characterized by voluntary recruitment and voluntary exit of its members, and its actions are aimed at securing power and obtaining political and material advantages for its members. It maintains a rigid definition of membership and imposes discipline and responsibility on its members. After the assumption of power, the totalitarian party becomes essentially nonvoluntary. Membership becomes coercive, based on the monopoly the party exercises over social opportunity and mobility. Exit becomes nonvoluntary as well.

The change from a "party of revolution" to a "party in power" is associated with profound changes in the functions, organization, and membership of the party. As the regime consolidates its power, the party becomes the central organizational instrument for penetrating and subordinating all potential centers of autonomous power in society. The *penetration of society* by the party is reinforced and with time may even be taken over by the coercive forces of the totalitarian regime. With the consolidation of totalitarian power, the party becomes bureaucratized and recruits specialized personnel to fulfill the increasingly complex tasks of governance. Such recruitment competes with vertical mobility as a basis for entry into the ruling elite. As a result, tension emerges between the totalitarian party's mass mobilizational role and its administrative role, between what is called in the Soviet case "reds" and "experts."

The center of power in a totalitarian regime is *monistic*, or concentrated in a single place, but not necessarily *monolithic*, or conflict-free. Conflicts in such regimes do not, however, arise out of society or take place between social groups and organizations. Conflict takes place between members of the ruling elite, who derive their power from membership in the elite itself, not from society. The conflicts between members of a totalitarian elite may reflect broader social or institutional categories of interest, but the elites themselves are neither accountable nor responsible to the society over which they rule.

The totalitarian regime does not necessarily call for either social ownership of property or a centrally planned economy. But the ideological commitment of all the Communist totalitarian regimes to at least some variant of Marxism led them all to carry out extensive socialization of property. Moreover, the decentralization of power and authority inherent in and necessary for the success of a capitalist market economy would be impossible to reconcile with the unconstrained power of a totalitarian ruling elite. At the same time, the total penetration of society by the instruments of command, their control by a highly centralized ruling elite, and the commitment to total mobilization for social revolution produce enormous pressure to establish central controls over economic activity even where ownership remains private. Thus, totalitarian regimes seem impelled toward at least the subordination, if not complete elimination of private prerogatives in the economy.

Finally, a totalitarian regime does not require the existence of a single leader. However, the features of the totalitarian order are clearly conducive to the emergence of such a figure, and the two archetypical totalitarian regimes—the Soviet Union and Nazi Germany—were, in fact, both led by autocratic figures, Stalin and Hitler. To the extent that compliance comes to depend on coercion instead of voluntarism induced by ideological commitment and material benefits, the tendency of the totalitarian regime to degenerate into tyranny becomes even stronger.

Stalinism and Nazism

The Organization of Command

Both the Stalinist and the Nazi forms of totalitarianism were characterized by the centralization of unconstrained power in the hands of the ruling elite and, ultimately, a single leader.

The Stalinist Organization   In the Soviet Union, the oligarchic, authoritarian Bolshevik party that had achieved only partial penetration of society by the late 1920s was replaced by a highly homogeneous, tightly organized and disciplined, personal organization surrounding the single leader, Stalin. This organization, Stalin's personal secretariat, served as the apex of the party, state, and police hierarchies that penetrated and subordinated every social organization and institution.[3]

The Bolshevik party was an authoritarian organization dominated by its leader, Lenin. But as late as the mid-1920s it could still be characterized by one of its other leaders as "a negotiated federation be-

---

[3]Niels Erik Rosenfeldt, *Knowledge and Power: The Role of Stalin's Secret Chancellery in the Soviet System of Government* (Copenhagen: Rosenkilde and Bagger, 1978).

tween groups, groupings, factions, and 'tendencies'."[4] This oligarchic tendency was suppressed by Stalin through deliberate attack. Stalin exploited the centralizing, authoritarian principles of party organization first advanced by Lenin in his prerevolutionary tract, *What Is to Be Done?* Stalin created new approaches to the management of party personnel more conducive to extending his personal influence over the whole party apparatus. He relied on spontaneous pressure to achieve party unity in the face of societal opposition to Bolshevik rule. He revised the ideology to strengthen its mass appeal, especially by making it more nationalist and less internationalist, and he addressed central issues of economic and political development in ways that appealed to critical sectors of society, especially the more radical communists. Finally, Stalin applied steadily increasing levels of coercion and violence against a steadily expanding scope of targets.

The totalitarian order was consolidated through the forced collectivization of the peasantry, the imposition of central economic planning, and the rapid industrialization of the country in the late 1920s and early 1930s. Collectivization was a violent process, which produced millions of deaths and widespread famine. The changes in the pattern of economic activity, the distribution of the population, and the role of various groups and institutions in society associated with industrialization amounted to a vast social revolution. It was directed by Stalin from above and carried out by the mass mobilization of the population, using material rewards, coercion, and the threat of coercion, the latter reinforced by the regime's demonstrated willingness to use force against its enemies and by its propensity to declare as enemies all who resisted its policies.

By the early 1930s, Stalin had brought the organizations of command—the party, state, and the secret police apparatuses—under his personal control, exercised through his personal secretariat. The basis of this control lay in the personal secretariat's monopoly over personnel assignments in all areas related to security, over access to the secret internal communications network of the party and state, and over the secret party archives, including personnel records. Stalin used these powers to appoint members of his secretariat as heads of key administrative bureaucracies such as the secret police and the network of political commissars who served as watchdogs over the military. These bureaucracies not only managed the economy but directly controlled vast resources, including human labor. The number of prisoners in labor camps under secret police administration, for example, skyrocketed, and their labor was mobilized for vast development projects.

[4]Nikolai Bukharin, quoted by Stephen F. Cohen, in "Bolshevism and Stalinism," in Robert C. Tucker (ed.), *Stalinism: Essays in Historical Interpretation* (New York: W. W. Norton & Co., 1977), p. 17.

Although united under Stalin's command, the party, police, and administrative bureaucracies were not yet integrated into a single organizational hierarchy at this time. Party members, for example, could be arrested by the secret police, but their punishment remained in the hands of party organs. However, in late 1934 Stalin began a violent campaign of arrests and executions that swept away all sources of resistance to central control and integrated the party, state, and police hierarchies into a single organization of command. This assault on society has come to be known as the period of "the great purges," or "the great terror." Beginning in 1935 and lasting until late 1938, Stalin and his closest assistants directed a massive campaign of arrests, deportations, and executions that affected many millions of people. Even today the exact number of victims is hotly disputed among Soviet historians and dissidents, with some estimates ranging in the tens of millions!

Unlike the violence that accompanied collectivization and, to a lesser extent, industrialization, this terror was also directed against the regime's own elites. The purges destroyed the overwhelming majority of the Soviet elite. Of the 1,966 delegates to the Seventeenth Party Congress in February 1934, 1,108, or 56.3 percent, were killed. Of the 139 Central Committee members elected at the Congress, 98 (70.8 percent) were killed; others committed suicide.[5] Eighty-five percent of provincial party secretaries perished in the purges. In the Red Army, one-third of the officer corps was executed, including three of five marshals, all but one of the fleet commanders, thirteen of fifteen generals of the army, all commanders of military districts, all corps commanders, almost all brigade and division commanders, and one-half of all regimental commanders. The military academies, the political commissars, and even the military intelligence networks were all swept by the purges.[6]

This campaign of terror was not simply the product of Stalin's madness, although any such campaign is, of course, *prima facie* evidence of madness. Nor can one discount the role of possible defects in Stalin's personal psychology in explaining it. But the terror also represented a conscious attempt by Stalin to consolidate his personal rule over the immense, centralized machinery of command, control, and communications that he had created. It destroyed the organizational autonomy of the vast bureaucratic hierarchies under his command and subjected them to his personal intervention. It prevented the entrenchment of lower officials and the creation of informal networks of communication, influence, and loyalties that might serve as the basis for resistance

---

[5]Figures revealed by Khrushchev in his denunciation of Stalin. Nikita S. Khrushchev, *The Crimes of the Stalin Era*, Special Report to the Twentieth Congress of the Communist Party of the Soviet Union [in closed session, February 1956] (New York: The New Leader, 1962).
[6]Robert Conquest, *The Great Terror* (London: Penguin Books, 1971), pp. 277–374.

to commands from above. It established what Aristotle called tyranny, for it gave to Stalin the power of life and death over his subjects, including even those in positions of authority.

As a result, Stalin enjoyed the use of an unprecedented machinery of societal penetration. He created what were, for his time, technologically advanced systems of communication, observation and monitoring, reporting, information processing, economic planning, resource mobilization, transportation, persuasion, and coercion. This did not mean, however, that Stalin decided everything in the Soviet Union. That would have been impossible. But it did mean that he could intervene in any process or make any decision without constraint.

The Stalinist Elite   Stalin did not have to decide each question personally because the totalitarian hierarchy of command was staffed with personnel who had been socialized to the official ideology and values of the regime. Through manipulation of centralized control over personnel, the ruling elite had been able to control access to elite status in the regime. After 1938, when the halt in the terror reduced elite turnover, appointment to responsible positions could be reserved for those who advanced vertically in the ranks, thereby reinforcing elite homogeneity and coherence.

Day-to-day administration of the economy was in the hands of the central state bureaucracies, personnel assignments to which were also controlled by the ruling elite. The number of state organs increased in number gradually from 1917 to 1936. Thereafter, a rapid proliferation of specialized state bureaucracies took place to meet the demands of overseeing the rapid industrialization of the 1930s and the mobilization and coordination of civilian and military tasks during the Second World War. By 1947, a hypercentralized, centrally planned economy administered by numerous highly specialized central state bureaucracies was firmly established. But these bureaucracies remained subject to supervision and intervention by parallel party and secret police organs. This pattern has lasted until the present day.

The existence of multiple overlapping administrative hierarchies within the organization of command provided a certain degree of adaptability to the Stalinist system. This was further enhanced by the fact that subordinate elites at lower levels of the hierarchies were unconstrained by rational, bureaucratic rules of procedure in the execution of their functions. They were free to use whatever means were available to fulfill the tasks assigned them by the central authorities, and they did. Thus, a great deal of corruption, black-marketeering, and other ostensibly illegal activities became routine methods of administration. This allowed the Stalinist totalitarian organization of command to maintain a relatively high degree of adaptability and responsiveness; but because the regime was at the same time a tyranny, that adaptability and responsiveness was not directed *below*, toward society, but *upward* toward the tyrant.

The end of the purges in 1938 marked the consolidation of the Stalinist totalitarian system. Although the tyranny he established could not survive him, many of the features of the totalitarian organization of command remained largely intact until Gorbachev's attack on it nearly fifty years later. The Stalinist form of totalitarianism was imposed on the East European satellite regimes in the post-World War II period and was adopted by the Chinese Communists after their successful seizure of power in 1949.

The Nazi Organization While the Stalinist organization of command was created long after the communist seizure of power and was composed of an integrated party/police/state organization, the Nazi organization of command was established prior to Hitler's assumption of state power in January 1933, and it encompassed many distinct and competing institutional and organizational structures. The most important of these were, of course, the Nazi party and its related organizations and the secret police hierarchy. These were then imposed on German state institutions. These hierarchies were controlled from above by Hitler, who never managed to establish the single, integrated hierarchy of command that Stalin was able to establish.

After Hitler took over leadership of the National Socialist German Workers Party (NSDAP), or Nazi party, in July 1921, he directed an immediate reorganization and expansion of the party's bureaucratic structure.[7] By 1928, the party had established core organizations throughout Germany, so that when the economic shock of the Great Depression intensified the domestic political conflict in 1929, Hitler stood at the head of a political organization ready to mount a nationwide campaign to seize power.

Upon his assumption of the chancellorship in January 1933, Hitler exploited its authoritarian powers to launch an accelerated attack on society, hiding behind the fiction that all his actions were "legal" and within the framework of the Weimar constitution's grant of emergency powers. The division of powers inherent in the federal system was destroyed, and power was centralized in the Hitler dictatorship. In February 1933, Hitler decreed a set of emergency measures that eliminated all civil liberties; in March 1933, he pushed through the so-called "enabling act," which transferred all legislative power from the Reichstag to Hitler's government; in April, he began an attack on the civil

---

[7]For an authoritative and detailed account of the development of the Nazi party and the construction of the Nazi totalitarian regime, see Karl Dietrich Bracher, *The German Dictatorship* (London: Weidenfeld and Nicolson, 1971). See also Franz Neumann, *Behemoth: The Structure and Practice of National Socialism* (New York: Harper & Row, N.D.) [reprint of the revised second edition first published by Oxford University Press in 1944].

service and judiciary by banning all non-Aryans, especially Jews, from employment; political opponents were simply arrested, and the secret police established camps for their detention; in July he outlawed all other political parties and established a legal one-party state.

With the support of the military and of the most conservative social elites, Hitler had in effect established a bureaucratic authoritarian regime. The political appointees of the republican years were removed from the state administration, and an alliance was forged with the bureaucrats, or "technocrats," who continued to administer the government under Nazi direction. But Hitler and the Nazis soon proceeded further. They relied on the organizational structure Hitler had created to penetrate and subordinate society, taking over or destroying all social organizations. A whole network of new associations was established: cultural associations, athletic organizations, philanthropic associations, literary clubs, guilds, and professional and educational associations. Within two years, Nazi organizations had mushroomed in every sector of the society, and all independent sources of information and opinions had been destroyed.

The Nazis successfully penetrated the trade unions and restructured their organizations. They destroyed the free press and restructured it. They totally penetrated the educational system and, together with their youth organizations, they penetrated the family and shifted the loyalties of children to the party, the Fuehrer, and the state. They penetrated home life by organizing leisure activities. They gained control of all agencies of the state through the direct assumption of office by Nazi officials and through indirect control by parallel party agencies.

This penetration of society was accompanied by the extension of the racist principles underlying the Nazi regime. The Nuremberg Laws adopted in 1935 "legalized" biological racism and anti-Semitism. The Nazis implemented these policies arbitrarily, but with a vengeance. They became the basis for internal persecution of Jews and non-Jews and, later, for the enslavement during World War II of the peoples of the occupied territories and the establishment of death camps in which millions of Jews and others were killed.

For a while, the army remained beyond the control of the party. It had formed a solid and autonomous organization with its own symbols and loyalties and a history that often had put it above the state itself. By 1934, however, officers were required to take an oath of loyalty directly to the Fuehrer. By 1938 many of the top generals were discredited and new ones were promoted by the Nazis. The regular army was gradually subordinated to the elite troops of the Nazi party, the black-uniformed SS formations, and the Nazi secret police, the Gestapo. Together, these organizations coerced the army into silence and obedience.

The force that amalgamated the people, the party, and the state into one entity was the leader. The authority of the entire Nazi command structure derived from the extraordinary, almost mystical, personal characteristics of the leader in the eyes of his followers—in short, it derived from Hitler's *charisma*. He possessed the ability to both command and represent; to elicit both full support and total obedience; to infuse the people, the party, and the state with will and give guidance to all. The leader commanded not as a "sovereign" who imposes his will upon others; on the contrary, "the Leader is the Party; the Party is the Leader," "the Leader is the opposite of Sovereign." These are not phrases taken from George Orwell's *1984*. They were the actual slogans used in Nazi Germany by Hitler and other leaders of the party. This is what became known in Germany as the *Führerstaat*, the leader-state. It reflected the starkest form of absolutism, cast in mystical terms.

The Nazi Elite The Nazis attempted, like the Stalinists, to fashion a new political elite that absorbed or subordinated others. But they were not as successful. The Nazis did not carry out a social or economic revolution. They were helped into power by older, more traditional elites among the military, the business community, the conservative political leaders and parties, and even the churches and the parliament. Many of these pre-Nazi elites were absorbed into the totalitarian ruling elite.

The Nazis focused special attention on the mobilization of youth. Every effort was made to shape young people's views as early as possible and socialize them into the new order. They established an elaborate network of youth organizations for children ranging in age from under ten up to eighteen. It was only at eighteen that membership in the party and a political career became open. Special schools were set up to train young people at this age.

The members of the Nazi party were selected on the basis of their courage, their unswerving loyalty to the leader, obedience to the higher authorities in the party, anti-Semitism, and racial "purity." The members of the ruling core of party administrators were drawn from among those with lower social and economic origins who had committed themselves to the Nazi party earliest and achieved the most rapid upward mobility within the party itself.

Mobilization, Coercion, and Consent

The mobilization of consent in a totalitarian regime involves an extraordinary degree of coercion and even terror. Thus, the meaning of "consent" is somewhat distorted in these regimes; it might be better perhaps to speak of "compliance" or "acquiescence." However, no regime can survive for long in the absence of at least some voluntary support, even if it is limited to narrowly instrumental support.

Coercion and Support Under Stalinism   The main foundation of Stalinist totalitarianism was coercion. Almost immediately upon seizing power, the Bolsheviks had established a network of extraordinary secret police organizations to arrest and execute perceived opponents of the new regime. With the consolidation of Bolshevik power, this network became a part of the People's Commissariat of Internal Affairs (NKVD), and certain formal legal restraints were imposed on it. But in practice, the secret police remained subject to few constraints, as it pursued class enemies, former political opponents of the revolution, and even the non-Bolshevik left.

The secret police undertook much broader tasks with the onset of collectivization and industrialization. It became the instrument for carrying out the arrests, deportations, and violence that accompanied the social revolution from above, and administered a greatly expanded network of forced-labor camps with a population in the millions. In 1934 the secret police took control over all instruments of coercion and control outside the military, in addition to all the functions of internal security. Control over the police was located in Stalin's personal secretariat. With the onset of the Great Purges, the police assumed unlimited power to terrorize the population. Although the fiction of "the leading role of the party" was maintained during this period, the NKVD was restrained only by personal instructions from Stalin. The terror appeared to be limitless and was so widespread as to give the impression that anyone could become its victim at any moment. The insecurities and anxieties that these conditions induced in the Soviet population destroyed the bases of potential resistance to commands from above and completed the penetration of society by the totalitarian organs of command.

In order to elicit the positive cooperation and support of key segments of society, the totalitarian elite in command of the Stalinist system balanced coercion with positive incentives consisting of status, privilege, wealth, and power. The new young scientific and technical intelligentsia—already the beneficiaries of the rapid turnover in elite positions produced by the purges—were rewarded for loyal performance with social status and privileged access to goods in short supply, from food to housing. This gave them the equivalent of wealth. Similar incentives were made available to the cultural intelligentsia willing to produce and enforce the official culture. For political functionaries, status, privilege, and wealth were reinforced by power.

A whole stratum of new elites, all of them in positions subject to control by the party's appointments process, was created. Not all individuals in such positions were rewarded equally, of course. The Stalinist system was characterized by substantial inequalities. Collectively, however, they came to be known as "the nomenklatura," after the lists of positions, or nomenklatura, under the control of the party. The nomenklatura under the direct control of Stalin's personal secretariat, working at times through the cadres department of the party secretariat, constituted the ruling elite of the Stalinist system.

The Stalinist system also produced benefits for those not part of either the nomenklatura or the scientific, technical, and cultural elites. Expanded educational opportunities in the prewar period brought near-universal literacy to the urban population and transformed a pre-dominately illiterate rural population into a predominately literate one. Rapid industrialization brought expanded opportunities for upward so-cial mobility, especially for those who acquired specialized secondary and higher education. The number of such "specialists" increased more than fourfold during the period of industrialization. Economic develop-ment was also accompanied by the establishment of an expanded public health system. These benefits played a major role in generating in-strumental support for the regime and contributing to its legitimization.[8]

Popular compliance and support were also encouraged through a comprehensive network of agitation and propaganda. Agitation com-prised party-led activities designed to elicit the participation of the populace in officially sponsored activities such as voting. The range of opportunities for involvement in such activities multiplied dramatically as soon as the Bolsheviks consolidated power, and the Stalinist leader-ship continued to create organizations to serve as the "transmission belts" through which it could spread its influence and control.

Propaganda work consists of imparting information to the popula-tion in such a manner as to lend support to the regime's policies, and organized lectures in workplaces, residential communities, and other locations constituted a major element of propaganda work. Such lec-tures provided an important alternative channel for informing the pop-ulation at large or selective elite groups within it of issues and de-velopments that the leadership wished to keep out of the mass media. To eliminate information and views inconsistent with those of the leadership, an elaborate system of censorship was established. Careful censorship of the Soviet media was accompanied by efforts to insulate the country from external influences. In this way, the Soviet Union became a "closed society."

Coercion and Support Under Nazism   The Nazi party mounted a mas-sive campaign to mobilize popular support in the period before its assumption of state power in January 1933. This campaign was based on a mixture of ideological appeals, symbolic manipulation, and coercion. But after Hitler was handed the chancellorship and the authoritarian

---

[8]On this point, see the results of a survey of former Soviet citizens who fled the USSR during World War II and settled in the West, reported in Alex Inkeles and Raymond Bauer, *The Soviet Citizen* (New York: Atheneum, 1968) [originally published in 1959 by Harvard University Press], pp. 233–254.

powers of the state, the emphasis of Nazi activity shifted to the imposition of central control through coercion. Mobilization became the instrument for penetrating society completely and subordinating all social forces to totalitarian control—or destroying them.

Nazi ideology consisted of a series of simplistic appeals to the extreme emotions of the alienated. Nazi appeals to emotion were always expressed in the most simple, direct, and provocative manner. They played upon the economic fears of the middle class, the frustration of German nationalism produced by military defeat and postwar humiliation, the romantic yearnings of youth for radical action, and mystical ideas about German superiority. The latter were expressed in unrestrained xenophobic racism. They were reinforced by the dramatic manipulation of such symbols as the swastika, brown shirts, and the "heil" salute; by the staging of mass gatherings cynically orchestrated to induce mass emotional identification with Nazi ideology and support for the Nazi party; and by violent attacks by the party's paramilitary SA units on the declared enemies of Nazism and Germany: Jews, communists, and others.

Contrary to their rhetoric, the Nazis did not impose domestic programs of social, economic, and political action to resolve the problems that so agitated the German people. Any specific proposal was bound to alienate some powerful group, and the object of Nazi action was to mobilize support across all social groups, except the Jews. Once the Nazis gained power, they made little effort to implement their ideological promises to the alienated. Almost all such promises were abandoned in favor of compromises with the status quo for the purpose of building and sustaining a war economy. As David Schoenbaum concludes from his study of class and status in prewar Nazi Germany, "objective social reality, the measurable statistical consequences of National Socialism, was the very opposite of what Hitler had presumably promised and what the majority of his followers had expected him to fulfill."[9] The only element of the ideology which the Nazis actually even attempted to fulfill was its racist, xenophobic, and especially anti-Semitic dimension. Thus, the class structure, the basis for wealth and privilege in Nazi Germany, was left largely intact.

As early as 1935 some fifteen concentration camps had been set up in Germany, and the number multiplied when the German armies moved into Eastern Europe. The Nazi regime quickly became a police state. Bracher points out that "we are dealing here not only with the external coercive measures of a dictatorship, but with the creation of ideological and racial policing powers that encroach on every aspect of human life. The establishment of concentration camps as instruments of

[9]David Schoenbaum, *Hitler's Social Revolution: Class and Status in Nazi Germany 1933–1939* (Garden City, N.Y.: Doubleday & Co., 1967), p. 285.

both reeducation and terror, and their development into pillars of mass arrests and mass extermination," he concludes, "were simply consequences of this totalitarian authority."[10]

Legitimation of the Totalitarian Regime

Even though emotional, affective, and ideological supports are important, the legitimacy of totalitarian regimes depends ultimately on their performance. The legitimation of the Nazi regime rested in large part on its ability to create a full-employment economy. For the millions of Germans who had been unemployed and the many thousands of young people who never had had the chance to become employed, the loss of freedoms entailed in the Nazi destruction of autonomous social and political organizations and the growing application of terror to Jews, dissenters, homosexuals, and other social categories identified in Nazi propaganda as alien were less significant than the employment, improved standards of living, and opportunities for social mobility that accompanied Nazi power.

Charisma—the extraordinary, irrational, almost supernatural appeal of a leader to his followers—is at the same time both the most powerful basis of regime legitimation and the least durable. Charismatic leaders die, and no successor can share in that charisma. The Nazi regime was destroyed by war, and we shall never know how long it could have survived the death of Hitler.

The Stalinist regime, in contrast, did survive the war, even if in greatly altered form. The war brought large numbers of refugees from the Soviet Union to the West, where thousands of them were later interviewed about the nature of the regime and their lives in it. Those interviews revealed that even disaffected former Soviet citizens continued to value "the system of public education and the socialized health services" and "the special benefits for workers" provided by the regime and would have wanted to retain them even if the regime were to be replaced. The American scholars who analyzed these interviews found that *"those who experienced arrest and those who had no contact with it, those who were forcibly evacuated and those who fled the Soviet authority of their own volition were alike in high support for the principles of the welfare state."*[11] The Stalinist regime, therefore, seems to have enjoyed significant levels of instrumental support and therefore at least some legitimacy.

Yet, the commitment to material development that generated instrumental support for the Stalinist regime also generated social changes

---

[10]Karl Dietrich Bracher, *The German Dictatorship* (London: Weidenfeld and Nicolson, 1971), pp. 355–356.
[11]Alex Inkeles and Raymond Bauer, *The Soviet Citizen* (New York: Atheneum, 1968) [originally published by Harvard University Press, 1959], pp. 236, 242 (emphasis in original).

that had profound effects on later political developments. Increasing material satisfaction and rising levels of education gave rise to new political demands in the Soviet population that eventually compelled Soviet leaders to alter the organization of consent in ways that would transform the Soviet Union into a post-totalitarian regime.

Totalitarian regimes need not necessarily submit to political demands generated by social modernization, however. The Chinese Communists led by Mao Zedong established a totalitarian regime on the Chinese mainland after completing their revolution in 1949. Although built on the historical and traditional cultural foundations of Chinese bureaucratism and authoritarianism, the Chinese Communist totalitarian regime closely emulated the Stalinist system. The Chinese collectivized agriculture, established state ownership of the means of production, centralized planning, and carried out the rapid industrialization of the country. They relied on extensive mobilization of the masses to carry out plans that, like their Stalinist predecessors, emphasized the achievement of quantitative goals over quality or efficiency. The regime was organized around an official ideology—Maoism—that served as a general guide to official policy.

Unlike the Soviet totalitarian regime, however, the Chinese under Mao refused to permit the forces of social modernization to alter the character of official ideology or the nature of the political order. Maoism was based on a primitive notion of egalitarianism. It opposed the functional specialization and resisted the emergence of social hierarchy inherent in the modernization process. Maoism emphasized the importance of political or ideological fidelity over technical expertise in the selection and assignment of elites. The gradual shift in the character of the Stalinist regime from radical or revolutionary to conservative was denounced as "revisionism." Mao personally used his charismatic authority, his organizational powers, and the coercive military force under his control to mobilize support for opposition to revisionism. This opposition took its most violent form during the "Cultural Revolution" of 1966–1976, when millions of officials, students, and others were subjected to violent political humiliation, internal political exile, and purge as so-called "capitalist roaders."

Harry Harding suggests that Mao

> retarded what, given the history of other communist states, would have been the normal evolution of the Chinese political system. He delayed the progress toward pragmatism, the routinization of charisma, the relaxation of totalitarian controls, and the emergence of a better-educated, technocratic elite that occurred in most other socialist countries in the post-Stalin era. Except for a brief period in 1956–57, Mao never accepted Khrushchev's notion that class struggle

would come to an end in a mature socialist state, or that the
dictatorship of the proletariat could be replaced by a "state of
the whole people." Instead, Mao insisted on the artificial
perpetuation of revolutionary struggle against ill-defined
"capitalist roaders" and "class enemies."[12]

Despite the apparent defeat of this mentality in the post-Mao era and the
rise to power of Deng Xiaoping and a group of leaders committed to
economic modernization, the Chinese leadership appears to remain
committed to preserving the basic outlines of the totalitarian regime.

When the most modern sector of Chinese society—its university
students, especially those who had experienced contact with or lived in
the West—organized a prodemocracy movement, Deng Xiaoping
orchestrated its violent suppression in the bloody attack on demonstrators in Tiananmen Square and the executions and purges that followed.
The reconstruction of the Chinese Communist party leadership in late
1989 strengthened its commitment to preserving totalitarian control over
society, even at the expense of achieving economic modernization.

Conclusion

Unless destroyed by external forces, totalitarian elites seem well-
equipped to preserve the power of the state over society. The programs
of economic development to which such regimes are committed produces for them the instruments of modern communications and coercion that reinforce such control. But the relationship between development and totalitarianism is a complex one. Material development tends
to be accompanied by social modernization; that is, by changes in the
nature of the population that makes the preservation of totalitarian
controls more difficult. Moreover, as the tasks of development become
more complex, totalitarian controls may begin to get in the way of
material progress. Thus, a conflict soon emerges between two strongly
held commitments in the totalitarian elite: the commitment to power
and the commitment to material progress.

The Chinese case demonstrates the ability of any totalitarian
leadership to choose power over progress. But the experience of the
Soviet Union in the 1960s and 1970s has demonstrated that even cau-
tious concessions to material progress produce changes that undermine
totalitarian controls. By the late 1980s, Mikhail Gorbachev, the inheritor
of power in the Soviet Union, was confronted with a stark choice
between preserving what remained of the totalitarian order and thereby
eroding the ability of the regime to achieve further material progress, or
setting off on the uncertain path of reform.

[12]Harry Harding, *China's Second Revolution: Reform After Mao* (Washington, D.C.: The
Brookings Institution, 1987), p. 28.

The situation that confronts Gorbachev is but one example of the conditions that can lead to regime change. The sharp contrast between Gorbachev's responses and those of the Chinese to internal unrest and protest underlines the importance of elite choices in the process of regime change. It is to the interrelationships among material development, social modernization, and elite decisions that we now must turn in order to study political change.

Bibliography

Allen, W. S. *The Nazi Seizure of Power: The Experience of a Single German Town.* Chicago: Quadrangle Books, 1965.

Azrael, Jeremy R. *Managerial Power and Soviet Politics.* Cambridge, Mass.: Harvard University Press, 1965.

Barnett, A. Doak. *Cadres, Bureaucracy, and Political Power in Communist China.* New York: Columbia University Press, 1967

Berman, Harold. *Justice in the USSR.* New York: Vintage Books, 1963.

Bialer, Seweryn. *Stalin's Successors: Leadership, Stability and Change in the Soviet Union.* New York: Cambridge University Press, 1980.

Bracher, Karl Dietrich. *The German Dictatorship.* London: Weidenfeld and Nicolson, 1971.

Cocks, Paul, Robert V. Daniels, and Nancy W. Heer (eds.). *The Dynamics of Soviet Politics.* Cambridge, Mass.: Harvard University Press, 1976.

Conquest, Robert. *The Great Terror.* London: Penguin Books, 1971.

———. *Power and Policy in the USSR.* New York: Vintage Books, 1967.

Fainsod, Merle. *How Russia is Ruled.* 2nd rev. ed. Cambridge, Mass.: Harvard University Press, 1963.

Friedrich, Carl J. (ed.). *Totalitarianism.* Cambridge, Mass.: Harvard University Press, 1954.

Friedrich, Carl J., and Zbigniew K. Brzezinski. *Totalitarian Dictatorship and Autocracy.* New York: Praeger, 1965.

Friedrich, Carl J., Michael Curtis, and Benjamin Barber (eds.). *Totalitarianism in Perspective: Three Views.* New York: Praeger, 1969.

Gregory, Paul R. *Soviet Economic Performance and Structure.* New York: Harper & Row, 1981.

Harding, Harry. *China's Second Revolution: Reform After Mao.* Washington, D.C.: Brookings Institution, 1987.

Inkeles, Alex and Raymond Bauer. *The Soviet Citizen.* New York: Atheneum, 1968. Originally published by Harvard University Press in 1959.

Meyer, Alfred G. *The Soviet Political System: An Interpretation.* New York: Random House, 1965.

Neumann, Franz. *Behemoth: The Structure and Practice of National Socialism.* New York: Harper & Row, N.D. Reprint of the revised second edition first published by Oxford University Press in 1944.

Nove, Alec. *An Economic History of the U.S.S.R.* New York: Penguin Books, 1984.

Rosenfeldt, Niels Erik. *Knowledge and Power: The Role of Stalin's Secret Chancellery in the Soviet System of Government.* Copenhagen: Rosenkilde and Bagger, 1978.

Schapiro, Leonard. *The Communist Party of the Soviet Union.* 2nd ed., rev. and enl. New York: Vintage Books, 1971.

Schoenbaum, David. *Hitler's Social Revolution: Class and Status in Nazi Germany 1933–1939.* Garden City, N.Y.: Doubleday & Co., 1967.

Schurmann, Franz. *Ideology and Organization in Communist China.* 2nd ed. Berkeley: University of California Press, 1968.

Tucker, Robert C. (ed.). *Stalinism: Essays in Historical Interpretation.* New York: W. W. Norton & Co., 1977.

Part Four

Introduction

If change—rapid or gradual, revolutionary or evolutionary—is common to all political regimes, performance is for all a matter of life or death. Regimes must simply, over time, provide the citizenry with a sense of security from internal and external violence, respond to demands coming from societal groups, provide critically needed services or at least see to it that they are provided, and above all create minimal conditions of participation for the citizenry so as to enjoy its trust. Very often change and performance are intimately linked. The structure and the organization of power often must change in order to meet or improve societal needs and services. When societal needs and demands require a radical overhaul of the power structure, their implementation produces a change of the regime.

After decades of apparent stability, the pace of political, societal, and economic change seems to be quickening in most authoritarian and Communist regimes today—in Eastern Europe, China, the Soviet Union, even Nepal and Mongolia. It is fairly obvious that they have been triggered almost everywhere by prolonged nonperformance; it is also quite clear that they aim at significant—at times radical—reforms amounting to a revolution in the organization of political power and the structure of the society. Where will the winds of change lead these regimes? Above all, will the reforms now in progress manage to improve performance and increase acceptance and satisfaction, i.e. legitimacy? These are the questions to which we now turn.

169

8

Change,
Liberalization,
Democratization

Introduction

Political regimes are not immutable. Societal changes produce new
forces that may affect the recruitment and composition of elites, the
scope and requisites of state action, the configuration of interests, and
the level of popular participation and consent. Regimes begin to change
when the established "rules of the game" become inadequate for ordering political relationships among existing or emerging groups and for
dealing with new interests and their demands. The authoritative distributions of goods and values no longer correspond to those expected
or demanded by the populace. The ruling elite—democratic, authoritarian, or totalitarian—must modify existing institutions of representation, decision making, and consent or create new ones, and it may
even have to expand the scope of rights guaranteed the populace in
order to distribute goods and values in accordance with its demands and
thereby sustain its legitimacy.

Regime change involves the concrete actions of political leaders,
especially the decision by authoritarian ruling elites to abandon violence
and coercion and turn toward persuasion as the main basis for the
mobilization of popular support. Such decisions may be taken by the
elite on its own initiative, as in the case of Yugoslavia under Tito after
1948, Spain after the death of Franco and under the leadership of Juan

Carlos, or the Soviet Union under Gorbachev. Or this decision may be imposed on the elite by the populace, either peacefully or violently. In Hungary for example, the decision to turn from totalitarian coercion to authoritarian persuasion came only after the armed uprising of the population in 1956. But the transition from authoritarian to democratic regimes has begun peacefully elsewhere. In Poland, complete economic failure led the Communist party to relinquish control of the government, and peaceful mass demonstrations in East Germany and Czechoslovakia forced the end of communist regimes in those countries. In Romania, mass violence produced the overthrow of the Ceausescu tyranny, but the nature of the successor regime remains uncertain.

Democracies also change. In many cases, democratic regimes have collapsed into authoritarianism. In Germany, the democratic interwar Weimar republic broke down under the impact of changing social conditions and the forces they produced, especially the impact of elite reactions and the nationalist forces spearheaded by the Nazis. In Turkey, democracy has proven to be very fragile, and the military has repeatedly intervened. In Greece, a military junta set aside the democratic order in 1967 and ruled until the restoration of democracy in 1974. Fragile democratic regimes in Latin American countries have repeatedly broken down. The pattern of events in these cases has been summarized admirably by Juan Linz under the label, "the breakdown of democratic regimes."[1]

The number and frequency of democratic breakdowns, right up to the early 1970s, led to much discussion of "the crisis of democracy" and to concern that democratic regimes were inherently flawed. Not even the conversion of formerly totalitarian and authoritarian regimes in West Germany, Italy, and Japan into functioning parliamentary democracies offered much basis for optimism about the future of democracy. These regimes were, after all, established under extreme conditions unlikely ever to be reproduced: defeat and unconditional surrender in total war and occupation by the armies of democratic regimes whose leaderships were committed to imposing democracy on them. Until the 1970s, only Venezuela seemed to have managed a "transition" from an authoritarian to a democratic regime on its own.

Since the early 1970s, however, new bases for optimism have emerged. Democratic regimes have replaced authoritarian military and civilian regimes in Spain, Greece, Portugal, Brazil, and Argentina. These transitions from authoritarian to democratic regimes have involved a complex process of democratization. This process also appears to be underway slowly in Mexico. It is very much in evidence in Poland and Hungary and in East Germany and Czechoslovakia as well. In the Soviet Union, some of the conditions of transition also appear to be present.

[1]Juan J. Linz, *The Breakdown of Democratic Regimes: Crisis, Breakdown & Reequilibration* (Baltimore, Md.: The Johns Hopkins University Press, 1978).

In none of these cases is there any guarantee that democratization will ever be complete or even that the process will not itself break down, leading to the restoration of an authoritarian regime. Indeed, the example of China, and the bloody reaction of that regime to the emergence of mass demands for democratization, stands as a clear reminder of the ever-present danger of an authoritarian reaction, or "breakdown." The East German Communist leadership, for example, seems to have considered adopting a "Chinese solution" to the growing unrest in that country before finally deciding to concede to mass demands for change and to open the Berlin Wall in November 1989.[2]

Breakdowns of Democratic Regimes[3]

The breakdown of a democratic regime is associated with and usually precipitated by a crisis of performance. The regime becomes unable to solve a major problem or series of problems, thereby demonstrating a loss of efficacy and ultimately inducing a loss of regime legitimacy. Simple policy failures do not bring on such losses. The regime's failure must involve a problem or problems of sufficient magnitude to induce the kinds of societal fears that lead to a frantic search for solutions "at any cost"; large proportions of the mass population, or at least such sectors of the elite as the military and the political leadership, must be led to conclude that the scuttling of democratic institutions is required.

Such a failure can be brought on when the democratic ruling elite loses its ability to adapt to changing circumstances, or when its ability to enforce its decisions is eroded. It can be brought on by the elite's failure to recognize the problem at hand or its unwillingness to adopt the measures required to solve the problem; perhaps out of fear of short-term political consequences such as the loss of electoral support. It may even be brought on by the simple incompetence of the political leadership.

Declining regime performance and the erosion of democratic legitimacy engenders the political fragmentation of the regime. Political views become polarized, and extremist groups arise and gain supporters. The institutionalized channels of participation fail to satisfy the demands of the population. Established democratic political parties, in particular, lose their ability to aggregate, articulate, and secure the satisfaction of emerging, radicalized interests. At the elite level, fragmentation becomes manifest in an inability to agree on policy or an unwillingness to implement agreed policies. At the mass level, the first

---

[2]*The New York Times*, November 19, 1989.
[3]Our treatment of this topic follows closely the definitive work of Juan Linz, *The Breakdown of Democratic Regimes: Crisis, Breakdown & Reequilibration.* (Baltimore, Md.: The Johns Hopkins University Press, 1978).

clear sign of incipient breakdown is the appearance of popular political violence, and the inability of the regime to control it. The onset of street violence, organized political intimidation, mass demonstrations, and terrorist attacks mark either the loss of a democratic regime's monopoly over coercive force or a fatal internal division in the elite that renders it unable to maintain order. Such a failure to maintain order accelerates its loss of authority and legitimacy. In short, the civic order begins to erode.

If the erosion of the civic order is the product of chaotic social forces unloosed by continuing crisis, then the democratic regime may give way to anarchy. If the civic order is, in fact, under organized attack by a disloyal opposition or antiregime parties or groups, who are willing to use force to overthrow the existing order and able to mobilize popular support for their actions, then the democratic regime may give way to an authoritarian or even totalitarian order. As we noted in our chapter on authoritarian regimes, however, in most cases the democratic regime gives way to some form of military intervention, either unilateral or in alliance with other elite groups and their supporters.

The breakdown of democratic regimes is also conditioned by the nature of a country's political history and its political culture. The existence of a strong "civic culture" is an essential bulwark against breakdown. The existence of statist, militarist, or authoritarian elements in the political culture on the other hand, contributes to the delegitimation of a democratic regime confronting social crisis, as it did in Germany in the 1920s and 1930s. The existence of multiple political cultures, usually associated with either sharp class distinctions or the presence of religious or ethnic diversity, also may contribute to the breakdown of a democratic order by intensifying elite and mass-level conflicts.[4]

But political culture by itself is not a sufficient explanation of the breakdown of democratic regimes. If it were, a change of regime, even a sudden one, would imply a change of culture. Instead, the comparative analyst must look primarily to the *interaction* of elite behavior, socioeconomic conditions, and mass political culture. In each case, political change involves the actions or inactions of ruling and other elites. They play a central role in managing the demands and conflicts that arise out of changing social and economic conditions. Indeed, many authors attribute the continuing operation of democratic regimes in even deeply culturally divided societies to elite behavior.[5] And other analysts of the "transitions" from authoritarian to democratic regimes have all pointed to the centrality of elite behavior.

[4]See, e.g., Alvin Rabushka and Kenneth A. Shepsle, *Politics in Plural Societies: A Theory of Democratic Instability* (Columbus, Ohio: Charles E. Merrill, 1972).
[5]See, e.g., Arend Lijphart, *Democracy in Plural Societies.* (New Haven, Conn.: Yale University Press, 1977).

"Transitions" from Authoritarian Regimes[6]

As in the case of democratic "breakdowns," the onset of regime change in authoritarian regimes has been triggered by widespread popular perceptions of a crisis of performance and of the inability of the existing regime to resolve it. This crisis is usually economic. But the defeat of a military regime in war may also constitute a sufficient crisis of performance to initiate the process of regime change. The Greek military junta, for example, collapsed in 1974 following Turkey's invasion of Cyprus, and the Argentine military regime collapsed after the attempt to seize the Falklands Islands failed.

Economic nonperformance produces political discontent more rapidly after a period of relative improvement in the standard of living. Material decline is interpreted as "crisis" more easily after a period of relative prosperity because popular expectations for the provision of consumer goods and services are greater. The economic performance of a regime may also be judged inadequate when the population begins to compare its own standard of living to that in other, more developed countries. Even if an authoritarian regime continues to provide a standard of living that had produced satisfaction among the population in the past, it may fall behind the standards set in other regimes. And, when the population becomes aware of the higher standards elsewhere, it is likely to become dissatisfied with its own. No authoritarian regime can insulate its people from international communications. Much of the East German population, for example, received West German television broadcasts, complete with their uncensored news of the world. Even Soviet citizens are exposed to communications from Finland, Western Europe, and the United States via shortwave radio. Even the most carefully censored films and television broadcasts, not to mention the regime's own television reportage on Western society, convey important information about the quality of life in the democratic regimes of the West. And this information generates dissatisfaction with domestic economic conditions.

Another sign of the onset of change in an authoritarian regime is what Crane Brinton called the "desertion of the intellectuals." Among writers, scientists, students, managers, and technicians, there emerges a growing demand for what we may call "information goods." The educated strata of society demand knowledge and its application to societal

[6]We have relied for our summary of the process of transition in authoritarian regimes on the following collections of studies: Enrique Baloyra, Ed., *Comparing New Democracies: Transition and Consolidation in Mediterranean Europe and the Southern Cone* (Boulder, Colo: Westview Press, 1987); James M. Malloy and Mitchell Seligson, Eds., *Authoritarians and Democrats: Regime Transitions in Latin America* (Pittsburgh: University of Pittsburgh Press, 1987); and Guillermo O'Donnell, Philippe C. Schmitter, and Laurence Whitehead, Eds., *Transitions from Authoritarian Rule*, 4 vols. (Baltimore, Md.: The Johns Hopkins University Press, 1986).

needs. They demand the free flow of information, including more open and informative media. The technological revolution spreads telephones, computers, fax machines, and other means of communication through the population and undermines the authoritarian regime's control over information and its dissemination. To continue to impose controls in the name of political orthodoxy impedes the cooperation of critically important groups in the creation of new technologies and, therefore, the achievement of further material progress. The granting of concessions to intellectuals, however, is likely only to produce demands for further concessions to intellectual freedom.

No group is more likely than intellectuals to manifest the paradox inherent in any effort to reform an authoritarian regime, noted more than 130 years ago by Alexis de Tocqueville in his study *The Old Regime and the French Revolution*. He observed:

> . . . it is not always when things are going from bad to worse that revolutions break out. On the contrary, it oftener happens that when a people which has put up with an oppressive ruler over a long period without protest suddenly finds the government relaxing its pressure, it takes up arms against it. Thus the social order overthrown by a revolution is almost always better than the one immediately preceding it, and experience teaches us that, generally speaking, the most perilous moment for a bad government is one when its seeks to mend its ways. Only consummate statecraft can enable a King to save his throne when after a long spell of oppressive rule he sets to improving the lot of his subjects. Patiently endured so long as it seemed beyond redress, a grievance comes to appear intolerable once the possibility of removing it crosses men's minds. For the mere fact that certain abuses have been remedied draws attention to the others and they now appear more galling. . . . [7]

Political Elites

Democratization begins when these conditions are accompanied by a willingness on the part of at least key sectors of the ruling elite to accept power-sharing arrangements, or even the loss of power, *and* a readiness on the part of the people to participate in the process and lend it their active support. In particular, democratization requires both those who must give up power and those who are to inherit it to accept the constraints on change inherent in the compromises that accompany the establishment of a democratic order.

[7]Alexis de Tocqueville, *The Old Regime and the French Revolution*, new translation by Stuart Gilbert (Garden City, N.Y.: Doubleday Anchor Books, 1955), pp. 176–177.

The transition from authoritarianism, and especially from its totalitarian variant, is conditioned on a decision by the ruling elite to turn away from simple coercion and toward persuasion as a means of securing compliance. This decision can be prompted by the uncertainties surrounding the death of the authoritarian or totalitarian leader and the absence of any institutionalized procedure for succession. Or it might be engendered by the realization that the individual creativity and initiative necessary to sustain a modern economy cannot be secured through coercion. Or it might reflect the failure of the leadership to achieve its goals through coercion alone. Whatever the reason, authoritarian regimes can begin to change only when popular fear of open political action declines.

Mass Political Activity

We can only outline the overall conditions under which authoritarian regimes (including totalitarian ones) may begin to change in the direction of democratization. Such a transition cannot be plotted in terms of a specific sequence of changes over a specific period of time. It involves a series of manifestations:

1. Limitations upon absolute authority
2. The expansion of tolerance for independent spiritual, economic, and other social activities by associations and individuals
3. The widening of the free flow of information and public debate
4. Increased participation of old and new groups in the political process
5. The development and legitimization of semiautonomous and autonomous centers of power
6. The emergence of demands to enforce the accountability of leaders to elected representative bodies
7. Decentralization of decision making
8. The formation of oppositional political associations that challenge the ruling elite and compete with it for political power

It involves the emergence of individual and associational rights and the establishment of limits on the ability of the state simply to coerce compliance.

When hundreds of thousands of miners across the Soviet Union strike to demand better living conditions, and when millions of Latvians, Lithuanians, and Estonians form a human chain across these Baltic territories to protest their annexation by the Soviet Union in 1940, we know that that regime has entered a transitional period. It is the decline of fear that makes possible the rise of such popular political activity and the transformation of societal changes into political pressure on the leadership. This rise of "social pressure" is facilitated by prior changes in the organization and distribution of values in "grass roots" society that spread support for democracy throughout the population.[8]

In the absence of socially based opposition forces in the form of opposition parties or popular "movements," real changes in the organization of command, and especially in the accountability and responsibility of ruling elites, is unlikely to occur. The ruling elite will retain its monopoly of power, merely changing those who hold political office without altering the regime. Thus, the ability of regime opponents to organize themselves into effective political forces is an essential element in any transition from authoritarian rule.

The rise of popular political activity in the authoritarian regime also creates the organizational bases for linking the masses to emerging institutions of representation, decision making, and consent. When the authoritarian leadership grants recognition to the parties, movements, and other organizations through which mass participation is activated, they create a basis for resolving the crises of participation and legitimation. But this requires a high degree of political skill on the part of the ruling elite, because preauthoritarian or pretotalitarian political identities are likely to reemerge and challenge the legitimacy of maintaining the existing state. This challenge is most obvious in multinational or strongly regionalized states, where ethnic or regional identities give rise to nationalist movements seeking independence rather than participation in a unified, democratized regime. But this can also be a problem when precommunist identities reemerge to challenge the maintenance of even a democratized socialist order.

Ethnic Conflict

A period of political transition in a multinational authoritarian regime provides new opportunities for the expression of ethnic grievances. The divisiveness of ethnicity is reinforced where linguistic, religious, and other cultural cleavages coincide with social and economic differences, such as regional levels of development. It is most powerful where the overarching political community—the multinational state—is perceived by the minority nationalities as having been imposed on them or as being an instrument for their domination by another ethnic group. In multinational Yugoslavia and the multinational Soviet Union, ethnic minorities in the most developed regions of the country have used the greater political freedom granted them to organize popular movements that are both nationalist and liberal, or democratic, in character.

[8]On the importance of mass support for democracy, see Daniel H. Levine, "Paradigm Lost: Dependence to Democracy," *World Politics* 40, 3 (April, 1988), pp. 377–394; and "The Transition to Democracy: Are There Lessons from Venezuela?" *Bulletin of Latin American Research* 4, 2 (1985), pp. 47–61.

Slovenes in Yugoslavia and the Estonians, Latvians, and Lithuanians in the Soviet Union have organized sophisticated, de facto opposition political parties that have mobilized mass support among their respective national communities for accelerating the process of democratization. Slovene action has inspired organizational activity among the Croats of Yugoslavia, and the activities of the Baltic peoples have inspired the formation of similar movements among all the other major ethnic groups of the Soviet Union, and many of the smaller ones as well! As with all ethnically based political movements, however, demands for changes within the system have rapidly escalated into demands for doing away with the system; that is, demands for reform have become demands for secession. The confrontation between Gorbachev and the Lithuanians unfolding as this book went to press is certain to be only the first of many political conflicts in the Soviet Union between Moscow and ethnonational movements in the non-Russian peripheries of the Soviet Union.

Ethnic mobilization of one group in a multinational state often leads to the activation of other groups, as well. Not all ethnically based political movements are democratic in their orientation. Nationalist movements among the Serbs in Yugoslavia and among the Russians in the Soviet Union, for example, each display pronounced authoritarian characteristics. As the largest groups in their respective regimes, Russian and Serbian nationalisms might be expected to provide support for the preservation of the existing state. But the nationalisms of politically dominant groups represent powerful challenges to a ruling elite that professes to represent all groups, as both the Yugoslav and Soviet communist elites do. The rise of such nationalisms threatens to drive popular movements among minority nationalities more rapidly toward secession and at the same time mobilizes support among the dominant group for authoritarian responses to the heightened unrest characteristic of transitional periods.

Political Culture

Even more than the actions of ruling elites, the nature of the political culture defines the character of political change in the authoritarian regime. As we have seen in our discussions of authoritarianism and the breakdown of democratic regimes, a participatory civic culture that allows for dialogue among societal actors and the state, wherein freedoms and rights are assured and limitations on the state are established, is no guarantee against the "breakdown" of democracy. Many democracies at different times have lapsed into authoritarianism. But the civic culture underlying the old democratic order remained alive in these regimes and provided the basis for a return to democratic practices. In fact, most of the democracies that had broken down since World War II have now begun, or even completed, the return to democracy, including Spain, Portugal, Greece, Argentina, Brazil, Chile, and Mexico. And in Eastern Europe, the transition to democracy has proceeded most smoothly in Czechoslovakia, the state with the strongest civic culture and the most successful prewar experience with democracy.

The status of social, cultural, and religious institutions such as churches and universities is an important element in the civic culture. The more established and legitimized their status, the more resistant they remain to the efforts of an authoritarian regime to control and absorb them, and the more likely they are to play a role in the revival of democracy. Under many authoritarian regimes, and even certain totalitarian ones, such institutions maintain a precarious independence—as was the case of the Catholic Church in Fascist Italy and in communist Poland. Even universities, which are often the targets of authoritarian repression, may retain a certain degree of independence. The existence of such institutions can play an important role in preserving or even creating a civic culture at the grass roots of society.

Where private ownership is maintained, economic and professional groups may also enjoy a certain degree of autonomy, especially in a market-based economy. Similarly, syndicalist or cooperative organizations among workers and farmers may manage to assert their independence. The fragility of many authoritarian regimes lies precisely in their inability or unwillingness to do away with autonomous forces in society. These forces undergo the most rapid social mobilization with the onset of crisis in the regime and contribute to the reassertion of participatory values.

Political change, and especially change toward democratization, is far more complex and different to achieve in societies where there is no participatory civic culture and societal forces are fully penetrated and placed under the control of the state. This is the case in most of the Soviet Union, with the exception of the previously independent Baltic republics, in China, and in Romania.

Liberalization

The onset of change in communist regimes is usually signaled by the adoption of economic reforms aimed at improving the performance of the centrally planned economy. Such reforms are intended to keep the basic political order intact by increasing the level of instrumental support for the regime. In Yugoslavia, the introduction of workers' self-management in the 1950s and creation of a limited market economy in the early 1960s were part of an ongoing effort by the communist leadership under Tito to secure popular support and legitimize one-party rule. Although accompanied by important political reforms as well, economic reforms were not permitted to threaten the communist political monopoly. When the combined forces of economic reform, political decentralization, and rising nationalisms among the Yugoslav peoples threatened to divide the country and perhaps even supplant communist control in one or more regions, Tito used the army to suppress these forces and put a halt to liberalization during the early 1970s. As Yugoslavia enters the 1990s, some of that country's communist leaders appear ready to renew the liberalization process and accept its most likely political consequence—democratization. But that readiness is not yet widespread, and resistance to democratization remains powerful in at least some regions of the country.

Until 1989, the most extensive sustained liberalization in Eastern Europe had taken place in Hungary, where the reforms of the New Economic Mechanism (NEM), introduced in 1966 and implemented in 1968, replaced traditional central planning with a "guided market." Production decisions were decentralized to individual enterprises, and profits became the chief indicator of enterprise success. Prices were adjusted to bring them into closer line with actual production costs and world levels. At the same time, the trade unions were given new power to represent worker interests, and local governments were given greater control—within centrally determined limits—over local budgets and plans. The NEM also included a commitment to the development of agriculture, including private agriculture, with the goal of establishing self-sufficiency and creating an exportable surplus.

The state retained control over all infrastructural and social investment as well as over all major investments in production in order to control the broad features of the economy. In fact, state control over the economy remained extensive because of informal influence patterns and outright conservative resistance to market principles from within the party and state bureaucracies. Nonetheless, the NEM represented a remarkable change from the Stalinist model, and its positive consequences for the economy and population were evident in a sharp improvement in the quality of life in Hungary in the 1970s, especially compared with conditions in neighboring East European countries.

The NEM was adopted as part of a broader strategy to establish regime stability and foster popular legitimacy in the post-1956 period by increasing opportunities for popular participation in the system, by inceasing the scope of permissible private activity, and by improving the standard of living. Under Kadar's leadership, these policies were implemented in exchange for a general depoliticization of Hungarian society. Conflicts among material interests were recognized as legitimate, but the Communist party retained a monopoly over the representation of *political* interests and the resolution of conflicts among them. Individuals or groups who failed to observe this restriction were subjected to repression.

By the late 1980s, however, the performance of even the reformed Hungarian economy began to decline. External debt doubled, domestic growth rates declined, inflation halved disposable incomes, and as a result, the living standards of the Hungarian people began to decline. By the late 1980s, one-fourth of the population was living in poverty. Many of these problems could be attributed to the refusal of the Kadar leadership to free the economy from remaining central controls for fear of unleashing uncontrollable political forces.

The failure to follow economic reform with political change generated unfulfilled expectations and increasing dissatisfaction in Hungarian society. This was compounded by declining economic performance in the 1980s and finally produced the ouster of Kadar in 1988. By the spring of 1989, the Hungarian communist leadership was divided between elements intent on accelerating both economic reform and political democratization along social democratic lines, and more conservative elements. The victory of those intent on accelerating reforms produced further changes that initiated the process of genuine democratization in Hungary in 1989: The opening of negotiations with the democratic opposition; abandonment of the party's claim to a political monopoly; the adoption of guarantees of civil liberties for the population; and the calling of democratic elections.

Democratization

The first stage of transition from authoritarianism to democracy involves the extension of guarantees of individual and group rights: civil liberties, political rights, electoral systems, and a legal order based on due process. During this period associational groups—professional organizations, cultural associations, religious groups, writers, doctors, managers and technocrats, workers' free trade unions, and other groups—consolidate themselves, legitimize their positions in society, and demand a dialogue with the ruling elite. They gain the freedom and control over resources to make their positions known to the political leadership and attempt to secure their interests by influencing public policies.

This stage amounts to establishing democratic rules of procedure for the organization of interests and rights, but it does not necessarily involve the establishment of either elite accountability or open competition for control of the state. The organization of command and its dependency on the organization of popular consent may remain unaffected.

The inauguration of an electoral process, even if it is not yet a completely open or competitive process, does create incentives for the ruling elite to become more responsive to popular demands and thereby increases the importance of representation and consent. This signifies the end of the monopolistic leadership of the single party, even if it were to continue to make such a claim. For, in essence, different points of view and different interests will appear within the party, making it more of a debating and deliberative society than an instrument of mass mobilization, command, and control. It will become with time increasingly representative of societal diversity until such time as rival parties are permitted to function freely, when the various factions that have operated under the one-party umbrella will divide into separate organizations.

The inauguration of elections also encourages cooperation between the ruling elite and those opponents of the regime most likely to benefit from a transition to democracy. The former seeks to retain as much power as possible, while the latter become unwilling to jeopardize their seemingly inevitable victory through radical action. These pressures produce the compromises and mutual concessions that are so much a part of the democratic political culture. They also produce the exclusion from participation of those groups and forces dedicated to more "radical" changes, who are unwilling to negotiate or abide by an agreed-upon set of "rules of the game."

For these reasons, it is not surprising that the transition process usually involves extensive political maneuvering among ruling elites, leaders of opposition parties and movements, and other key actors concerning the issues of participation and representation in the emerging regime. Transitions in Latin America and elsewhere have involved the drafting of new constitutional arrangements as well as the formulation of agreements, or "pacts," that require the support of authoritarian leaders for the emerging democracy in exchange for guarantees concerning their personal and political fate under a democratic regime characterized by the rule of law.

In Eastern Europe, the onset of democratization has involved varying periods of negotiation between communist leaders and various opposition groups. In Poland, formal negotiations between solidarity and the communists under the leadership of Wojciech Jaruzelski produced a formal agreement establishing an electoral reform that resulted in an overwhelming victory for Solidarity. Solidarity's control of the Polish parliament, or Sejm, led to the creation of a Solidarity-led government under Prime Minister Tadeusz Mazowiecki and the beginnings of a democratic political order in September 1989. In Hungary, negotiations among competing factions within the communist leadership and several opposition groups produced an agreement to proceed toward democratic elections. Held in March 1990, these produced the overwhelming defeat of the communists and a victory for a conservative nationalist opposition party, the Democratic Forum. In Czechoslovakia, negotiations between the communists and opposition groups produced the very rapid disintegration of the ruling party and its replacement by representatives of the democratic opposition. Perhaps the most striking change in all of Eastern Europe during the tumultuous year of 1989 was the election of Vaclav Havel, the leader of the democratic opposition and former political prisoner, as president of Czechoslovakia in late December 1989.

Completion of the democratization process involves not only the institutionalization of elite accountability and responsibility but also the peaceful transfer of political authority from incumbents to their opponents through constitutional means: primarily, competitive elections or parliamentary defeat. And it also involves the laying to rest of the threat of intervention by military or other elements of the old authoritarian elite. When access to state power is restricted to constitutional means and that power has been transferred successfully from incumbents to opponents, democratization can be said to have taken place.

Much depends, of course, on the resolution of the underlying crisis that triggered the transition—the crisis of economic performance. The political leadership, and especially those elements of the leadership who advocate democratization, must improve economic performance so that at least for the greater part of the population the benefits of change outweigh the hardships as the process of transition unfolds. If they are able to do so, popular consent and support for change will increase. The emerging democratic order will become legitimized. If, however, changes associated with the transition to democratization increase popular hardships, mass resistance to change may increase, and the appeal of democracy may be eroded. This, for example, is the central challenge confronting the new democratic leaderships of Poland and Brazil, each of which has moved rapidly to adopt resolute economic policies.

Since authoritarian ruling elites are most often led to give up power by extraordinary crises of performance, the tasks of economic revival or reform are in most cases of authoritarian transitions going to be extremely daunting. Where democracy is valued by the population for its own sake, that is, where elements of a civic culture exist, the inevitable hardships associated with recovery from crushing international debts, domestic austerity programs, rampant inflation, unemployment, and the transition from central planning to a market economy may be at least partially balanced by the satisfactions derived from democratization.

The rapidity of change in Eastern Europe may very well be explained by the survival of elements of a civic culture in Poland, Hungary, and Czechoslovakia and by the exposure of millions of East Germans citizens to the cultural and political influence of West German democracy. But the transition from authoritarianism to democracy may be a matter of decades. During such a long period, internal or foreign crises may upset the delicate process of legitimization and provoke a quick return to authoritarian practices, especially where societal support for democracy is already weak. The Soviet Union under Gorbachev appears to have reached precisely that moment in the process of transition when the regime is on the threshold of democratization, but the door can still be slammed shut.

The Soviet Regime in Transition

From Totalitarian to Authoritarian Regime

The Stalinist regime survived the war but could not survive the internal crisis of succession; the death of the totalitarian leader was followed by a struggle for power that undermined the concentration of power, set limits on the coercive powers of the regime, expanded the definition of the ruling elite, and introduced elements of heterogeneity into it. At the same time, postwar modernization increased the level of social differentiation and specialization in Soviet society, made the regime more dependent on the population for skills vital to sustain the regime performance that produced instrumental support, expanded the scope of expectations in the population, and made the population less susceptible to both mobilization and coercion. The totalitarian organization of command remained intact for more than ten years beyond Stalin's death. But these changes in both the ruling elite and the society eventually produced changes in the organization of interests and consent, which altered the regime from a totalitarian to an authoritarian one.

The death of Stalin left intact the vast network of totalitarian control he had created. None of the surviving leaders, however, enjoyed enough personal authority or political power to assume control over the entire apparatus. A struggle to secure such a dominant position began among them almost immediately. To prevent this struggle from becoming violent and potentially even fatal, the post-Stalin leadership agreed to put an end to the use of violence within the elite. They reinforced this decision by dispersing the power Stalin had concentrated. They separated leadership of the party organization from leadership of the state administration and assigned these two posts to separate individuals.

Intra-elite violence is readily abandoned by a totalitarian autocrat's lieutenants upon his death. Even if this is only a simple collective act of self-preservation, it has important consequences for the nature of politics in the regime. Members of the leadership are compelled to build coalitions and gather political support both inside and outside the top elite. This pushes the leadership toward greater collectivity in the decision-making process and reinforces the establishment of patron-client relations with forces outside the elite. This erodes elite homogeneity. As members of the ruling elite establish such relations with social groups and forces, greater influence—albeit still indirect influence—

devolves onto them. This process becomes reflected in concessions to bureaucratic and organizational interests created or institutionalized in the totalitarian era. Thus, instruments of penetration and control now also assume the role of institutionalized channels for the expression of a limited range of social interests. By allowing the limited representation and participation of these interests in the policy-making process, the post-totalitarian regime secures consent.

Nikita Khrushchev, who had inherited leadership of the party and extensive control over the nomenklatura system after Stalin's death, attempted to build up his personal power and authority and thus free himself from the constraints of "collective leadership." A central component of this campaign was the open rejection of the Stalinist terror and an attempt to discredit all those associated with it, including his main opponents in the Presidium. De-Stalinization led to a political "thaw" and increased intellectual unrest. It also raised an implicit political threat to the chief beneficiaries of the terror: the entire generation of incumbent officials who had entered the elite as the result of the purges.

By June 1957, Khrushchev's opponents in the Presidium had secured a majority and attempted to force him to resign. Khrushchev refused. Instead, he made the unprecedented demand that the Central Committee, which had formally "elected" him, be convened to decide the issue. There he enjoyed broader support, and he defeated his opponents. Khrushchev's reliance on the Central Committee in 1957 strengthened its role as a central legitimizing institution in elite politics. Khrushchev later used open policy debate in the Central Committee to overwhelm his opponents in the Presidium, inviting supportive, nonmember experts to participate in Committee deliberations. This helped to transform the Committee into a semi-parliamentary body through which representatives of various organizational, regional, and functional interests achieved limited participation in the central policy-making process.

By 1964, Khrushchev had suffered a series of foreign policy defeats and had introduced domestic changes that alienated the very core of his domestic political support, the regional party secretaries and central party functionaries who composed the ruling elite of the system. In October 1964, the other members of the leadership—many of them appointed by Khrushchev himself—carried out a swift and peaceful coup. They convened a meeting of the party Presidium, demanded that Khrushchev resign, and convened a meeting of the Central Committee the next day to ratify their demand. The course of events had changed since 1957, and Khrushchev now enjoyed little support in the Committee.

The post-Khrushchev leadership reaffirmed and strengthened the dispersion of power and authority adopted after the death of Stalin and established a truly oligarchical regime. The Politburo was gradually transformed into a cabinet-like body. The senior party secretaries, key regional party leaders, the heads of the most important governmental ministries, the military and security chiefs, and other key figures were gradually incorporated into its membership. The Politburo rapidly became the indisputable most important policy-making body in the Soviet Union.

The establishment of an oligarchy centered in the Politburo and resting on shared control of the nomenklatura institutionalized the devolution of power and authority that had been taking place since the death of Stalin and reaffirmed the division of functions between the state and party. Central state bureaucracies reassumed control over the day-to-day management of the economy. The central party apparatus exercised oversight over the operations of state institutions to ensure the implementation of party policies and served as an alternative source of expertise in the policy-making process. The broader party organization retained its role in the mobilization of popular effort. But the oligarchy retained policy-making authority. The Politburo set careful limits on the degree of institutional autonomy and enforced them through their control over the nomenklatura. Meaningful participation was strictly limited to official, institutionalized channels.

The post-totalitarian leadership turned away from mass violence or terror as an instrument of mobilization or control. It was abandoned largely as part of the elite's own effort at self-preservation. But it was also abandoned because in order to achieve their developmental goals the leadership had to encourage the creative efforts of key sectors of society, especially the scientific and technical intelligentsia. Those who chose to engage in unofficial or dissident activity, however, were subjected to brutal suppression, including imprisonment in harsh labor camps and even psychiatric torture. For the population at large, obedience was purchased through moderate enhancements in the social welfare policies of the regime and greater emphasis on, and investment in, the production of food and consumer goods.

The ruling elite maintained its monopoly on political power. No competing political organization was permitted to exist. Neither autonomous opposition parties nor autonomous groups that advocate putting an end to this monopoly were tolerated. All social interests had to be expressed through officially sanctioned organizations and institutions that enjoyed only limited autonomy.

By November 1982, when Leonid Brezhnev, Khrushchev's successor, died at the age of 76, the Soviet system had been transformed from a totalitarian to a post-totalitarian regime with many of the characteristics of bureaucratic authoritarianism. However, the monopoly of power enjoyed by the oligarchy and the almost complete penetration of society by the party continued to distinguish the Soviet regime.

Modernization and Crisis of Performance

The complex set of social changes accompanying the modernization process also produce a "revolution of rising expectations" in the population. The social foundation of this revolution is to be found in the spread of education, especially higher education. This produces changes in the distribution of values in the population, to which a regime must respond. The dual process of structural differentiation and functional specialization at the heart of the modernization process multiplies the number and variety of interests in society and increases the role and social value of specialized skills in the economy. This makes any ruling elite whose legitimacy depends primarily on the satisfaction of material demands more dependent on specialized functional groups for the maintenance of performance and the retention of power. Over time, the demands of such groups change and, if satisfied, escalate. This is the meaning of "the revolution of rising expectations" in the Soviet Union as in every other modernizing regime.

Modernization rendered other characteristics inherited from the totalitarian period obsolete. In the centrally planned economy, economic growth is predicated on the mobilization and investment of abundant natural, capital, and human resources, without much regard for the efficiency with which they are used. Relatively high levels of economic growth were sustained on this basis throughout the 1950s and 1960s. But by the 1970s, the regime's ability to mobilize increasing resources was exhausted. This destroyed the basis on which the post-totalitarian elite had sustained the operation of the Stalinist economy, and it contributed to a sharp decline in economic performance in the 1970s and 1980s.

Social modernization eroded the ruling elite's ability to solve these problems by traditional totalitarian means. Large portions of the Soviet population, and especially the functionally specialized groups on which the regime was dependent to maintain performance, had become less susceptible to physical dislocation and coercion. By the 1980s, the population had become more highly urbanized, better educated, and therefore more sophisticated and demanding with respect to its working conditions and other "quality of life" issues. Even the nature of work itself had changed. The proportion of the labor force employed in white-collar and skilled jobs increased, while the proportion engaged in unskilled manual labor declined. In short, an urban professional and semi-professional middle class had emerged that could withhold its services from the regime in retaliation for any attempt to coerce it.[9]

[9]On the process and consequences of social modernization in the Soviet Union, see the two complementary analyses by Gail Warshofsky Lapidus: "Social Trends," in *After Brezhnev*, edited by Robert F. Byrnes (Bloomington: Indiana University Press, 1983), pp. 186–249; and "State and Society: Toward the Emergence of Civil Society in the Soviet Union," in *Politics, Society and Nationality Inside Gorbachev's Russia*, edited by Seweryn Bialer (Boulder, Colo.: Westview, 1989), pp. 121–148.

The modernization process had also produced a "revolution of rising expectations" in the Soviet populace. Popular satisfaction with the present and expectations for the future had long been based on comparisons with the dismal prewar Soviet past. By the 1980s, however, the new urban middle class and, to a great extent, the Soviet political elite itself was coming to judge Soviet accomplishments, as well as their own personal condition, against higher standards. The present was coming to be measured against the performance standards established in the 1950s and 1960s. And with the expanded international role and increased openness of the Soviet Union in the 1970s, knowledge of the vastly superior material standards of living in the developed West raised expectations still further. All these factors combined to increase the standards of material performance against which the regime was being measured.

The modernization process also produced a redistribution of values in the Soviet population. Sociological research conducted by Soviet scholars revealed not only widespread aspirations for material affluence and social status, it showed that the younger, more highly educated population was growing impatient with the regimentation of state controls and wanted greater personal freedom. The frustration of these aspirations contributed to the alienation of the Soviet populace.

Popular alientation was compounded by the failure of the regime to produce consumer goods. The Stalinist economy could not produce enough food and housing to satisfy demand and still meet its industrial production quotas. And the consumer goods it did produce were of such poor quality that consumers found many of them unacceptable even under conditions of extreme scarcity.

The technological revolution that was sweeping the West, Japan, and other countries had bypassed the Soviet economy. Unless it developed a domestic high-technology sector of its own, the Soviet Union would be condemned to eternal economic inferiority. The technological revolution in the West was made possible by three antecedent conditions: the creation of scientific and technical cadres capable of developing new technologies; widespread research and development activities carried out by entrepreneurial individuals and organizations; and the information revolution, which created a virtually free flow of ideas. Entrepreneurial research and the information revolution fueled and were themselves facilitated by the revolution in personal computing.

Social modernization since World War II had already created the first condition in the Soviet Union by the time Mikhail Gorbachev came to power. That the second condition could be met was suggested by the highly successful research and development effort in the military sector and the space program. But this activity was neither widespread nor independent. And the information revolution characterized by the free flow of information, and especially the widespread distribution of personal computers in private hands, had not even begun.

No serious economic recovery could take place, however, until the leadership accepted the necessity of introducing radical changes in the organization of command, consent, interests, and rights in the Soviet Union. Powerful political actors within the ruling elite of the post-totalitarian regime had to take concrete actions to change the regime from within. In the absence of such internal support for change, the coercive power at the command of the elite remained far too great to be overcome by pressure from below alone. But in order to solve the regime's problems, the leadership of the Soviet regime seemed compelled to undertake changes that would push it into a transitional condition between authoritarianism and democracy.

Soviet Authoritarianism in Transition

Gorbachev began to lay the foundations for change by calling for "glasnost," or publicity, in discussions of the shortcomings of the old order. Glasnost appears at first to have been an attempt by Gorbachev to mobilize the support of those who wished to see rapid changes introduced within the framework of the existing order. But it was greeted most enthusiastically by Soviet intellectuals, who seized the opportunity to subject a broad spectrum of issues to critical reevaluation. The new "openness" gave rise to an explosion of popular political activity. Hundreds of groups concerned about particular social, economic, political, religious, environmental, and even ethnic issues and interests began to organize themselves and produce scores of independent publications.

Not only conservatives but even Gorbachev himself has shown a certain degree of discomfort about these developments. Nonetheless, the public expression of radical demands for change has aided Gorbachev by making his own calls for reform seem less threatening. In the economic sphere, he has advanced plans calling for reducing the level of detail subject to central planning; giving economic enterprises increased control over their product mix, wages, investments, and eventually prices; requiring enterprises to finance themselves out of their own earnings; increasing the role of workers in enterprise administration through a form of workers' self-management; permiting private individual and cooperative economic activity; and even creating opportunities for peasants to obtain long-term leases for control over the land, thereby reducing the role of the collective farm to service cooperatives among the leaseholders.

But even a limited economic restructuring is impossible to achieve in the context of Stalinist authoritarian controls over individual thought and behavior. Enterprise managers and private entrepreneurs must be given substantial freedom of action. The media must be permitted to report critically on polices that don't work. Mechanisms must be created to compel enterprises and policymakers to respond to changing conditions. Popular enthusiasm and support, and especially creative energies, must be mobilized. Gorbachev has therefore also called for the "democratization" of political life.

In order to encourage popular participation and increase the accountability of public officials, he has introduced multiple-candidate elections and opened positions of authority to nonparty members. The centerpiece of these changes has been the creation of a new, constitutionally supreme representative body, the Congress of People's Deputies, consisting of 2,250 delegates elected from local districts, from the national territories, and from the party and party-controlled organizations such as the trade unions. In elections held in March 1989, competition between party-supported candidates and independent opponents produced decisive defeats for many party candidates and the election of numerous independent delegates to the Congress. As a result, opposition to the inclusion of delegates handpicked by the party leadership grew rapidly and, within a year, the practice was rejected. Thus, after the next round of elections, the Congress will consist only of delegates elected from local districts and national territories. This change promises a further diminution of the already declining control of the party over this body.

The Congress of People's Deputies elects a smaller body, the 542-member Supreme Soviet, to conduct the actual legislative business of the state. While the earlier Supreme Soviet had functioned merely as a rubber stamp for the party leadership, lending the facade of democratic legitimacy to its decisions, the newly reconstituted Supreme Soviet has become an increasingly important institution for the representation of societal interests and the exercise of social control over the institutions of government. It is far less subject to control by the party leadership than the Congress, and its members subject the Prime Minister and other members of the government—whom it elects—to careful scrutiny and often, powerful criticism.

These changes have led to ·the emergence of genuine "interest group" politics in the Soviet Union, focused on the legislative organs at the local, regional, and national levels. These have begun to function as genuine institutions for the representation of societal forces in the authoritative decision-making process and as institutions through which the government can secure the legitimation of popular consent.

But these changes have unfolded against the background of a simmering conflict between popular groups and forces attempting to break down all constraints on political activity and conservative forces growing increasingly uneasy about their activity. Up to now, the most pronounced resistance to change has come from social and political "conservatives" concerned about the loss of old values. Members of the vast network of ideological and educational workers trained under Stalinist conditions and socialized to Stalinist values, including the thousands of teachers of "Marxism–Leninism" courses at all levels of the educational system; members of the cultural and academic intelligentsias whose careers were established under the old system and for whom the new conditions of openness and competition threaten to overturn the prestige of their past work and personal status; and members of the party and state apparatuses for whom "perestroika" means the loss of power and privileges all represent important sources of support for resistance to change.

Prominent members of the political and cultural elite staked out positions far more conservative than those advanced by Gorbachev at a June 1988 party conference. And their positions were reinforced in later months by government actions to restrict the activities of private entrepreneurs and by calls for restrictions on the activities of independent political groups. Conservative reservations about the speed and scope of changes have continued to find expression at party meetings and in the open press. The formation of a separate Russian party organization in June 1990 and its immediate capture by conservatives created an important political bastion of opposition to change. The Russian party became the voice of conservative and nationalist—Russian and Soviet—forces. At the Congress of the Soviet Communist Party held in Moscow in July 1990, Gorbachev and his supporters in the party came under fierce attack, and were put on notice that they could not rely on the party as an instrument of reform. If they are to push reforms through, Gorbachev and his supporters will have to rely on the institutions of the state instead. And these are presently in considerable disarray.

Underlying many conservative complaints has been an increasing concern on the part of some members of the leadership about the growing potential for mass unrest among the Russian urban industrial work force. For the common citizen, "perestroika" meant a perceptible worsening of material conditions, including simultaneous price increases and widening shortages of food and consumer goods. Moreover, economic reform put an end to the job security heretofore enjoyed even by the least productive workers. For some Soviet workers, unemployment—long criticized by official propaganda as an evil of capitalist exploitation—had already become a reality. Such conditions contributed to the rise of worker unrest and the creation of the Solidarity movement in Poland. And while Russian workers are very different from Polish workers, the formation of an independent worker's party faction in Leningrad in July and widespread strikes among miners across the Soviet Union in the summer and fall of 1989 clearly increased fear in the leadership of the emergence of a Solidarity-like organization.

Popular activism in general has increased in the Soviet Union in recent years. Tens of thousands of informal groups of various kinds are reported by the official Soviet press to be active in the Soviet Union. This includes environmental groups, disarmament groups, cultural groups, groups based on shared nonpolitical interests, mass movements among the non-Russian peoples, Russian nationalist groups, and explicitly political clubs, parties, and other groups. In January 1990, for example, a democratic opposition group, or faction, called the "Democratic Platform," was formed within the Communist party itself.[10] The onset of transition in the Soviet Union has thus produced both the pluralization and the fragmentation of society.

In apparent reaction to continuing resistance to change from conservative forces, to the fragmentation of Soviet society, and especially to the onset of interethnic violence, Gorbachev has gradually expanded his own power to impose change on the Soviet system. In March 1990, he mobilized his control over the many party-selected delegates to the Congress of People's Deputies to push through the creation of a more powerful Soviet presidency. And he secured his own appointment as President for a five-year term, without having to stand for popular election. The newly reconstituted presidency gives Gorbachev the power to declare martial law, to impose policies by decree, and to veto actions of the Supreme Soviet. His closest advisors suggested, in interviews with the Western media following Gorbachev's assumption of the presidency, that he would soon use his new powers to implement a program of radical economic reforms establishing a market economy in the Soviet Union. But he has repeatedly shied away from doing so, apparently out of fear of the social unrest such action might provoke, and the political consequences thereof.

Paradoxically, his seeming effort to accelerate the liberalization process met with resistance from some liberal intellectuals, who otherwise had been its strongest supporters. As Gorbachev increasingly accumulated personal power and began to reconstruct the central organs of government, some intellectuals grew concerned about creating conditions for the potential reemergence of a dictator. Others, in the ethnic peripheries, appear to have grown wary of the centralization of decision-making power in Moscow, which is inherent in proposals for constitutional reform. Still others appear to have grown inpatient with Gorbachev's continuing refusal to permit the creation of opposition parties.

Ethnic Conflict and Political Change

The most destabilizing development in the era of glasnost, however, has been the rise of nationalist movements among the non-Russian peoples. Local aspirations for increased autonomy have formed the basis for organized public protest across the Soviet Union. In the Baltic republics of Latvia, Lithuania, and Estonia, long-suppressed popular resentment of the Soviet annexation of these previously independent countries, and

---

[10]Julia Wishnevsky and Elizabeth Teague, " 'Democratic Platform' Created in CPSU," *Report on the USSR* 2,5 (February 2, 1990), pp. 7–9.

their subjection to culturally alien Russian rule, has given rise to mass movements seeking to establish independence from Moscow. These movements are able to mobilize tens of thousands of people for street demonstrations in support of their positions. They have become de facto opposition political parties, nominating and electing their own candidates to local and national political office and advancing their own platforms for political reform.

Similar mass movements have emerged among Moldavians, Uzbeks, Kazakhs, Turkmen, and Ukrainians. The economic and political importance of Ukraine and the Ukrainians makes the prospect of a mass nationalist, separatist movement among Ukrainians particularly unsettling. In the Caucasus, rising nationalist sentiments have led to a long and violent territorial struggle between Armenians and Azerbaidzhanis and to a tragic confrontation between Georgian demonstrators and the military.

The depth of nationalist emotions and the scope of popular support in the peripheries for demands for autonomy appear to have inclined Gorbachev toward making concessions. He began in early 1987 by conceding that policy toward the nationalities required "special tact and care," and suggested the need to ensure the representation of all groups in leading positions in the party, state, and economy. In June 1987, he included ethnic group interests among those that would have to be taken into account in the policy-making process. And in early 1988 he elevated the nationalities question to an issue of "vital" importance and called for increasing the role of the national republics in the Soviet state political system, according them representation in central political organs. A much-delayed party platform on the nationalities question, finally adopted in September 1989, suggests an attempt to win back ethnic loyalties through concessions to local autonomy. But liberalization—and the prospect of democratization—of the Soviet system under Gorbachev appears to have produced powerful societal forces for the confederalization of the Soviet political order along ethnic lines and even its complete disintegration into separate national states.

The evolution of the Lithuanian popular movement, Sajudis, from support for perestroika to proponent of outright independence for Lithuania reflects the acceleration of demands associated with liberalization and, especially, democratization in an authoritarian regime. As de Tocqueville suggested, the changes introduced by Gorbachev to redress past grievances and mobilize support for a new Soviet order have produced instead demands for further, more rapid changes, including demands for the complete overthrow of the Soviet system. Mass political movements paralleling the Lithuanian Sajudis are already active in every region of the Soviet Union and among every ethnic or nationality group, large and small. In elections held in February and March 1990, many candidates backed by these movements won impressive victories, including the winning of majority control in the cities of Moscow, Leningrad, Kiev, and Lvov. Elections scheduled for later dates in other regions hold out the prospect of similar victories elsewhere. Thus, the confrontation between Gorbachev and the Lithuanians, which followed Lithuania's declaration of independence in March 1990, is surely only the beginning of local and regional challenges to Moscow's control— challenges that will be intensified by ethnic differences between Moscow and the peripheries.

Nationalist unrest in the Baltic republics; among Georgians, Armenians, and Azerbaidzhanis in the Caucasus; in Byelorussia, Moldavia, and the Ukraine; and in the republics of Central Asia has been paralleled by the rise of Russian nationalist sentiments in the central regions of the country and especially in the large cities of European Russia. The views expressed by nationalist Russian literary and cultural figures range from the most liberal to the most reactionary. The group which has drawn the most widespread popular support, however, has been the Russian nationalist organization "Pamyat," or "memory." "Memory" is both chauvinistic and anti-Semitic and has adopted behaviors reminiscent of German and Italian fascism of the interwar period, including the adoption of a uniform of black shirts. The cultural, economic, and environmental issues it raises reflect the accumulated resentments of Russians who view the developmental benefits that have accrued to the non-Russian peoples and territories under Soviet rule as having come at the expense of Russia and the Russian people. And it unites the two most powerful sources of resistance to perestroika: cultural conservatism and political neo-Stalinism. Russian nationalism thus represents a potentially powerful basis for the mobilization of reactionary forces willing to slam the door shut on regime change in the Soviet Union. The formation of a separate Russian Communist party organization, and its capture by extreme conservative forces, would appear to be a major step toward the realization of this potential.

Leaderships of the national movements, and the most active elements of their memberships, tend to be drawn from the intellectual strata and to be highly concerned with issues of individual freedom and democracy and national cultural survival. The mass populations in the republics, in contrast, tend to be far more concerned with economic issues and the material conditions of everyday life.[11] The increasingly open elections that took place in the spring of 1990 nonetheless produced decisive victories for the democratic opposition at the expense of more conservative forces. It remains to be seen, however, whether popular support for democracy will survive the challenges of economic hardship.

[11]David Marples, "A Sociological Survey of 'Rukh,' " *Report on the USSR* (January 12, 1990), pp. 18–20.

The Soviet Union is now characterized by numerous instances of unrest stimulated by food shortages, housing scandals, discontent with local communist leaders resistant to change, and growing demands from within the party itself for democratization. Crime of all types, including violent assaults, has been increasing dramatically. At the same time, pessimism about the future is becoming more widespread among the Soviet populace. According to a public opinion survey conducted by a leading Soviet weekly, the proportion of Soviets who expected next year to be better than last decreased from 34 percent in 1989 to only 4 percent in 1990, while the proportion of those expecting conditions to get worse increased from 6 to 14 percent.[12] Popular discontent found public expression at the traditional May Day celebration on May 1, 1990, when crowds of protesters jeered Gorbachev and the other members of the leadership assembled atop the Lenin mausoleum in Red Square and loudly called for Gorbachev's resignation. This growing popular discontent promises to make introduction of the genuine reforms that are required to establish a viable economy in the Soviet Union even more difficult. Indeed, fear of mass unrest in reaction to the rising prices, sharp increases in unemployment, and a further plunge in living standards that would accompany any effort to move rapidly to a market economy appears to lie behind the continuing reluctance of Gorbachev to impose on the Soviet economy the kind of radical, rapid, "shock" therapy adopted with at least initial success by the Poles.

Prospects of Democratization

The 1980s have seen the gradual emergence of mass society as a partially autonomous force in Soviet politics. This process accelerated under conditions of glasnost. Gorbachev is attempting to mobilize the support of those forces seeking reform for a major reorganization and reduction in power of the party and state bureaucracies. However, Gorbachev continues to reserve to the Communist party alone the right to define the direction and parameters of change, and political opposition—especially competing political parties—is still forbidden. Thus, the changes Gorbachev has introduced do not add up to the "democratization" of the Soviet Union, at least not as we have defined it in this volume. Rather, they appear to aim at "modernizing" the one-party system.

Gorbachev has grown increasingly ambivalent about the speed and scope of reform as the consequences of changes already in place give rise to unintended and uncontrollable developments. He has vacillated on

---

[12]Cited in *Report on the USSR* (April 27, 1990), pp. 35–36.

the question of permitting the emergence of a formal multiparty system. But he has been unable to prevent it from emerging in fact. As a result, the Gorbachev leadership appears to have attempted to co-opt forces inside and outside the party that are pressing for democratization. Prior to the March 1990 elections, for example, the party newspaper *Pravda* published a roundtable discussion with the leaders of the "Democratic Platform" faction of the party in an effort to win popular support for party candidates. At the same time, local party officials began to join opposition groups in an effort to penetrate their leaderships and turn them toward cooperation with the regime. Such efforts have had little success. The March 1990 elections produced widespread electoral victories for democratic opposition groups. The opposition won control of city governments in Moscow, Leningrad, and other large cities and established, for the first time, institutionalized bases for the politics of opposition in the Soviet Union. And this opposition is likely to grow even more powerful if the "Democratic Platform" splits from the Communist party and forms an open, opposition party.[13] But, by the time of the Twenty-eighth Congress of the CPSU, held in July 1990, it had not yet gathered the courage and support to do so.

By spring 1990, the range of independent political groups in the Soviet Union included:[14]

1. National "popular fronts" of the non-Russian peoples of the Union republics and other territories, focused on securing national independence
2. "Popular fronts" in the Russian republic, encompassing large cities or regions of the republic and Western or leftist in orientation
3. Movements among ethnic minorities such as Crimean Tartars and Jews
4. Movements among the Russians living in non-Russian republics, opposed to independence for these republics and highly conservative in orientation
5. Russian nationalist groups
6. Independent groups within the CPSU, usually called "clubs," established in over 100 cities across the Soviet Union. Such clubs form the basis of the democratically inclined "Democratic Platform" group and the orthodox communist "Marxist Platform" group
7. Parliamentary groups, or factions, of delegates elected to national and regional parliaments; these include groups of all political orientations, from the most radical to the most conservative

---

[13]For further discussion, see Vera Tolz, "The Emergence of a Multiparty System in the USSR," *Report on the USSR* (April 27, 1990), pp. 5–11.
[14]*Ibid.*, pp. 9–11.

8. Independent workers' groups and trade unions, including those organized spontaneously by striking workers in the summer of 1989 and those organized by conservative party officials attempting to siphon working class support away from opposition movements
9. Anti-Stalinist groups, the best-known of which is the Moscow-based "Memorial" group
10. Ecology groups, including the antinuclear movement in Kazakhstan, part of a burgeoning "Green" movement across the Soviet Union
11. National-cultural groups formed to defend the ethnic and cultural heritages of their respective nations
12. Religious groups
13. Veterans' groups and military trade unions organized to defend the interest of veterans and enlisted men, which have formed cooperative relationships with either conservative or democratic opposition groups
14. Self-declared political parties, whose numbers are growing each day, but whose membership and influence remain small

With each new session, the Congress of People's deputies provides a more open forum for the expression of popular sentiments and for the exercise of pressure on the central leadership from below. This has given it enormous importance as an institution for the legitimation of Gorbachev's attempt to reform the system. Delegates in the Congress have coalesced into several "blocs" that constitute loose opposition parties. The formation of opposition parties was given a considerable boost in February 1990 when the party formally relinquished its constitutional guarantee of a monopoly of political power. But this act had greater symbolic importance than real effect. The ability of the Congress to hold Gorbachev and his leadership accountable remains severely restricted. Despite the fact that the Congress has rejected several nominees for ministerial positions and has empowered representatives of popular political movements to limit the freedom of the leadership simply to impose its choices, the Congress remains under the considerable influence of the institutions of command.

The rules of procedure, the domination of the Congress and its agenda by a Presidium composed of Gorbachev's hand-picked supporters, and the continuing presence of numerous representatives of the old party machine all inhibit the Congress' development into an effective institution of representation and consent, and especially its development into an institutionalized channel for imposing accountability on the organs of command. A major step toward such development was taken in late 1989 when the Congress made a decision to do away with the reservation of one-third of its seats for representatives of social organizations dominated by the party apparatus. If this decision is implemented and all seats in the Congress are subject to popular vote at the next scheduled nationwide election in 1994, the representation of opposition forces will increase and central control over this institution will erode even further. As a result, the ability of the Congress and the smaller Supreme Soviet it elects from among its own members to influence the organs of command and hold them accountable will increase dramatically. Such a development would create an important counterweight to the strengthening of the central executive organs that took place with the redefinition of the presidency adopted in March 1990.

After considerable debate in the party and the Congress, constitutional amendments establishing a new executive presidency of the Soviet Union were adopted in March 1990, and Gorbachev was elected President by the Congress of People's Deputies. Although there was strong sentiment in favor of direct election of the President by the people, this step was delayed until the end of Gorbachev's term. Presented by Gorbachev's supporters as an attempt to break, once and for all, the power of the party over the political order, the establishment of the presidency concentrated a number of powers in the hands of a single leader in order to permit him to counteract the disintegration of public order on the one hand, and to push through more radical economic and political changes on the other.[15]

The new president enjoys the power to declare war and has the status of commander-in-chief of the armed forces. The president also appoints the leading members of the government, subject to confirmation by the Congress of People's Deputies and the Supreme Soviet. The most distinctive, and inherently controversial, powers granted to the president by the constitutional reforms of March 1990 are the power to veto legislation passed by the Soviet Union Supreme Soviet and the requirement of a two-thirds vote of the Supreme Soviet to overturn such a veto; the ability to issue decrees that have the force of law on the entire territory of the Soviet Union and that cannot be overturned by the legislature as long as they are ajudged constitutional; the power to dissolve the Supreme Soviet in certain circumstances; and the ability to impose martial law on areas of the Soviet Union.

A new "presidential council" has also been established, and a reorganization and redistribution of executive authority and functions has allowed it to operate as a kind of cabinet-like advisory body to the president. Together with the plan to submit the presidency to direct popular election in the future, these changes have brought the Soviet Union closer to the establishment of a strong "semi-presidential" system of government. However, in the absence of a clearer separation of

---

[15]See Elizabeth Teague and Dawn Mann, "Gorbachev's Dual Role," *Problems of Communism* 39,1 (January–February 1990), pp. 1–14.

powers among the branches of government, and especially a strengthening of representation, consent, and accountability, the danger that a strengthened presidency has created conditions for a reversion to authoritarianism in response to disintegrative pressures from below remains very real.

The increasing accumulation of personal power by Gorbachev appears to be part of a dual strategy for increasing popular support for changes that will make one-party rule economically more efficient and socially less repressive, increase its popular legitimacy, and thereby strengthen its ability to resist forces calling for its overthrow. On the one hand, he appears intent on accumulating sufficient personal power to reduce and reconstruct the party and state bureaucracies in Moscow and limit their power over the economy and society. On the other, he appears intent on mobilizing popular participation and channeling it into more active representative organs of government while subordinating these organs to the relegitimated political authority of the party and its leader.

Pursuing the first strategy, however, brings him into direct conflict with the party apparatus and the state bureaucracies, and the use of his power to impose economic reform brings him into conflict with a whole stratum of managerial elites whose power and privileges are threatened by the prospect of worker self-management and the imposition of objective, efficiency-based performance criteria. Soviet managers accustomed to dealing with central decision makers in the context of a planned economy will have to develop entirely new skills for dealing with labor, controlling costs, and marketing products to demanding consumers. For party apparatchiks and state bureaucrats, the transfer of even limited decision-making authority to autonomous enterprises represents a major loss of power. As reform proceeds, provincial party secretaries in particular will begin to lose power to successful enterprise managers and other entrepreneurial actors in their territories. And the revitalization of local institutions of representation and consent promises to subject them to even greater direct popular pressures.

Alienation of the party apparatchiks at the center and the party secretaries in the provinces is potentially very dangerous. These are the very groups most heavily represented in the Central Committee and whose discontent over similar threats to their positions contributed to the overthrow of Khrushchev in 1964.

At the same time, pursuing the second strategy requires Gorbachev to continue to support glasnost and the expanded opportunities for popular political action that that creates. Gorbachev appears to be gambling that popular demands can be accommodated within the framework of a reformed Soviet political system. Ultimately, it is the balance of popular opposition and support that will determine the fate of perestroika, for real change depends on changes in mass values and behavior; that is, on changes in the dominant political culture. In the absence of such change, perestroika must fail. As such change takes hold, it will be increasingly difficult to oppose. But as opportunities for meaningful political participation increase, and if such participation produces the satisfaction of popular demands, the legitimacy of institutions of representation and consent will increase, as will support for the regime. Such institutionalization of popular participation might strengthen the legitimacy of the Soviet system sufficiently to permit it to withstand higher levels of everyday political activity, including political conflict. In effect, Gorbachev is gambling on the emergence of a "civic culture" in the Soviet Union.

However, increasing the opportunities for independent political activity while the economic crisis confronting the regime remains unresolved raises the prospects of worker unrest arising out of worsening material conditions, nationalist conflict arising out of ethnic competition for scarce resources or straightforward demands for political autonomy, oppositional activity by intellectuals seeking more radical changes, and other forms of behavior likely to prompt a conservative backlash. For Gorbachev to succeed, therefore, he must contain popular political activity within limits acceptable to conservatives.

Thus, Gorbachev is engaged in a political balancing act. He must create a new set of political forces and institutionalize them in power at a rate faster than he dismantles the old order. To institutionalize a new political order, however, he must reduce the power of the old one. Yet he cannot allow the old order to be weakened too rapidly, lest the new political forces slip out of control. For his goal is to save the Soviet system, not destroy it.

Transitions in Eastern Europe

While change has come to the Soviet regime from above, the onset of democratization in Eastern Europe has been produced by pressure from below. In most cases, this pressure had been building up for decades and was released finally by Gorbachev's unequivocal statements precluding Soviet intervention to shore up collapsing regimes. In Poland, however, widespread dissatisfaction had produced repeated confrontations between the state and society in the past and produced a mass-based resistance movement, Solidarity, in 1979. After failing to destroy resistance through repression, the near-collapse of the economy finally forced the Polish regime to permit at least partially democratic elections, through which Solidarity finally broke the communists' political monopoly. The formation in August 1989 of a new government headed by Solidarity, but with communist participation, ushered in a period of expanding freedom and the institutionalization of individual rights. This new government faces enormously difficult economic challenges and must rely on the affective, or emotional, support of the Polish people for democracy if it is to survive, for it can provide little in the way of material benefits. Indeed, while the economic austerity program imposed on the country by Prime Minister Mazowiecki in January 1990 has produced full shelves in the country's food stores for the first time in many years, it has also produced the impoverishment of the Polish people. The survival of this government, and the success of the democratization process in Poland, thus seems to depend on whether the people can endure the hardships that will ensue before their material conditions can be improved.

In Hungary, declining economic performance led to conflict within the communist political elite over the future course of reform, and this conflict soon spilled over into society. Under the pressure of increasingly frequent and growing demonstrations demanding democratization, the communist leadership rapidly fragmented, and the party disintegrated. By spring 1989, it was clear that a new, more democratic, and more pluralistic order was emerging in Hungary, as opposition groups coalesced into parties. In an attempt to break with its own past, the Hungarian Communist party changed its name and negotiated an agreement with opposition forces on the calling of free elections.

Events in Poland and Hungary fueled popular impatience with authoritarianism in East Germany and Czechoslovakia. Thousands of East Germans fled to West Germany in 1989. At the same time, mass demonstrations calling for democratization took place in Leipzig and other cities. Although some in the communist leadership contemplated violent repression of this unrest, more moderate views prevailed. A new Communist leadership took over the country and attempted to win popular support by making dramatic concessions to the people's desire to travel, including the opening of the Berlin Wall. These concessions only served to whet the appetite of the East German people for true democratization. Continuing demonstrations forced the resignation of the Communist party and governmental leaderships, clearing the way for the emergence of a noncommunist regime in East Germany as well. The electoral victory of democratic conservatives in East Germany in March 1990 released forces that have already produced the monetary union of the two Germanies and will inevitably produce their political unification as a single, democratic German state. Thus, communist authoritarianism not only collapsed, but has effectively been replaced by the existing West German democracy.

The pace of change accelerated in Eastern Europe throughout 1989. In Czechoslovakia, mass demonstrations beginning in mid-November 1989 toppled the communist leadership by the end of December! And in Romania mass demonstrations overthrew the Ceausescu tyranny in a few short days before Christmas! The dizzying changes in Eastern Europe in 1989 and 1990 are summarized in Table 8.1.

The demise of Communist authoritarianism in Poland, Hungary, East Germany, and Czechoslovakia was made possible by the changes that had already taken place in the Soviet Union, especially the public disavowal by Gorbachev of any intention of intervening to stop such changes. Communist regimes were artifically imposed on these societies by the Soviet Union and maintained in power by the presence of Soviet troops. Soviet forces had been used repeatedly to shore up East European regimes: in East Germany in 1953, in Hungary in 1956, and in Czechoslovakia in 1968. With the threat of intervention laid to rest, the danger of engaging in oppositional activity radically declined. Despite the efforts of local communist leaderships to gain legitimacy, their political subordination to a foreign power made demands for change synonymous with demands for national independence—just as had been the case with the liberal uprisings against Austrian domination in many of these same lands in the middle of the nineteenth century.

Even more important than this, however, is the fact that several of these countries had experienced independent democratic existences in the historically recent past. Between the world wars, for example, Czechoslovakia had been a stable parliamentary democracy. Despite the efforts of the communist leaderships to seal these countries off from the West, Western values had already become embedded in their political cultures. This factor, more than any other, explains the rapidity with which events have unfolded in Eastern Europe.

Liberalization, Democratization, and the Western Experience

A number of facile generalizations are often used in studying democratization and the liberalization of authoritarian and totalitarian regimes. The most common is to evoke "Western experience"—that is, the transition in some countries of Western Europe from absolutism to democracy two to three centuries ago—and to link the transition to democratization with the emergence of industrialization, individual entrepreneurship, and the free market economy; in short, capitalism. But there are a number of caveats that must considered when we evaluate the prospects of change in today's world.

First, there is no a priori reason to assume that the Western experience, limited as it is to only a few countries, will be replicated. Second, there is no causal relationship between capitalism and democracy. There is at best a correlation that may very well prove to be spurious. In fact, rapid capitalist, industrial development was linked to democracy only in England, the post-Civil War United States, and perhaps France. Histor-

TABLE 8.1   1989 and 1990: Tumultuous Time of Transition in Eastern Europe

JANUARY 1989   *Poland*   Communist party agrees to negotiations with Solidarity opposition

Hungary   Communist party leaders promise multiparty system

APRIL   *Poland*   Communist leader Wojciech Jaruzelski and Solidarity leader Lech Walesa reach agreement on partly democratic elections to parliament

MAY   *Hungary*   Demolition of "iron curtain" begins with removal of barbed wire from Hungarian–Austrian border

JUNE   *Poland*   Solidarity wins overwhelming victory in first partly free parliamentary elections; gains control of strengthened parliament

Hungary   Imre Nagy, hero of 1956 anticommunist uprising executed by the communists, is reburied as national hero

JULY   *Poland*   Communist leader Wojciech Jaruzelski elected president of Poland as part of agreement negotiated with Solidarity; communists prove unable to form government coalition capable of winning parliamentary majority

AUGUST   *Poland*   Solidarity-led government is elected by parliament, with Tadeusz Mazowiecki as prime minister. Noncommunists lead social and economic ministries, communists head military and security ministries with noncommunist deputies, and Jaruzelski remains as president

SEPTEMBER   *Hungary*   Hungarian leadership opens its borders with Austria, permitting exit of East Germans seeking refuge in West Germany

OCTOBER   *East Germany*   Flow of refugees to West Germany, through Hungary, Poland, and Czechoslovakia continues as internal demonstrations for change increase in size and frequency; longtime communist leader Erich Honecker is replaced by Egon Krenz

Hungary   Communist party reorients itself toward more liberal political program and renames itself Socialist party; parliament revises constitution to end communist political monopoly, allowing multiparty system

Czechoslovakia   Arrest of playwright and opposition figure Vaclav Havel prompts protest by thousands, broken up by police

Bulgaria   Protest rally leads to promise of reform by communist leadership

NOVEMBER   *East Germany*   Shakeup of communist party leadership fails to stem either flow of refugees to West or rise of internal unrest; politburo resigns; Berlin Wall is opened and free travel to West permitted; Krenz promises free elections

Czechoslovakia   Hard-line speech by party leader Milos Jakes prompts increased dissatisfaction with continued communist rule; mass protests break out, and opposition groups form "Civic Forum" alliance; demonstration by 350,000 people in Prague forces Jakes to resign; despite efforts by communists to retain power through concessions, opposition forces prevail; millions of people participate in national strike on November 27; party renounces monopoly of power and concedes need for free elections

Hungary   Voting in a referendum, Hungarian people reject attempt by communists to structure electoral process so as to hold on to power; stage is set for free, competitive parliamentary elections

Bulgaria   Longtime communist party leader, 78-year-old Todor Zhivkov, is ousted; replaced by 53-year-old Petar Mladenov, who begins to carry out a program of modest political liberalization

DECEMBER	*Czechoslovakia* New government, with noncommunist majority is formed; Vaclav Havel elected president of Czechoslovakia by parliament; Alexander Dubček, leader of the communist reform movement crushed by the Soviet invasion of 1968, is elected head of the parliament
	East Germany Communist party replaces Krenz with new reformist leadership, but does not break completely with the past; round-table discussions among communist party leaders, leaders of other parties, and democratic opposition leaders lead to agreement to hold free elections
	Romania Local protest against harassment of ethnic Hungarians escalates, with support from ethnic Romanians, into mass demonstrations against Ceausescu tyranny; popular hatred for the regime turns official Bucharest rally into anti-Ceausescu demonstration; military leadership refuses to obey orders to shoot demonstrators, as soldiers join demonstrators; as battle between military and security forces erupts, opposition figures form provisional government; Ceausescu and wife are arrested and executed
JANUARY 1990	*Yugoslavia* The League of Communists (Communist party) of Yugoslavia convenes an extraordinary Congress at which it renounces its constitutional monopoly of political power and endorses a multiparty political system; conflict between Slovenia, seeking rapid reforms, and more conservative Serbian forces fuels secessionist sentiments in Slovenia
	Poland Communist party (Polish United Workers Party) formally disbanded and reconstitutes itself as a noncommunist but socialist-oriented party known as Social Democracy of the Republic of Poland in an attempt to win popular support; a dissident group of reformist communists establishes another, separate party, the Social Democratic Union of the Polish Republic
FEBRUARY	*Yugoslavia* Slovenian League of Communists declares itself an independent party, widening rift between that republic and the rest of Yugoslavia
MARCH	*Bulgaria* 26 opposition groups form coalition to oppose Communist party in elections scheduled for June 1990; Communist party and opposition conclude agreements easing transition to democratic political order
	Hungary First free multiparty elections produce electoral victory for democratic opposition; the moderate-to-conservative "Democratic Forum" wins 24.7 percent of vote, the more radical Alliance of Free Democrats wins 21.4 percent, and the Independent Smallholders' party wins 11.8 percent
	East Germany First free multiparty elections produce electoral victory for alliance of conservative democratic opposition; the "Alliance for Germany" wins 48 percent of the vote to the Social Democratic party's 22 percent; the leading force in the Alliance is the conservative East German Christian Democratic Union, which secured 41 percent of the vote; the former Communist party, the Party of Democratic Socialism, won 16 percent of the vote
APRIL	*Yugoslavia* Free, competitive elections for regional parliament in Slovenia results in victory for DEMOS, a coalition of the democratic opposition groups in that republic; in elections for President of Slovenia, Communist party leader Milan Kucan wins 58 percent of the vote and defeats the candidate of the democratic opposition; in Croatia, republic elections produce overwhelming victory for the conservative alliance of opposition forces, led by former nationalist leader and political prisoner, Franjo Tudjman
	East Germany Conservative democratic coalition government takes power

ically, the emergence of capitalism was almost everywhere associated with strong centralized state controls—with absolutism. In the first half of the twentieth century, industrialization and capitalism flourished, but did not produce democracy, in Japan and Germany. And in the later twentieth century, industrialization and capitalism have failed to bring democracy to South Korea or Taiwan.

Third and perhaps most relevant in an era of tumultuous and rapid changes in the Soviet Union and Eastern Europe, it is important to remember that where the process of democratization succeeded, it took a long time! It was not until the beginning of the twentieth century that the hereditary House of Lords lost its powers. In France, the struggle between conservative and authoritarian forces on the one hand and liberal and democratic forces on the other was not resolved until the very end of the nineteenth century. Some might say not until after 1945! In the United States, some might argue that mass democracy was not secured until after the Civil War, while others rightly point to the successes of the civil rights movement in the 1960s as the consolidation of democracy in America.

With the benefits of historical hindsight reaching back at least to the end of the seventeenth century, one can point to a great number of signposts along the road to democracy. But the democratization of each of these regimes was a staggered and uneven process with victories and setbacks; not a smooth march. It is therefore downright silly to expect the present transitions of authoritarian regimes to be completed in a matter of years or even decades.

Our final caveat concerns the importance of national unity and legitimacy to the process of democratization. The early democratic regimes in England, the United States, and France were buffeted by extremely disruptive social forces and severe economic dislocations unleashed by the industrialization process. The conflicts they produced were cushioned and contained in these countries only because national unity had already been achieved, and political institutions for the resolution of group conflicts had already been consolidated. In virtually all other countries—including Germany, Italy, early twentieth-century Russia, and later Japan—the forces unleashed by industrialization contributed to the breakdown of the democratization process.

The consolidation of the early democracies before the onset of industrialization allowed democratization to take place during a long period of increasing material prosperity and to unfold gradually. We should not expect the authoritarian regimes of Latin America, the Soviet Union, and Eastern Europe to follow the same pattern. Indeed, none of the later democracies has duplicated it. Democratization may be more difficult to achieve in totalitarian than in authoritarian regimes. Indeed, Soviet and East European experience suggests that loosening the controls of the totalitarian order may produce an authoritarian regime. But democratization requires the overthrow of the old order in its entirety. All we might expect is that knowledge of these earlier experiences will allow Soviet, Polish, Hungarian, Brazilian, Argentine, and other reformers to define their own successful paths to democracy.

At present, however, the political landscape in most of these countries remains inchoate. By spring 1990, for example, more than thirty new political parties had come into existence in Czechoslovakia, more than fifty in Hungary, and more than one hundred in Poland![16] Thus, the onset of democratization has brought a process of political fragmentation of society in these states. This has been counterbalanced in some cases by the pressure to form alliances created by the prospect of electoral competition. The March 1990 elections in East Germany, for example, saw the formation of an alliance of conservative democratic parties, called the Alliance for Germany. The Alliance comprised the Christian Democratic Union, the German Social Union, and the Democratic Awakening, was backed by West Germany's Christian Democratic Party, received the campaign support of West German Chancellor Helmut Kohl, and won a decisive victory, with 48 percent of the vote. In other cases, however, electoral politics may not lead to alliance formation.

In Hungary, for example, the onset of liberalization and democratization intensified divisions among various elements in the democratic opposition. The more conservative and more nationalist-oriented Hungarian Democratic Forum party waged a particularly emotional campaign against its more radical competition in the opposition, the Alliance of Free Democrats. The resort to nationalistic and anti-Semitic tactics on the part of some in the Democratic Forum in an attempt to discredit the Free Democrats suggests that the Forum's commitment to the norms of tolerance characteristic of liberal democracies may not be very strong. Moreover, the victory of the Democratic Forum in the March–April 1990 elections in Hungary may enable the party to control parliament and establish a government on its own, further reducing its incentives to uphold such norms.

Even in a unified Germany, the consolidation of democracy in the formerly communist territories may be difficult to achieve. Economic dislocations and their attendant social problems are certain to result from the rapid introduction of a capitalist, market economy in the East, and these may give rise to political forces inimical to German democracy.

In Eastern Europe and the Soviet Union, the establishment of democratic norms, a "civic culture," is made still more difficult by the recent resurgence of nationalisms in this region. Demands by ethnic groups in the Soviet Union for national independence (such as those of

---

[16]"Political Parties in Eastern Europe," *Radio Free Europe Research* (February 10, 1990).

the Lithuanians and other Baltic peoples), as well as age-old ethnic rivalries that cut across both internal and international boundaries (such as the conflicts between Hungarians and Romanians in Romania or Armenians and Azerbaidzhanis in the Soviet Union), make agreement on new "rules of the game" difficult to reach through consensus. And it is very difficult to imagine the establishment of democracy through the authoritarian practices which often accompany attempts to suppress ethnic or political minorities!

Bibliography

Baloyra, Enrique (ed.). *Comparing New Democracies: Transition and Consolidation in Mediterranean Europe and the Southern Cone.* Boulder, Colo.: Westview Press, 1987.

Bialer, Seweryn (ed.). *Politics, Society, and Nationality Inside Gorbachev's Russia.* Boulder, Colo.: Westview, 1989.

Brown, Archie. "Gorbachev: New Man in the Kremlin," *Problems of Communism* 34, 3 (May–June 1985), pp. 1–23.

Colton, Timothy J. *The Dilemma of Reform in the Soviet Union.* rev. ed. New York: Council on Foreign Relations, Inc., 1986.

Friedberg, Maurice, and Heyward Isham (eds.). *Soviet Society Under Gorbachev.* Armonk, N.Y.: M. E. Sharpe, Inc., 1987.

Goble, Paul A. "Gorbachev and the Soviet Nationality Problem," in Maurice Friedberg and Heyward Isham, Eds., *Soviet Society Under Gorbachev.* Armonk, N.Y.: M. E. Sharpe, Inc., 1987, pp. 76–100.

Gustafson, Thane, and Dawn Mann. "Gorbachev's Next Gamble," *Problems of Communism* 36, 4 (July–August 1987), pp. 1–20.

Hammer, Darrell P. *The U.S.S.R.: The Politics of Oligarchy.* 2nd ed. Boulder, Colo.: Westview, 1986.

Hough, Jerry. "Gorbachev Consolidating Power," *Problems of Communism* 36, 4 (July–August 1987), pp. 21–43.

Lapidus, Gail. "Ethnonationalism and Political Stability: The Soviet Case," *World Politics* 36, 4 (July 1984), pp. 555–580.

Levine, Daniel. "The Transition to Democracy: Are There Lessons from Venezuela?" *Bulletin of Latin American Research* 4, 2 (1985), pp. 47–61.

———. "Paradigm Lost: Dependence to Democracy," *World Politics* 40, 3 (1988), pp. 377–394.

Lijphart, Arend. *Democracy in Plural Societies.* New Haven, Conn.: Yale University Press, 1977.

Linz, Juan J. *The Breakdown of Democratic Regimes: Crisis, Breakdown & Reequilibration.* Baltimore: The Johns Hopkins University Press, 1978.

Malloy, James M., and Mitchell Seligson (eds.). *Authoritarians and Democrats: Regime Transitions in Latin America.* Pittsburgh: University of Pittsburgh Press, 1987.

Odom, William. "How Far Can Soviet Reform Go?" *Problems of Communism* 36, 6 (November–December 1987), pp. 18–33.

O'Donnell, Guillermo, Phillippe C. Schmitter, and Laurence Whitehead (eds.). *Transitions from Authoritarian Rule.* Baltimore: The Johns Hopkins University Press, 1986.

Rabushka, Alvin, and Kenneth A. Shepsle. *Politics in Plural Societies: A Theory of Democratic Stability.* Columbus, Ohio: Charles E. Merrill, 1972.

Rigby, T. H. "The Soviet Leadership: Towards a Self-Stabilizing Oligarchy?" *Soviet Studies* 22, 2 (October 1970). pp. 167–191.

Skilling, H. Gordon, and Franklyn Griffiths (eds.). *Interest Groups in Soviet Politics.* Princeton, N.J.: Princeton University Press, 1971.

White, Stephen. "Elites, Power, and the Exercise of Political Authority in the USSR," in David Lane, Ed., *Elites and Political Power in the USSR.* Aldershot, England: Edward Elgar 1988, pp. 269–287.

9

In Lieu of
a Conclusion:
Political Performance

Political Performance

This book has surveyed characteristics of political regimes—their institutions and structures, and the political processes that unfold within them. In order to draw conclusions for this survey, however, one must undertake the daunting task of *evaluating* the performance of these regimes.

There are at least two levels at which regime performance can be measured and evaluated. The first is functional. How well does it perform the major functions it must perform in order to survive? Does it maintain order? Can it prevent disruptive internal behavior? Has it gained enough recognition and acceptance to be legitimized? Has it developed adequate capabilities to make and implement decisions? Has it managed to safeguard a modicum of material well-being for the citizens? Is it in a position to defend its citizens against hostile forces from without? Harry Eckstein[1] suggests four basic criteria for evaluating performance: *decisional efficacy, civil order, legitimacy,* and *durability.* To these we add *inclusiveness.*

These criteria can help us weigh performance, but only in functional terms. They may tell us how well a given regime has functioned over

[1]Harry Eckstein, *The Evaluation of Political Performance: Problems and Dimensions* (Beverly Hills, Calif.: Sage Publications, 1971).

time or how well it is functioning in the present. However, they tell us very little about the purpose of the regime and the values it implements. This is the second and more difficult level of analysis—the normative level—which subjects the purpose of a regime, the goals it sets forth and the values it maintains, to critical evaluation.

The normative approach stipulates that the criteria of evaluation are outside the regime and its functioning and that it is but an instrument to implement a higher moral purpose. Functioning is not in itself enough to measure performance. Rather, the yardstick of performance lies in measuring the extent and the degree to which it conforms to and implements generally accepted and universal values, or at least those values prized by those carrying out the evaluation. What is the sense of knowing that trains run on time, as the Fascists proclaimed in Italy, unless we know where they take us? To Shangri-La or to a concentration camp?

Let us now turn to how the regimes we surveyed compare at these two levels of analysis. First, a functional evaluation.

Decisional Efficacy

The institutions of a regime, in order to perform well, must be *adaptable, responsive,* and *inclusive.*

Adaptability Like all other institutions, political regimes must adapt to new conditions, adjust to new constraints, and use new opportunities. It is with regard to adaptability, one can argue, that democracies function more effectively than authoritarian/totalitarian regimes. Democracies have the institutional framework for changes that sometimes amount to a revolutionary reallocation of powers and services. The statement that in democracies "people agree on how to disagree" makes the point. In democracies people agree on translating their disagreements into policies, and one side (the majority) wins over the other (the minority). When the lines are not clearly drawn, there are incremental changes and compromises. Thus, as we pointed out in this book, there is room not only for adjustment and compromise but also for change and experimentation. Democracy provides for changes *in* the polity, not *about* the polity, changes *in* the constitution, not *about* the basic rules of the constitution.

The history of democracies shows how adaptable they have been. England, the Scandinavian countries, and the United States have made vast changes (in political participation, voting rights, the powers of the directly elected legislative assemblies, the role of political parties, the allocation of powers between the central governement and the states in federal systems or between the central government and local units) without changing the regime. Even more significantly, basic structural changes have been made on economic and societal matters. The nationalization of industries in France, England, and elsewhere, the development of the welfare state, economic planning, the enormous expansion of education and health care—they all took place *in* democratic regimes, or to put it negatively, they did not necessitate a change of regime.

Can authoritarian/totalitarian regimes make similar changes without undergoing radical regime change? The question is no longer "academic" or speculative—it is right before us. Will authoritarian and communist regimes allow free elections, and will leaders accept the popular verdict so that the process may become legitimized over a period of time? One election—as in Nicaragua, Chile, Argentina, the Philippines, Hungary, Czechoslovakia, or the Soviet Union and its various republics—is not enough. Just as one swallow does not make a summer, one election does not assure us that democracy has been legitimized. Similarly, will authoritarian regimes, especially communist regimes, truly decentralize economic controls and open the way to the privatization of state enterprises and individual economic freedoms? Again, it may take some time before we can be sure, even though there is evidence to indicate that some authoritarian regimes are beginning to do so in Eastern Europe and even the Soviet Union. These reforms, if made, will be just as revolutionary as the adoption of universal suffrage was in many European democracies in the nineteenth century, and as the massive nationalizations of industry and the welfare redistributive income systems were in others in the twentieth.

The answer is that of course authoritarian and totalitarian regimes can make reforms and that in fact some of them are already in process of doing it. In so doing, however, they are losing their authoritarian or totalitarian character—they are becoming more democratic. The substance and the organization of the regime is being transformed, and so are its values and ideology.

Democracies, we have argued, can adapt to new conditions and circumstances. Totalitarian/authoritarian regimes, however, both because of the homogeneity and cohesiveness of the elite and the concentration of political powers it holds, are less responsive to new circumstances and less adaptable. The official ideology may be so rigid and one-sided as to fail to allow for the consideration of new demands; it cannot face new circumstances, both at home and abroad. Change, as a result, may be brought about only by violence or the collapse of the ruling elite and its ideology. Change in the authoritarian regime, if sustained, therefore produces a change of regime. In terms of openness to change, experimentation, modification of power relations, and governmental structures, democracies perform better.

Responsiveness Decisional efficacy also involves *fulfilling demands*. To the extent that a regime is able to fulfill the demands that come from the people and various interests, it is able to generate *instrumental support* and gradually build up *affective support*.

Governments and governing elites must be able to gauge demands accurately if they are to fulfill them. Responsiveness, therefore, requires that interests be articulated and conveyed to the ruling elite. And this depends in large part on the extent to which interests are organized and allowed to participate in the policy-making process, and on the linkages between them and the command structures—the bureaucracy, political parties and representative assemblies, or even neocorporatist institutions. However, even the extensive organization and participation of interests is no guarantee of decisional efficacy.

Democratic regimes, if the government is overresponsive to all demands, may become victims of their responsiveness in a number of ways. By trying to satisfy all demands, they may satisfy none. By putting the emphasis on responding to individual and group claims, they may lose sight of larger priorities and functions, such as generating commonly shared goals, maintaining civil order, or providing for the common defense. Excessive responsiveness may act as an accelerant, provoking more and more demands that may drown the governmental machinery, paralyzing decision makers and incapacitating the regime as a whole in times of crisis. Some authors claim that excessive responsiveness to rising expectations produces new demands that cannot be met, causing a crisis of performance.[2]

Authoritarian and communist regimes we have surveyed, in contrast, seem more likely to suffer from a lack of responsiveness. Because of the concentration of power in the authoritarian elite, such regimes are likely to ignore demands from below. The limits placed on the organization and participation of interests in authoritarian regimes suppress the articulation of demands and make it more difficult for the elite even to be aware of them, let alone anticipate and cope with them. Paradoxically, however, the emphasis in these regimes on modernization and material development inevitably produces an increase in the volume and scope of demands from below. Authoritarian regimes, therefore, are more likely to experience a buildup of suppressed demands until they reach crisis proportions—the crisis, indeed, that is now spreading among most of them.

Inclusiveness   Another consideration in assessing decisional efficacy is the degree and the extent to which the command structure and the governing elite penetrate the societal forces and the degree to which the government reaches out into society to reshape them and to keep them under its constant supervision and control, so that they will stay in step with its policies. Regimes that have strong penetration are supposed to

[2]Samuel P. Huntington, et al., *The Crisis of Democracy* (New York: New York University Press, 1979).

perform better than democracies where the societal forces maintain their autonomy and various groups can go their own way. This is particularly relevant in the control of the economy, either through nationalizations, direct or indirect planning, or outright state management. The economy follows government directives and the government faces no hindrances from independent units in issuing them. In this sense, a great number of authoritarian governments, including communist regimes of course, could be expected to perform better than democracies, where not only are cultural, religious, and political associations immune from governmental penetration but also the economy and key industrial decisions about production, prices, and interest are in the hands of autonomous units.

But inclusiveness is a two-edged sword with respect to performance. The very burden of control and the very scope of state penetration may jeopardize rather than enhance performance. Penetration leaves no safety valves for spontaneous activity, incentives, and experimentation; it makes little room for the many small mistakes inherent in many decisions. The Ford Motor Company could produce the famous Edsel car that proved to be a huge loss, but the economy as a whole and even Ford survived it. The American farmers suffer when they produce more than the market consumes (some may go bankrupt), but the economy as a whole survives and even prospers. Entrepreneurs, manufacturers, and other businessmen go bankrupt every day in the capitalist market economies of the advanced industrial democracies, but few call for overthrowing the democratic regime because of it. The same mistakes, however, committed by nationalized industries and in state-administered economies ("command economies," as they are called) are rightly viewed by the people as failures in regime performance and directly affect the level of popular support for these regimes; i.e., their legitimacy. Inclusiveness and penetration, in other words, are no guarantee of performance!

Legitimacy

Legitimization is the process by which a population comes to accept and comply with the command structure, the ruling elite, and the decisions they make. In effect, legitimization amounts to the population giving its consent to be governed by the ruling elite. But *legitimacy* is more than this alone. It is also the belief of the population that the regime is endowed with a *right* to rule.[3]

Legitimization comprises the processes that link the command structure (those who make decisions) with the people at large. We

---

[3]For an extended discussion of the concept of legitimacy, see Reinhard Bendix, *Max Weber: An Intellectual Portrait* (Garden City, N.Y.: Doubleday and Co., 1962).

emphasized that the major criterion of legitimization is consent: the acceptance by the governed of the authority of those who govern. We discussed the processes of legitimization in terms of participation, socialization, respresentation, the political parties, and elections. We found that in totalitarian regimes the emphasis is on mobilization. The single party and the official ideology are the mobilizing forces. Authoritarian regimes, on the other hand, rely heavily on administrative and coercive mechanisms to ensure obedience rather than to inculcate consent. As a result, legitimization is warped in authoritarian regimes because consent and supports are uncertain. They cannot easily meet crises; their emphasis on maintaining order is so great that they allow for no alternative but complete disorder, such as acts of violence and anti-regime uprisings.

We have argued that consent in democratic regimes, whatever the strength of the socializing ideology, is relatively open and spontaneous. Obedience to those who issue orders stems from participation, elections, representation, and ultimately, rules that make the officials responsible to the electorate. In a sense, consent and supports to the regime are, to use a famous expression, a "daily plebiscite." In totalitarian regimes, legitimization is also the product of a socializing ideology. At times it can generate supports far more powerful than can be found in any democracy, as, for example, in Nazi Germany. But without open procedures for registering acceptance, one can never be sure how strong the supports are at any given time and how much consent there is for the regime or its policies. In contrast, in democracies supports are constantly tested (and testable). The opposition to the war in Vietnam by Americans or the war in Algeria by the French, to nuclear weapons, and to energy and environmental policies proves the point. But we have no way of testing legitimacy in totalitarian and authoritarian regimes except when they collapse, as they seem to be doing now. If they do not, compliance should not be presumed to indicate acceptance and legitimacy.

Civil Order

If a political regime is to maintain order, it cannot allow an excess of social disruption and especially not organized violence by dissenting groups. Disruptive acts undermine the performance of a regime, and conversely, their absence indicates at least some level of positive performance. Which of the regimes surveyed—democratic, totalitarian, or authoritarian—performs better in maintaining order?

If we view violence only in terms of private persons or groups pitted against public authorities, then it would appear that democratic regimes experience over time a great deal of violence—strikes, demonstrations, gang warfare, crime, among other forms. However, if we include the use of organized force by public authorities against private persons and groups in our definition of violence, we might then conclude that authoritarian regimes experience more violence, indeed much more. The degree, the persistence, and the comprehensiveness of repression is much greater, on any scale of measurement that might be devised than the acts of organized violence in a democracy. The resort to repression must be considered an indication of the failure (i.e., nonperformance) of a regime. Harry Eckstein makes the point forcefully when he argues that "the persistent coercive repression of large social collectivities surely denotes political failure of some sort; if it is reasonable to expect polities to reduce private conflict, it is also reasonable to expect them not merely to displace it onto the public level."[4]

Order, and the rules in force to sustain it, are greatly affected by two fundamental aspects of societal life that also relate directly to legitimacy and consent: the *distribution of values*, and the *distribution of goods*.

The Distribution of Values   Values are things, ideas, attachments, ways of life, to which people commit at least some degree of their support. People want these values respected and protected. Family values, religious freedom, linguistic freedom, freedom of association, political autonomy, and creative or artistic freedom are only some of the values people treasure. They appear to be intangible, and it is no easy task to place a price tag upon them. But for many they are the very cornerstones, the very essence of our lives.

One has only to think of the group conflicts taking place at present within such multiethnic states as Yugoslavia, the Soviet Union, India, and Sri Lanka or the religious wars that swept through Europe in the seventeenth and eighteenth centuries. In the United States, the intensity of political conflicts over women's rights and especially abortion rights reveals that, even in modernized societies, the profound emotional attachments associated with fundamental values can give rise to powerful and sometimes violent political conflict.

Order obtains when individuals and groups are guaranteed the preservation and peaceful expression of the values they hold dear. There are some societies in which such guarantees have become part of the political culture—the "civic culture." Some of these are homogeneous societies whose populations share a single ethnic identity, language, or religion; where there is an overwhelming attachment to a set of shared values. Others are societies in which important differences exist with regard to these basic values, but in which, over the course of time (often centuries) agreement has been reached to accept these differences and mechanisms have been established to guarantee the free expression of diverse values.

[4]Eckstein, *The Evaluation of Political Performance*, p. 37.

In the great majority of cases, however, differences persist with respect to both values and the mechanisms for preserving and expressing them. Such differences give rise to persistent demands for government action. For it is the government, as we noted earlier, that has the power to enforce rules, through coercion if necessary. Such demands, when they threaten the values held dear by others, endanger the existing political order, unless the regime is able to develop mechanisms for accommodating conflicting values. And, where the values of dominant and subordinate groups are seen by each as incompatible, dissolution of the shared regime—peacefully or by violence—may ensue.

The Distribution of Goods The distribution of goods relates to material goods and access to them. It raises squarely the question of equality, whether of opportunity or of the relative satisfaction of material wants. With the onset of economic development, such wants grow almost exponentially to include such things as job security, health care, and pensions. In many regimes—democratic, authoritarian, and even totalitarian—the provision of such benefits has been transformed in the minds of the populace from a privilege of development to a right of citizenship. The more widespread the availability of material goods, the more widespread and greater the ensuing satisfaction of the population.

Many centuries ago, however, Aristotle emphasized the need for material equality as well as satisfaction. "The cause of sedition is always to be found in inequality," he wrote.

> There are some who stir up sedition because their minds are filled by a passion for equality, which arises from their thinking that they have the worst of the bargain in spite of being the equals of those who have got the advantage. There are others who do it because their minds are filled with a passion for inequality (i.e., superiority), which arises from their conceiving that they get no advantage over others (but only an equal amount, or even a smaller amount) although they are really more than equal to others. (Either of these passions may have some justification; and either may be without any.) Thus inferiors become revolutionaries in order to be equals, and equals in order to be superiors.[5]

At the founding of the American republic, James Madison also singled out sharp inequalities as the source of factional disputes that might destabilize the democratic regime. He wrote:

> the most common and durable source of factions has been the various and unequal distribution of property. Those who

[5]*The Politics of Aristotle*, ed. and trans. by Ernest Barker (New York: Oxford University Press, 1962), p. 207.

hold and those who are without property have ever formed distinct interests in society. Those who are creditors, and those who are debtors, fall under a like discrimination. A landed interest, a manufacturing interest, a mercantile interest, a moneyed interest, with many lesser interests, grow up of necessity in civilized nations, and divide them into different classes, actuated by different sentiments and views.[6]

Many have sought the foundation of civic order in the establishment of a numerous and strong "middle class," in which the extremes of wealth and poverty are avoided. The wider and more equitable the distribution of goods in society, it is argued, the more stable the political order. Conflicts and disagreements over material goods will be moderated, hence susceptible to compromise.

In all societies, except perhaps for some of the least developed, conflict over goods and services, over "who gets what," remains what politics is all about. Political order is generally in danger when there are widely shared perceptions of gross inequalities and discrimination in material well-being. We say "perceptions" because there are no objective criteria against which we can judge the political significance of such inequalities. The poor and underprivileged can live a long time in their poverty. But poverty becomes politically significant only when the poor gain an awareness of their position, when they become conscious of their *deprivation* and demand redress; in short, when they become *mobilized*. Similarly, the relatively better-off segments of a society may develop expectations of further advance that prove impossible to fulfill and become the basis of their own feelings of *relative deprivation* and their own mobilization in support of demands for political change. With social modernization, and particularly the spread of education, the scope of popular demands in all segments of society expands with respect to both material needs and the range of values held dear.

Successful political regimes are those that have been able to devise instrumentalities to cope with the mobilization of social groups in support of demands concerning the distribution of values and goods. Changes are agreed upon as government responds to new demands: The franchise is extended to broader social groups, social welfare legislation is adopted, education is universalized, wealth is redistributed more equitably, and the center of decision making gradually shifts to popularly elected officials and institutions as citizen participation increases. Nothing illustrates better the cumulative, transforming effects of the gradual adaptation of a regime than the political history of Great Britain. In the United States, the adaptation to new demands has also occurred gradually over the last two centuries.

---

[6]James Madison, *The Federalist Papers*, No. 10, (New York: New American Library, 1961), p. 79.

Civil Disorder

Political order gives way to political disorder when a regime is unable or its elites are unwilling to devise institutions to accommodate and respond to new demands and reconcile conflicts about them. Adaptation is virtually impossible where there is an absence of participatory institutions and the freedoms required for their effective use. This is the case with all authoritarian regimes. However, vestigial participatory institutions, such as opposition parties and legislatures, survive in many authoritarian regimes. When a crisis occurs, these can be turned into channels for the representation of interests, the expression of demands, and the organization of consent.

Of course, political disorder in the form of demonstrations, acts of violence, and demands for participation in authoritarian regimes may simply be suppressed by force by the ruling elite. But where disorder is the product of emerging social and economic forces, its suppression will undermine performance. It erodes the informational and recruitment bases of the elite, alienates the people's support, antagonizes new interests, and blocks state/society interaction. Declining decisional efficacy, in turn, will make it very difficult for any regime to continue to produce the kinds of benefits to the population that engender instrumental support and consent. The requisites of regime performance, therefore, call for the creation of institutionalized channels for the participation of emerging social forces.

Conclusion Keeping the criteria we suggested in mind, the student may try to assess the performance of political regimes undergoing change. In terms of durability, we find that despite the present crisis, authoritarian and many communist–totalitarian regimes managed to survive for a long period of time—over seventy years in the Soviet Union, over forty years (and still going) in China, over thirty-five years in Cuba, to mention some of the most important communist regimes. As for authoritarian ones, their longevity is remarkable too (see Table 9.1). Many that are undergoing democratization, especially in Latin America, have not as yet shed some of their authoritarian and militarist traits. But durability alone should not be equated with legitimacy. A regime may endure because it has imposed itself on the populace through intimidation and force. There is no test like that of democracy: open and free elections. For some of these regimes, however, the test has at long last come. In Nicaragua, after ten years of authoritarian rule the Sandinistas were turned down in an open election in favor of the opposition. In Chile, the military dictator lost to a civilian presidential candidate who assumed office in 1990. In East Germany, the communist monopoly was reduced in the election of March 18, 1990, to a mere 16 percent of the vote! In Hungary, not even a new name and program could garner the former Communist party more than 9 percent of the vote in free elections held in March and April 1990. Even in the Soviet Union the

TABLE 9.1 Durability of Authoritarian Regimes and Leaders	
Franco (Spain)	1935–1973
Salazar (Portugal)	1927–1965
Alfredo Stroessner (Paraguay)	1954–1989
Bourguiba (Tunisia)	1958–1989
Ne Win (Burma)	1962–
Argentina (military junta)	1966–1973; 1976–1983
Sekou Tourè (Guinea)	1958–1984
Houphouet-Boigny (Ivory Coast)	1962–
Qaddaffi (Libya)	1969–
Trujillo (Dominican Republic)	1930–1961
Mexico (IRP—single party)	1940–1990 (?)
El Salvador (military)	1932–1983 (?)
Algeria (military and party)	1964–
Uruguay (military rule)	1974–1985 (?)
U.S.S.R. (Communist party)	1917–1990 (?)
Castro (Cuba)	1958–
Sandinistas (Nicaragua)	1979–1990
Marcos (Auth./Mil.) (Philippines)	1946–1986
China (Communist party)	1949–
Poland (Communist)	1947–1989
Albania (Communist)	1946–
Romania (Ceausescu)	1951–1989
Yugoslavia (Tot./Communist)	1945–?
Hungary (Communist)	1947–1990

monopoly rule of the party and the communist regime itself is being rejected at the polls as elections become freer and more competitive. Not even the extensive changes outlined in Chapter 8 appear capable of saving the authoritarian order in the face of popular insistence on democracy. Legitimacy, therefore, cannot be presumed, even when a given regime has been in power over a long period of time.

The Normative Question

If there are difficulties in evaluating political regimes in terms of their performance, the difficulties of judging them in normative terms are much greater. Long ago Aristotle pointed out that the purpose of a political regime was not mere material satisfaction and functionality. The purpose of the state was to provide for the best possible life. In other words, what is "administered best" must also be judged in terms of what *is* best. What criteria shall we use? Freedom? Equality? Abundance? Order and protection? Justice and happiness for all?

All regimes, even authoritarian ones, set forth normative goals to be attained in the future. Communist totalitarian regimes and democratic regimes have shared, by and large, some of the same ultimate goals: to bring about individual freedom, to give people all the opportunities to realize themselves and their talents, and to build a world of cooperation and peace. But it is not enough to set forth the goals. A regime must infuse values into its political institutions and structures, in accord with the goals. It must give them life and meaning so that the goals become *operative*.

In both democracies and authoritarian regimes there has been considerable (at times very great) disparity between ultimate goals and operative institutions and practices. Democracies have ignored the very strong linkages between equal rights and equal opportunities on the one hand and equality of living conditions and income on the other. There is still truth in the argument that in democracies many of us are free only to be homeless and hungry. But totalitarian regimes have blatantly ignored the links between political and individual freedoms and the material equalities to which they are committed. Without the former, there is no guarantee that material equalities (even if they exist) can be preserved. There is no assurance that equals are free to develop their talents or participate in the political process and jointly share in the formation of common goals and common pursuits. A society of equals (in the sense of material and physical increments of wealth) may consist of persons living in a permanent state of subjection. All slaves are equal to each other! And, as recent revelations about the lifestyles of former communist leaders in Eastern Europe, and as well-known facts about the privileges of the Soviet communist elite suggest, these regimes failed to provide even equality, let alone prosperity.

Equality and freedom remain the two major normative values against which all regimes may be judged. Regimes must be evaluated in terms of the institutions and practices they establish to protect individual freedom and ensure equality. The processes set up to attain them can give us some clues that we can observe and study. Difficult as their assessment may prove to be, they at least provide a handle for evaluating performance in these normative terms.

Freedom and equality, both material equality and equality of opportunity; civil order and domestic tranquility in our persons and properties; and a real opportunity for all people to work and live their lives in a society that provides rewards for their respective talents—these are the conditions that make up justice. Can political regimes by compared on the scale of justice? Which regimes provide it best? What operative ideas, institutions, and practices—not simply abstract ideological propositions—implement it? Where does justice infuse the structures, the forms, and the institutions we surveyed? Without justice, what is "administered best" may be the worst. "Kingdoms without justice, how like they are to robber-bands," wrote St. Augustine. His plea continues to challenge us all.

Index